DATE DUE

SEP 0 6 2016		
OCT 0 1 2016		
OC 1 1 16		
MAY 1 5 2017		
		PRINTED IN U.S.A.

DIMESTORE

 This Large Print Book carries the
Seal of Approval of N.A.V.H.

DIMESTORE

LEE SMITH

THORNDIKE PRESS
A part of Gale, Cengage Learning

GALE
CENGAGE Learning·

Farmington Hills, Mich • San Francisco • New York • Waterville, Maine
Meriden, Conn • Mason, Ohio • Chicago

LIBRARY OF CONGRESS CATALOGING-IN-PUBLICATION DATA

Names: Smith, Lee, 1944- author.
Title: Dimestore / by Lee Smith.
Description: Large print edition. | Waterville, Maine : Thorndike Press, 2016. |
  © 2016 | Series: Thorndike Press large print biographies and memoirs
Identifiers: LCCN 2016011907| ISBN 9781410490681 (hardcover) | ISBN 1410490688
  (hardcover)
Subjects: LCSH: Smith, Lee, 1944—Childhood and youth. | Novelists,
  American—20th century—Biography. | Grundy (Va.)—Biography. | Grundy
  (Va.)—Social life and customs. | Large type books.
Classification: LCC PS3569.M5376 Z46 2016b | DDC 813/.54—dc23
LC record available at http://lccn.loc.gov/2016011907

Published in 2016 by arrangement with Algonquin Books of Chapel Hill, a division of Workman Publishing

Printed in Mexico
1 2 3 4 5 6 7 20 19 18 17 16

the *New York Times* as "Given Tools, They Work the Language," 1996.

"Driving Miss Daisy Crazy," originally a talk, then published as the introduction to *New Stories from the South,* 2001.

"Good-bye to the Sunset Man," originally published in the *Independent Weekly,* October 2004.

"A Life in Books," based on an Associated Writing Program keynote address (and then printed in the *AWP* magazine/newsletter) and a piece named "Everything Else Falls Away" written for the collection *Why I Write: Thoughts on the Craft of Fiction,* edited by Will Blythe, Little, Brown, 1998.

"Angels Passing," originally published in the *Independent Weekly.*

"The Little Locksmith," in the *Raleigh News and Observer,* 2002.

"Heritage," in *From the Mountain, From the Valley: New and Collected Poems* by James Scill, edited by Ted Olson, published by the University Press of Kentucky, March 2005.

Excerpts from *The Wolfpen Notebooks: A*

Record of Appalachian Life by James Still, published by the University Press of Kentucky, July 9, 1991.

"Salvation," in *The River Hills and Beyond* by Lou Crabtree, published by Sow's Ear Press, 1998.

"Song to Oysters," in *Soupsongs/Webster's Ark* by Roy Blount Jr., published by Houghton Mifflin, 1987.

With gratitude to the original publishers of Lee Smith's work quoted herein: *The Last Day the Dogbushes Bloomed,* Harper and Row, New York, 1968. Oral History (1983) and Fair and Tender Ladies (1988), G. P. Putnam's Sons, New York. The story "Tongues of Fire," in *Me and My Baby View the Eclipse,* by Lee Smith, G. P. Putnam's Sons, New York, 1990.

For my grandchildren,
Lucy, Spencer, Ellery, and Baker

Writing fiction has developed in me an abiding respect for the unknown in a human lifetime and a sense of where to look for the threads, how to follow, how to connect, find in the thick of the tangle what clear line persists. The strands are all there: to the memory nothing is ever really lost.

The events in our lives happen in a sequence in time, but in their significance to ourselves they find their own order, a timetable not necessarily — perhaps not possibly — chronological. The time as we know it subjectively is often the chronology that stories and novels follow: it is the continuous thread of revelation.

— *One Writer's Beginnings,*
Eudora Welty

CONTENTS

PREFACE:
RAISED TO LEAVE: SOME
THOUGHTS ON "CULTURE"

I was born in a rugged ring of mountains in southwest Virginia — mountains so high, so straight up and down, that the sun didn't even hit our yard until about eleven o'clock. My uncle Bob Venable — they lived across the road — used to predict the weather by sticking his head out the window and hollering back inside, "Sun on the mountaintop, girls!" to my cousins. The only flat land in the county lay in a narrow band along the river where we lived, about a mile from town. Though we all ate out of the garden, real farming was impossible in that hard rock ground. The only thing it produced was coal. We never thought of our jagged mountains as scenic, either, though we all played up in them every day after school. We never saw a tourist, and nobody we knew hiked for fun.

I will never forget the first time I ever saw a jogger: my mother and I were sitting on

15

the front porch stringing beans and watching the cars go up and down Route 460 in front of our house, when suddenly one of these VISTAs we'd been hearing about, a long-haired boy with great legs, came running right up the road. We both stood up, and watched him run out of sight. "Well, for heaven's sakes," my mother said. "Where do you reckon he's going, running like that?"

He was going back to where he came from, eventually; but most of us weren't going anyplace. We were closed in entirely, cut off from the outside world by our ring of mountains. Many of the children I went to school with had never been out of Buchanan County. People still described my own mother as "not from around here," though she had spent most of her life teaching their children and "trying to civilize you and your daddy!" as she always joked, but it was a challenge.

So I was being raised to leave.

I was not to use double negatives; I was not to say "me and Martha." I was not to trade my pimento cheese sandwiches at school for the lunch I really wanted: cornbread and buttermilk in a mason jar, brought by the kids from the hollers. Me and Martha were not to play in the black river behind our house, dirty with coal that would stain my shorts. I was to take piano lessons from the terrifying Mrs. Ruth Boyd even though I had no aptitude for it. I was to play "Clair de Lune" at my piano recital, wearing an itchy pink net evening dress.

I was not to like the mountain music that surrounded us on every side, from the men playing banjo and mandolin on the sidewalk outside my daddy's dimestore on Saturdays, to Martha's father playing his guitar down on the riverbank after dinner, to Kitty Wells singing "It Wasn't God Who Made Honky Tonk Angels" on our brand-new radio station, WNRG. But here, my mother ran into serious trouble. For I loved this music. I had been born again to "Angel Band," sung high and sweet at a tent revival that I had to sneak out to go to; and I had a dobro-playing boyfriend, with Nashville aspirations.

Even my mother enjoyed going to the drive-in theater on Saturday evenings in the summer to hear two brothers from over in Dickenson County, Ralph and Carter Stanley, play and sing their bluegrass music on top of the concrete-block concessions stand. "I never will marry, I'll take me no wife; I intend to live single, all of my life," Ralph wailed mournfully, followed by their fast instrumental version of "Shout, Little Lulie." Old people were clogging on the patch of concrete in front of the window where you bought your Cokes and popcorn; little kids were swinging on the iron-pipe swing set. Whole families ate fried chicken and deviled eggs they'd brought from home, sitting on quilts on the grass. My boyfriend reached over and squeezed my sweaty hand. The Stanley Brothers' nasal voices rose higher than the gathering mist, higher than the lightning bugs that rose from the trees along the river as night came on. When it got full dark, the Stanley Brothers climbed down off the concession stand and we all got into our cars and the movie came on.

I loved that music, just as I loved my grandmother's corn pudding and those scary old stories my Uncle Vern told. But this hillbilly music didn't have anything to do with "culture," as I was constantly being reminded. No, "culture" was someplace else, and when the time came, I would be sent off to get some. Culture lived in big cities like Richmond, and Washington, and Boston and New York — especially in New York, especially in places like Carnegie Hall.

Forty years later, I stood on my hundred-dollar balcony seat in Carnegie Hall and screamed as seventy-four-year-old Dr. Ralph Stanley and the rest of the traditional musicians and singers from the phenomenally successful *O Brother, Where Art Thou?* soundtrack played to a sold-out house. Elvis Costello was the emcee; Joel and Ethan Coen, the filmmakers who made the *O Brother* movie, were in the audience, along with T Bone Burnett, its musical director. The Coen Brothers had written this note about the music in the program, aimed at their New York audience: "These songs were for the most part created by people whose lives were hard and horizons narrow. Their lives were not like ours. All that urges their music on us is its humanity . . . And yet, this soundtrack went platinum without receiving any airplay: pop stations considered it too country, and country stations considered it too . . . country."

On stage at Carnegie Hall, the Fairfield Four sang their stark treatment of "Po' Lazarus." Dan Tyminski tore it up on "I Am a Man of Constant Sorrow." The Cox family, fresh from Louisiana, brought down the house with "Will There Be Any Stars in My Crown." Reigning bluegrass princess Alison Krauss fiddled up a storm, then sang "When I Go Down to the River to Pray" in tight harmony with Gillian Welch and Emmylou

19

Harris. They sang so sweet, they could have been angels. The little Peasall sisters — Sarah, age thirteen, Hannah, age ten, and Leah, age eight, wore patent-leather shoes and bows in their hair to sing "In the Highways and the Hedges, I'll Be Somewhere Listening for My Name." Gillian's husband, David Rawlings, teamed up with her on "I Want To Sing That Rock and Roll."

But the night belonged to Ralph Stanley, who came out last, all by himself, and took center stage to give his famous a capella rendition of the terrifying "O Death," with all lights black except for a single spotlight trained directly on him. "O Death, O Death, won't you spare me over for another year?" His high, haunting voice filled the huge dark hall. The song lasted for five minutes, followed by almost a full moment of total silence. Then the stage lights went up, the house lights came on, the other performers rushed out on stage, and the standing ovation went on and on.

Although he loves to poke fun at his own success — recently referring to the movie as "O Brother, Where Art Thou *At*" — Dr. Ralph Stanley has come a long way from the top of the concession stand at the Grundy Drive-In Theater. A six-time Grammy nominee and a Grand Ole Opry member, Stanley was the first recipient of the National Endowment for the Humanities' Traditional American Music Award, and he performed at the inaugurations of both Jimmy Carter and Bill Clinton. He has been awarded the Library of Congress Living Legend Medal.

Dr. Ralph's Carnegie Hall appearance symbolized something that has happened to Appalachian culture as a whole. Now, everybody in the region realizes that we don't have to go anyplace else to "get culture." Every little town has its own little festival, celebrating itself with local music, food, and crafts, whether it's called a "blackberry festival," or a "ramp festival," or a "wooly worm contest," or "gingerbread day," or a "hollering contest," or a "fiddling convention." Fueled by a national, politically-correct appreciation of whatever is still ethnically or geographically or culturally distinct, America as a whole is coming to appreciate and value its differences. Everybody understands that our own Appalachian culture is as rich, and as diverse in terms of history, arts, crafts, literature, folklore, and music, for instance, as any area in this country.

But in fact, we are far richer than most. Our formidable geography acted as a natural barrier for so long, keeping others out, holding us in, allowing for the development of our rich folk culture, our distinctive speech patterns, our strong sense of tradition, and our radical individualism. Appalachian people are more rooted than other Southerners. We still live in big, extended families that spoil children and revere old people. We will talk your ears off. We still excel in storytelling — and I mean everybody, not just some old guy in overalls at a folk festival. I mean the woman who cuts your hair, I mean your doctor, I mean your mother. Our great music is country music — which was always working-class, from its beginnings in the old-time string bands and ballads right up through honky-tonk and the high lonesome sound of bluegrass to present-day glitzy Nashville, and then all the way back around to the current revival of more old-time, traditional music.

Look at Dolly Parton, now a national icon: "I had to get rich to sing this poor," she has said, referring to the success of her albums *The Grass Is Blue,* her take on traditional bluegrass, and *Little Sparrow,* which is old-time, or what Dolly calls her "blue mountain music." Look at Lucinda Williams and Steve Earle and Patty Loveless. And the big national stars just keep on

22

coming, like Kenny Chesney, Florida Georgia Line, Eric Church, and Miranda Lambert . . . country music is mainstream American music now.

But what about our literature? No one could deny that there is a veritable explosion of Appalachian writing today. A lot of it is hitting the best-seller lists, too — this means it is being read, and widely read, outside the region. I'm talking about Charles Frazier's Civil War novel *Cold Mountain* and Ron Rash's amazing *Serena,* for instance, both set in western North Carolina; about Barbara Kingsolver's *Prodigal Summer,* which takes place near Emory, Virginia; about Sharyn McCrumb's Ballad Novels and Robert Morgan's *Gap Creek,* which even got "Oprah-fied," as did Gwen Hyman Rubio's eastern Kentucky novel *Icy Sparks.* I'm especially talking about Adriana Trigiani's lively comic novels from my own neck of the woods, *Big Stone Gap, Big Cherry Holler, Milk Glass Moon.*

Big Stone Gap has recently been filmed in Big Stone Gap, Virginia, starring Ashley Judd and directed by Adriana herself. *Cold Mountain* was a hit film even though they shot most of it in Romania, to Charles Frazier's dismay. So was *Walk the Line,* which chronicled the Carter Family and Johnny Cash. *Nashville* is a popular television series. The film *Songcatcher* traced the adventures of a Boston musicologist who comes to visit her crusading sister at a settlement school in Madison County, North Carolina, and sets about "catching" — or transcribing all the local ballads. The darker film *Winter's Bone,* based upon the novel of the same name by Daniel Woodrell and set in Arkansas, deals with the pervasive drug problem in the mountains, as does Ron Rash's *The World Made Straight.*

Newer Appalachian writers such as Silas House, Ann Pancake, and Wiley Cash deal with mountaintop removal mining and other energy and ecological problems besetting the region now. In *Flight Behavior,* Barbara Kingsolver makes it clear that such Appalachian issues are global issues, too. Widespread Appalachian literature courses, festivals, and writing workshops ought to ensure the fine new crop of young writers — and activists — continues.

Clearly, I could go on and on, and I'm not even really getting into visual arts, or poetry, or design, or drama, or documentary film. My point is that mainstream American culture has become "Appalachian-ized." No matter what you think of NASCAR, for instance — arguably our most successful Appalachian export — it's everyplace now.

I'm of two minds about all this. I was country, remember, when country wasn't cool. I don't really like to see my favorite places and people be "discovered." I'd rather hear Sheila Adams sing a ballad on a mountaintop in Sodom, North Carolina, than on her latest CD. I'd rather eat at Cuz's in Pounding Mill, Virginia, than Cracker Barrel.

Even though I sometimes wish I could be back in the simpler, saner, safer world of my childhood, eating a piece of fried chicken on a quilt at the drive-in theater while Ralph Stanley plays music on top of the concession stand, I know I can't. The drive-in is long gone, and so am I. But I'll tell you something else — I was mighty proud to be there the night Dr. Ralph played at Carnegie Hall.

DIMESTORE

Grundy nestled in its mountains "like a play-pretty cotched in the hand of God," as an old woman once described it. Surely I could always count on these mountains, this river behind our house, this town where I grew up in my father's dimestore and across the street in my grandfather's office at the courthouse and in the Methodist Church and in my grandparents' house just across Slate Creek, right next to my school. "Honey, the only thing you can count on in this world," my granddaddy used to say, "is death and taxes." But that couldn't be true, I felt. This was my geography. It would be like this forever. My daddy knew. He called it his "standing ground."

I could drive that road with my eyes closed, or almost — twisty Route 460 as it wound up through the mountains of southwest Virginia. I turned at Claypool Hill, passed Richlands, and went over the heart-stopping Shortt Gap. I passed the huge Island Creek coal tipple; innumerable "yard sales," held in no yard but right along the roadside; a storefront with a big sign that said WE BUY GINSENG; several houses turned into the kind of freelance churches where you get to scream out and fall down. Like a vision of Hell itself, the coke ovens appeared as I crossed the bridge over the Dismal River, brick chimney after chimney belching red flames into the sky. We used to drive up there and park when I was a teenager — it was the most exciting thing to do on a date (also the only thing, except for the revivals and the movie that changed once a week). There was a lot of traffic as I got closer to Grundy, where the large hollers spill out into the main road: Garden Creek, Big Prater, Little Prater, Watkins Branch, and Hoot Owl Holler, just beyond the house I grew up in. Somebody was sure to greet me by rolling down the window of his truck and yelling, "Hi, Lee, when did you get in?"

I was always struck by that preposition *in.* Driving into Grundy was like heading into a bowl, producing that familiar sense of enclosure that used to comfort me and drive me wild all at the same time when I was a teenager. These mountains are so steep that the sun seemed to set about 3 p.m., so steep that a cow once fell off a cliff straight down through the roof and landed in my Aunt Bess and Uncle Clyde's kitchen in downtown Grundy, close to the courthouse. This is true.

Founded at the confluence of the Levisa Fork River and Slate Creek, Grundy became the county seat of Buchanan County in 1858, enduring cycles of fire and flood, bust and boom, as lumber and coal businesses came and went. Perhaps its isolation and its constant struggles were what made its citizens so close to each other, so caring and generous — "the best people in the world," my daddy always said, and this is true, too. Even after Mama died, I could never get him to retire and leave Grundy.

"No, honey, I need me a mountain to rest my eyes against," Daddy always said.

My very first memory is of downtown Grundy. I'm standing up in my crib, gripping its spool railings, looking out an upstairs dormer window of my grandparents' house at the flickering colored lights of the Morgan Theater, reflected in the waters of Slate Creek. First green, then yellow, then blue and red and green again, they twinkle through the distance like fairy lights in an enchanted kingdom, promising everything. In my mind's eye, I can see them still, mysterious, beautiful, and always too far away. I've been told I watched them steadily for hours, and it must be so, for that memory is indelible, as is the somber striking of the courthouse clock that marked the passing of every hour.

It is 1945. I am one year old. My father, Ernest Smith, is away in the Navy. My mother, Virginia Marshall Smith (nicknamed "Gig"), has left her job teaching home economics at the high school and is working at the Ration Board. She and I are living with my grandparents until my daddy returns. Then we will move into our own house up the river at Cowtown and Daddy will open the Five and Ten Cent Variety Store with the financial help of his uncle Curt Smith (who was actually Daddy's own age — it was that kind of family). Though the store will later become a Ben Franklin, it would always be known in town as simply "the dimestore."

Many of my favorite memories of Grundy take place in this dimestore. As a little girl, my job was "taking care of the dolls." Not only did I comb their hair and fluff up their frocks, but I also made up long, complicated life stories for them, things that had happened to them before they came to the dimestore, things that would happen to them after they left my care. I gave each of them three-part names: Mary Elizabeth Satterfield, for instance, and Baby Betsy Black. Their lives were very dramatic.

Upstairs in my father's office, I got to type on a typewriter, count money, and talk to Roberta Ratliff, pale, blonde, and pretty as a princess in a fairy-tale book. She would later become the manager. I spent hours and hours upstairs in that office, observing the whole floor of the dimestore through the one-way glass window and reveling in my own power — nobody can see me, but I can see everybody! I witnessed not only shoplifting, but fights and embraces as well. Thus I learned the position of the omniscient narrator, who sees and records everything, yet is never visible. It was the perfect early education for a fiction writer.

I always went down to check on the goldfish in their basement tank. And every spring I looked forward to the arrival of the pastel-colored Easter chickens. But my favorites were the little round turtles with roses painted on their shells. I used to wear these turtles to school on my sweaters, where they clung like brooches. I liked to visit with John Yuhasz, a very kind man, on my trips to the basement to "help" him put up stock. Clovis Owens, in charge of maintenance, could fix anything, and his wife made the best pound cake in the world. She always sent me a piece, wrapped in wax paper.

Up on the main floor, I chatted with the dimestore "girls" who had all been working there for as long as I could remember — sweet Ellen Clevinger in children's wear; Viola, back in piece goods, who always hugged me; floor supervisor Ruth Edwards; and Ruby Sweeton, supposedly in toiletries, who seemed to be everywhere. With bright red spots of rouge on her cheeks, Mildred Shortridge presided over the popcorn machine and the candy counter at the front of the store, whispering the craziest things in my ear. She made me laugh and laugh. I always bought some of the jellied orange slices and the nonpareils, those flat chocolate discs covered with hard little white balls of sugar. My friends were surprised to find that I never got anything free at the dimestore; despite my protests, I had to save my allowance and pay just like everybody else.

I was allowed to run free all over town, which was filled with our relatives, not only Smiths, but Dennises and Belchers as well.

Russell Belcher ran the Rexall drugstore. Uncle Curt Smith owned the Lynwood Theater and lived with his wife Lyde and her sister Nora Belcher in a shotgun apartment above it, reached by a long, dark staircase. I was fascinated by this apartment, where the rooms were all in a row and Lyde cooked a big hot lunch in the middle of every day. Uncle Vern Smith (longtime member of the Virginia State Legislature) and his son Harold had opened the first Ford Agency. Uncle Clyde Dennis ran the insurance agency. Uncle Percy Dennis, Sr., was the Superintendent of Schools, while Percy Dennis, Jr., operated the Mingo lumber yard across the river. My grandfather's alcoholic brother, piano-playing Blind Bill Smith, often came over from West Virginia to play boogie-woogie piano for dances. My grandparents Chloe and Earl Smith lived across Slate Creek from town in a big old brick house reached by a scary swinging bridge that I crossed each time with my heart in my mouth.

I went to town every single day when school let out, across that swinging bridge and then the real bridge they built later on. First I went to the dimestore and got some candy from Mildred and did my homework upstairs in the office, or crossed the street to the old stone courthouse and did my homework in my grandaddy's treasurer's office, eavesdropping all the while. In the dimestore I learned who was pregnant, who was getting married, who had got saved, who had got churched for drinking, who was mean to her children or made the best red velvet cake. In the courthouse I'd hear a different kind of story — who was in jail, who had gone bankrupt or shot his brother or tried to short his employees, who was out of a job or had set his house on fire just to collect the insurance money. I also liked to go around the county politicking with Granddaddy on Sunday afternoons, sitting down to eat some Sunday dinner with everybody. I liked to stand out on the courthouse corner with him on Saturdays when he gave out dollar bills. Men would be smoking and shooting dice and "loafering around telling lies," as Grandaddy said, on the courthouse bench, and boys would be shining shoes. Somebody would always be playing music, guitar and fiddle and maybe banjo, out on the sidewalk in front of the dimestore.

Next to the dimestore was the Rexall drugstore, where as a teenager I gossiped with my girlfriends, bought Maybelline makeup, ate mysterious "meat sandwiches," and read *Teen* magazine with its articles like "How to Talk to Boys (Tip: Learn about Cars)." Then came Russell's Men's Store where I held Christmas jobs during high school; and finally, Uncle Curt's Lynwood Theater which I attended virtually every time the movie changed during my entire life in Grundy.

Here, for the cost of a mere quarter, the big silver screen brought us the rest of the world. Here we formed our notions of bravery, of glamour, of danger and sophistication, of faraway places and people like no people we had ever seen. Western theme music swelled our hearts. Our ideal of heroism came from stoic John Wayne; of beauty, from Jane Russell and Marilyn Monroe. Was anything ever as scary as *Hush . . . Hush, Sweet Charlotte*? Or as sad as *Imitation of Life*? We found Ma and Pa Kettle hilarious, and howled at the Three Stooges, the Marx Brothers, and later, Jerry Lewis. Our first dates took place at the Lynwood ("Nice girls do not sit in the balcony!" our mothers decreed) where we grimly held our dates' hands in a kind of death grip throughout the whole show, afraid we'd hurt their feelings if we stopped for even one minute to wipe off our sweaty palms.

The movies taught me that place can be

almost as important as personality, and that actions really do speak louder than words. Plot is all-important; beginning, middle, and end is the most natural and satisfying sequence of events. Most important of all: something has to happen. People in a movie do not just sit around thinking all the time, the way I did in real life — "mooning around," my mother called it, disgustedly.

From Main Street, it was only a stone's throw to our little Methodist Church. With its chiseled stone exterior and beautiful stained-glass windows, it looked totally different from every other church in town — much more holy, I felt! Its slightly damp, mildewy smell was a holy smell, too. At Christmas, each child received a paper bag containing an orange, an apple, some walnuts, and a Hershey bar. In the Christmas pageant, I was first an animal, then a wise man, and finally an angel, but never the Virgin Mary. The Virgin Mary could not have curly hair. On Mother's Day, you wore a red carnation corsage to church if your mother was still alive and a white carnation if your mother was dead, something I could not imagine. Everybody wore a corsage on Easter Sunday. Summer's Vacation Bible School featured Lorna Doone cookies and red Kool-Aid in paper cups. We made lanyards and sang, "Red and yellow, black and white, they are precious in his sight, Jesus loves the little children of the world," though we had never seen any of those other ones. Later, at Youth Fellowship, we made pizza, which we called "pizza pie." We had learned about it on our summer trip to Myrtle Beach. "Ju-ust as I a-am, without one plea," we sang tremulously at revivals, where I always rededicated my life, to my mother's embarrassment. "A nice girl does not rededicate her life at the drop of a hat," she said. We ate three-bean salad and coconut cake at church suppers.

From church we crossed Slate Creek on the swinging bridge to my grandparents' house. A low stone wall separated their front yard from the road in front of it. I remember the paw-paw trees by the gate, the pungent smell of the pods rotting on the ground. I remember looking up from the yard to watch a long, slow line of people carrying a casket up Hibbetts Hill for burial in the town cemetery. "Oh where is my dear brother? Oh where is my dear sister? Day is a-breaking in my soul," they sang.

My grandmother's flower garden, to the right as you faced the porch, was her pride and joy, perhaps the purest expression of herself — for she had an innate artistic bent, a love of beauty and poetry, that had nothing to do with her own biography: an isolated childhood up on Fletchers Ridge, marriage at sixteen, and a lack of formal education. But she never stopped learning. In her later years, she attended summer courses at Lake Junaluska, the Methodist version of Chautauqua. Their house was filled with books and catalogs that she had sent off for. She sent off for some of her plants, too, which bloomed in astonishing variety and profusion. Her garden was like an English garden, its flowers planted in clusters rather than rows. A clematis-covered white lattice arch shaded two benches and a table. In curlicue lettering, an iron placard proclaimed:

The kiss of the sun for pardon,
The song of the birds for mirth,
I am nearer God's heart in a garden
Than anywhere else on earth.

The living room was too dark and too formal for me as a child, with its flowered carpet, velvet armchairs with fancy lace antimacassars on their backs and armrests, the hissing radiator behind them, and the piecrust table with its tiers of dainty knickknacks that I was just dying to break, particularly that white china lady from Japan. My grandmother would sit in a wine velvet wingchair, all dressed up in some kind of filmy voile dress with matching brooch and earrings. She seemed to have hundreds of these sets. When she died, I was astonished to learn that they were all fake. Grandmother — for this is what we were instructed to call her at all times — received a steady stream of visitors. Years later, I learned that my own mother had first developed serious colitis "about the time I realized that I was expected to visit your grandmother every day."

Still, Mama and my Aunt Lois often brought me and my cousins Randy and Melissa over there in the summertime: in my memory, the mothers are always sitting on the porch sewing or stringing beans, watching to see who'll come up the road or stop in for a glass of iced tea. We loved the big swing and the comfortable wicker furniture. The whole family came over on Sunday afternoons. Most of the men were in politics, yellow-dog Democrats always running somebody for office or politicking and agitating about something. They were all big talkers. They'd drink some whiskey out behind the house and after a while they would bet good money on just about anything, even which bird would fly first off the telephone wire, and then everybody would stay out on the porch talking and telling stories until it got dark and we could all see the fairy lights of the Morgan Theater's marquee over in town. I usually fell asleep on somebody's lap, looking at those lights and hearing those stories, told by somebody that loved me, so that my sense of a story is still very personal. Even today, when I'm writing, stories usually come to me in a human voice; often it is the voice of a character, but sometimes it is the voice of the story itself.

My sweet granddaddy, a kind man with a Humpty Dumpty figure in later years, always wore a suit and a hat to town. He loved children, often serving as ringmaster for our circuses in the yard. He also loved the Cincinnati Reds, listening avidly to their games on his giant Philco radio upstairs in the bedroom by the side window.

Grandmother, too, spent many hours before her own side window right below, sitting on the blue tufted sofa with all those little covered buttons. The view from their respective windows symbolized the changes that were taking place in Grundy: originally, my grandparents looked out upon their own vegetable garden, the barn and various outbuildings, the chickens and the cow, the woods and the mountains. Later they could see the narrow-gauge railroad headed for West Virginia, and the growing town just down at the mouth of Slate. In their final years, this view was cut off by the first modern supermarket in Grundy, Jack Smith's Piggly Wiggly, which he built right next to my grandparents' house on the biggest piece of unoccupied flat land in the downtown area, where land was suddenly at a premium. "Progress" triumphs over nature every time, and Grundy was no exception. The late sixties and early seventies were boom times for coal and expansion years for business in Grundy. In those years, of course, nobody even considered the effects of unregulated growth upon the environment.

I went to school right on the other side of my grandparents' house, in the stately old school building that is now the Appalachian School of Law. Here I encountered the terrifying Miss Nellie Hart, with her bright white hair, foghorn voice, and beautiful skin, who could diagram any sentence, even sentences so complex that their diagrams on the board looked like blueprints for a cathedral. It was an ability I aspired to. I loved English, flunked math, and admired my gorgeous and sophisticated French teacher, Anita Cummings, who wore her hair appropriately in a French twist, and gave us quiche lorraine to eat in class. Astonishingly, she was married to the football coach. I liked funny Mrs. Garber, in whose class I made a spectacularly ugly yellow blouse with darts that went the wrong way. I approached my job as football cheerleader with utmost seriousness, practicing endlessly at home, though I never knew the first thing about the game. I could do a cartwheel and land in a split, however. I remember the yellow-tiled cafeteria where I surreptitiously picked up all the Peppermint Pattie wrappers ever touched by the football player I had a crush on, then saved them at home in little silver stacks in my dresser drawer. My girlfriends and I decorated that cafeteria with endless rolls of crepe paper for dances where I slow-danced with the Peppermint Pattie boy to "The Twelfth of Never," our song.

I remember the auditorium where study hall was held and where to everyone's shock I was once crowned Miss Grundy High in spite of my amazingly awful outfit: a red velvet ribbon tied around my neck like a noose; a white strapless dress with about two hundred rows of tacky little net ruffles

marching all the way down its ballerina-
length hoop skirt to my red high heels. This
outfit was my own concept entirely. I won a
rhinestone tiara, a glittery banner proclaim-
ing MISS GRUNDY HIGH, an armful of real
red roses, a steam iron, and a set of white
Samsonite luggage, which my cousins had
to lug home because my date wouldn't give
me a ride. Now, he said, I'd "get too stuck
up." I cried all the way home. My parents
were out playing bridge with the Beinhorns,
and missed the whole thing. "A nice girl
should not win a beauty contest" was my
mother's opinion.

When I think of Mama, she is always at
home, holding forth in her kitchen, and
somebody is always there visiting. Most
often it's Ava McClanahan, who helped her
for years, or one of her many friends or
neighbors: Stella Burke, Margaret Prit-
chard, June Bevins, or Dot Trivett, for
instance. The kitchen is filled with cigarette
smoke, the smell of coffee perking, and
whatever's baking in the oven; often it is
Mama's famous loaf bread. The women lean
forward, over their coffee cups, and lower
their voices. Writing or drawing at my own
little table in the corner, I perk right up.
Now they are going to *really* talk, about
somebody who "has just never been quite

right, bless her heart," or somebody who is "kindly nervous," or somebody else who's "been having trouble down there." *Down there* is a secret place, a foreign country, like Mexico or Nicaragua. I keep on drawing, and don't miss a word. Mama takes the loaf bread out of the oven and gives us all a piece, crusty on the outside and soft on the inside, with butter melting into it. It is the best thing in the world. Country music plays softly on the countertop radio, tuned to our brand-new station, WNRG; in my mind it's always Johnny Cash, singing "Ring of Fire." The Levisa River flows out back, with the railroad on the other side, carrying Norfolk & Western trains loaded with coal.

How I loved the mournful whistle of those trains as they roared past several times a day! Often I ran out and stood there on the riverbank watching them pass, wondering where they were going. On the edge of the riverbank sat the little "writing house" that my daddy built for me and then had to build back again after every flood.

My mother had been raised at Chincoteague Island, on Virginia's far Eastern Shore; she had just graduated from Madison State Teachers College when she met my father at a family wedding; her older sister, Marion, married his uncle John

Dennis, creating some kind of complicated cousins I never could figure out. As a girl, Mama was beautiful and light-hearted — silly, even. She loved to dance. Daddy fell hard. With both the time and the inclination for courting, he would not be put off, arriving in Chincoteague ten days later, only to learn that she had to leave immediately for Harrisburg, Pennsylvania, her first teaching job. She'd scarcely been there a week when — to her surprise — Ernest Smith showed up. He took a room at a local boardinghouse near her own rented quarters, then appeared bright and early each morning to drive her to school, and at the end of every school day, he'd be waiting by the gate with a bunch of roadside flowers and a big grin on his face. This went on for months. The whole town took a fancy to it. By Thanksgiving, he had worn her down; at Christmas vacation, they eloped.

Thus Mama came to Grundy, where she taught home economics, quitting after many years to "raise me." When I was little, she read aloud to me constantly; I believe it is for this reason that I came to love reading so much, for I always heard her voice in my head as I read the words on the page. She never got used to the lack of a horizontal horizon or the fact that the sun couldn't reach our yard before 11 a.m., not enough sun to really grow roses, though her roses looked okay to me. Still, she loved Grundy almost as much as Daddy did, despite the floods that twice destroyed her house and yard. They built it all back each time. My mother loved that house, as she loved her roses and her crafts. My own North Carolina home today is filled with quilts and afghans she made, furniture she refinished, and pictures she decoupaged. "Hell, Gig will decoupage anything — she'll decoupage a chair while you're sitting on it!" neighbor Dr. Burkes was heard to say.

Cowtown was a wonderful neighborhood to grow up in, roaming from house to house with our gang of neighborhood kids — my best friend Martha Sue Owens, Melissa and Randy and other visiting cousins, Rowena and Bill Yates, Cathy and Russ Belcher, Jimmy Bevins and little Terry Trivett, the Boxley boys who came to stay with their grandmother in the summertime. I ate supper at all their houses. Gaynor Owens made the best cream gravy and cornbread, but the Trivetts ate the most exotic things, even foreign things, such as lasagna and chop suey. I learned to swim in their backyard pool.

Martha Sue and I started a neighborhood newspaper named *The Small Review,* which we wrote out laboriously by hand and sold door to door for a nickel. I got in lots of trouble for my editorials, such as "George McGuire Is Too Grumpy," or my opinion that "Mrs. Ruth Boyd is a mean music teacher. She hits your fingers with a pencil and her house smells like meat loaf all the time." We also wrote news items such as the following: "Miss Lee Smith and Miss Martha Sue Owens were taken by car to Bristol, Virginia, to buy school shoes. They got to look at their feet in a machine at Buster Brown and guess what. Their bones are LONG AND GREEN."

We kids formed dozens of clubs, each with its secret handshake and code words. We ran our mountains ridge to ridge — climbing trees and cliffs, playing in caves, swinging on grapevines, catching salamanders, damming up creeks, building lean-tos and lookouts, playing Indians and settlers with our handmade slingshots or the occasional Christmas bow-and-arrow set. Every day after school we'd throw down our books and "head for the hills." We'd stay there until they rang the bell to call us home for supper.

Back in my own yard, I spent a lot of time

sitting under a giant cluster of forsythia bushes, which I called the "dogbushes" because I took an endless series of family dogs under there with me — my Pekingese, Misty, and our boxer, Queenie, come to mind — along with an entire town full of imaginary friends. My two best friends in that dogbush town were Sylvia and Vienna (who was named for my favorite food, the Vienna sausages in the nice flat little cans that I used to take under there with me to eat, along with some of those little cellophane packets of saltine crackers). My friend Vienna was very beautiful, with long, red curly hair. But my friend Sylvia could fly. I also spent hours down by the river, where I had a wading house — the understory of a willow tree — which would find its way into my first novel, *The Last Day the Dogbushes Bloomed.*

I wasn't allowed to play in the Levisa when it ran black with the coal they were washing upriver. But once Martha Sue and I made rafts out of boards tied on to inner tubes and floated down past the Richardson Apartments and under the Hoot Owl Bridge, around the bend at the hospital and under the depot bridge, all the way to town, where we landed in triumph behind the dimestore. Here we were greeted by a sizable crowd including my daddy, alerted by enemy spies. We were quickly returned, dripping wet, to our worried mothers for a spanking.

The Levisa seemed so tame then. Impossible to imagine that this friendly stream could become a raging torrent as it had done in 1937 and then again in the great flood of 1957, when I found a huge catfish flopping down the dimestore stairs into the water-filled toy section. My little dead turtles were floating everywhere, with roses on their shells. After it flooded again in 1977, I came home to help. I remember gathering up floating pieces of the parquet floor in my mother's dining room to keep as building blocks for my little boys back in North Carolina. The muddy water had risen above the countertops in Mama's kitchen. That flood killed three people, devastated 90 percent of the downtown businesses, and caused $100 million in damage countywide. Those were the "twenty-year floods," but there were other floods, too — Grundy had had nine major floods since 1929. Daddy never slept when it rained. He was always out back with his flashlight, "checking the river." He had an enormous steel flood door constructed for the back of the dimestore, which was put into place each time the river started rising.

Daddy finally closed his dimestore in 1992 due to lack of business, despite everyone's pleas that he keep it open. I thought he should, too. Since my mother's death four years earlier, I couldn't imagine what he would do when the dimestore was gone. Its popular lunch counter had made it not only a store but also a gathering place, a landmark. But Daddy was too good a businessman to "run a losing proposition," as he put it. The town population had been declining for years due to the floods and the failing coal industry. There had been 35,000 people in Buchanan County when I was growing up there; the population had fallen to around 28,000. Three thousand people had lived in Grundy alone during the coal boom days of the early 1970s; now there were fewer than a thousand. Unemployment had soared to 16 percent.

Watching my father close his dimestore after forty-seven years in business was one of the saddest things I have ever witnessed; in a way it was fitting that he died on the last day of his going-out-of-business sale. He was eighty-two.

I had been visiting him for a week. Everybody we ever knew had come by the store to pay their respects and buy something, one last thing from the dimestore. All the merchandise had been sold, and some men had come from Bluefield to take away the fixtures, which had been sold, too. They loaded their big truck and drove off. Daddy and I walked out of the store together; he turned off the light and locked the door behind us. I headed back down to my home in North Carolina, and Daddy went back to his house in Cowtown, where he ate the supper which one of the girls had sent home with him, read the paper and the mail, and at some point fell to the kitchen floor, breaking several ribs.

He lay there all night, until Ava McClanahan came by to check on him and fix him some breakfast the next morning. I was back in North Carolina, getting ready for school, when the hospital called. My father was okay, the doctor told me, but they were going to keep him until I got there. I canceled my class, jumped back in the car, and drove that road I knew by heart. I was already planning to bring him back to North Carolina with me for a while, willing or not.

I found Daddy sitting up in bed, ready to go home as soon as they would let him. "I tell you what," he said, handing me a $50 bill. "These nurses have been so sweet to me, I want you to go over to the Piggly Wiggly right now and buy them some candy, about six boxes. Buy some real good candy, like Whitman's Samplers. Go on right now, they're fixing to close." Behind him, one of those nurses smiled indulgently, shaking her head. Everybody knew what Ernest Smith was like. And I knew better than to argue.

I came back with the candy to a very different scene, the hospital room suddenly filled with frantically busy people, Daddy's bed surrounded, the doctor running down the hall toward us, his white coat flying out behind him. "Code Blue in Room 112, Code Blue in Room 112," the loudspeaker kept repeating. "Hit's a hemhorrhage, honey," a nurse said, pulling me back, "from his stomach. Why don't you just stay out here with me." I knew this nurse from high school.

After that, things happened very fast.

And then very slowly, as Grundy turned into a ghost town. An ambitious plan for flood-proofing the town was said to be in the works, but it was a long time coming. One by one the old stores closed. New businesses would not move into the empty buildings of the flood plain; they became increasingly dilapidated. We gave the dime-store to the community, which used it as a much-needed teen center — one of the few downtown buildings in use at all. Traffic slowed, then nearly ceased. Parking places stood empty. The last car dealership closed. With the coal business in decline, Grundy was being kept alive mostly because it was the county seat; government continued in the old stone courthouse across the street.

The new Appalachian School of Law, which opened its doors in 1995, had brought some much-needed new energy and ideas to town despite the fact that it was very difficult for faculty or students to find housing, meals, or merchandise in Grundy — both of the closest towns, Rich-lands, Virginia, and Pikeville, Kentucky, were at least forty-five minutes away.

I drove that twisty road again when I went to say good-bye to old Grundy in 2005, a few weeks before they would blow up the dimestore, which I found already boarded up. I got out my camera and took a picture of it. The dimestore would be demolished along with three dozen other Main Street stores and a score of homes as part of the drastic and daring $177 million Grundy Flood Control and Redevelopment Project, which was finally under way, a historic collaboration among the U.S. Army Corps of Engineers, the Virginia State Department of Transportation, and the Town of Grundy itself, population by then 1,100. They planned to move the railroad and rebuild U.S. 460 on top of a fourteen-foot levee running where the buildings once stood.

"New Grundy" would rise on the newly created moonscape I stood looking at across the deceptively docile Levisa River: thirteen astonishingly flat acres where a mountain had once stood until very recently, when they had blasted away 2.3 million cubic yards of it. The idealistic concept of "raising Grundy" reminded me of that old gospel song, "Lord lift me up and let me stand, by faith on Heaven's table land . . ." Now a 300-foot wall of rock rose straight up behind the flat area, Heaven's table land. I took several pictures of the site. New bridges would connect the "new town" with the older Walnut Street and historic courthouse area, I was told.

"Doesn't it make you sad?" friends asked.

Well, yes and no.

Of course I felt sentimental and nostalgic, but then I hadn't been driving 35 miles one way to buy a shower curtain. And I'm a merchant's daughter, remember. Unfailingly civic, Daddy always loved Grundy, and I knew he would have supported any plan to save it.

But . . . *Walmart?*

Grundy may be one of the only towns in the United States that has ever actually invited Walmart into its downtown area, instead of organizing against it. The moonscape's new "retail center" would be anchored by a unique Walmart Supercenter sitting on the third floor of a 500-space parking building. Shoppers would take their carts up and down on a giant escalator. A three-story Walmart with a giant escalator! Looking at those muddy acres, it sounded like science fiction to me.

The town fathers had made this unilateral decision themselves; no public referendum or vote was ever held. Though some local opponents formed a group called People Allied for Grundy, led by lawyer Mickey McGlothlin, they didn't get anywhere. Some merchants simply pocketed their government payouts and closed forever. Some had already moved out of town. Others were moving up the hollers or into a metal-shell building up the road, known as the Grundy Mall. The town offices and *The Virginia Mountaineer* newspaper were already there, along with Elaine's Boutique and the

Street Law Firm. Terry's Tobacco had gone online.

"We had to look at it for the betterment of all the people," Town Manager Chuck Crabtree told me earnestly at the time. "We had to think, how do you bring the people in? We want to reenergize the town and bring the people back. We want to give them a revitalized town to come to, a place to stop and shop. It's not Walmart that kills your town, it's the location of Walmart. So we're bringing it downtown. Our tax base will skyrocket. It'll be the best thing that's ever happened to this community. I have staked my whole life and my reputation on this."

I took a few more pictures of the empty main street and all the boarded-up stores before I left. I was glad my father had not seen this. He never wanted to retire or leave Grundy, and I could not imagine how he would have spent his days when his beloved dimestore was gone.

Now, I realized, his kind of business could be gone forever.

May 2012: I haven't been back home in a couple of years. For one thing, I don't have any relatives living here now; I go to Abingdon to visit most of them. But today I'm heading up that twisty Route 460 toward Grundy where I will present a program commemorating the fiftienth anniversary of the Buchanan County Public Library; my mother was on its founding board. And also — I have to admit — I am very curious to take a look at that three-story Walmart, which has just opened (finally!) with much fanfare.

The muddy moonscape with its forlorn little sign reading WALMART COMING SOON stood empty for so many years that many people ceased believing in it altogether. Instead of Walmart, the recession came, then deepened. Funding slowed down. Everything stalled. That optimistic town manager disappeared. A huge boulder rolled down off a mountaintop to crush the area's one remaining movie theater, so — outside of school activities — there'd been absolutely nothing for teenagers to do. They couldn't even make out up at the coke ovens — they'd closed, too. An entire generation of children had grown up in the town of Grundy, which was no town at all — there was simply nothing there.

But this is a gorgeous Appalachian spring day, with redbud and sarvis and dogwood blooming on the pale green mountainsides and a deep blue sky arching overhead.

Speaking of those mountainsides, they look different, I suddenly realize as I drive along. The Beatrice mine tower is gone, along with the other old tipples and trolleys. I remember the slag heaps often smoking near the tops of the mountains, and the little frame houses clustered on the steep slopes below — where are they? And what about the old company towns, gone too? Where is Raven? I wonder as I leave Richlands. Where is Red Jacket? And what was the name of that big company town with the large houses over in the bottom by the river? Deel! What has happened to Deel? To Vansant? All the outlying communities seem to have disappeared as I approach Grundy. Signs read WE BUY GOLD AND SILVER now, instead of WE BUY GINSENG. Sleek metal coal trucks have replaced the old self-owned and decorated trucks with personal signs like DON'T LAUGH, IT'S PAID FOR and names like "Tennessee Stud." The coal company offices have disappeared or been turned into "energy" companies, i.e., gas, with Consol Energy predominating. I note several locations. The coke ovens are burning again, but now run by SUNCOKE ENERGY, JEWELL OPERATIONS, a sign proclaims. The former bowling alley is a well-drilling business. Big pipes for pipelines lie in stacks everywhere. At

Oakwood, the old Garden High School has become the new Appalachian College of Pharmacy, and there's the impressive Twin Valley Middle School, too.

The closer I get to Grundy, the heavier the traffic is; we crawl along bumper to bumper on the newly widened and raised Rt. 460, which is still under construction. Huge machines lift red dirt and rocks into huge trucks; dust fills the air. My old neighborhood, Cowtown, looks totally shocking. Only my own house has not been raised up to the level of the new highway (it can't be, I later learn, due to its frame construction). It looks fragile and dingy, so much older and smaller and lower than the other houses, each of them sitting up on its own divot of earth, like toy houses set up on stands for display. At the end of the driveway behind "my" house, I catch sight of the last incarnation of my writing house, poised on the riverbank with a glint of the river behind. The mountainside across 460 where we used to run so wild and free has been sheared off, a red wound with rock at the top.

Finally the traffic crawls around the bend of the Levisa to Hoot Owl Holler, filled with personal meaning for me as the setting for my novel *Oral History.* A new green road sign reading POPLAR GAP PARK, FOURTEEN MILES points across the Levisa River Bridge and up the mountain, where a large mesa created by mountaintop removal mining has now — in a brilliant stroke of public relations — been turned into a public park. It boasts picnic facilities, athletic fields, playgrounds, tennis courts, and the state-of-the-art Consol Energy Stage for large events such as concerts. Sunsets viewed from atop Poplar Gap are said to be spectacular. Operated by the county, the park was much needed and is heavily used for everything from the "Race for the Cure Relay" to fireworks and horse shows. I have been reading about it in *The Virginia Mountaineer,* to which I have always subscribed.

Slowly I pass the attractive Comfort Inn at the bend of the river, a new Italian restaurant, and the 24-hour Waffle Shop. I don't check into the Comfort Inn yet, afraid that with all this traffic, I won't have time to see "the new Grundy" before my program begins at the library. There's only the one road, route 460, to get anyplace. Finally the traffic inches down the hill and Walmart comes into view, a behemoth on its big flat lot. It is enormous! Any letter on its sign WALMART is taller than any of the tractor-trailer trucks bringing it merchandise. It looks more like a huge alien spacecraft than like a building. Traffic flows across its bridges, a steady stream in and out of it, back and forth from town, which is still a construction site, though the existing stores and buildings on Maple Street and the courthouse area are busy. The sidewalks are thronged with people, all kinds of people! I don't see one single person that I know. Finally I find a parking place in the public lot where the old stone Methodist Church once stood. I have to grin as I remember our singing "red and yellow, black and white, they are precious in his sight" — Grundy actually has some diversity now.

"There's not another town in the nation that has undergone this much change this fast," my friend Debbie Raines, still the senior high school English teacher, has told me. "It is a totally unique situation. You're still here, but your town is gone . . . and when you go to the grocery store now, you see all these strangers," referring not only to the folks who have come in with Walmart but to the influx of new people who have moved in with the Appalachian School of Law and the University of Appalachia's School of Pharmacy. A new optometry school is planned. Whoever would have thought of Grundy as a college town? The college students are involved in community service projects everywhere, from teaching kids soccer to weatherproofing houses. Newcomers are scrambling to find anyplace at all to live; apartments are going up all over the place. "Psychologically, it's hard to undergo this much change," Debbie said. "So many different ideas are being brought into this community, our whole small-town value system is changing. It's very threatening to our older, more conservative residents. It makes it easier to leave here now."

But I have to admit, I enjoy the latte I buy at the new coffee shop, Perks, which has opened up in my Aunt Bess and Uncle Clyde's old house — that same house where the cow fell through the roof. I take a picture of this coffee shop, to send to my cousin Randy in Denver.

I have to hurry in order to make my program. I find myself gritting my teeth as I cross the Levisa and follow the signs into the mammoth three-story Walmart which looks even bigger, if possible, close up. Its scale is more suited to Charlotte, or New York. I am directed up to the second parking level, which is nearly full. I park and just sit in the car for a minute, not sure whether I can do this or not.

Finally I get out and walk over to ride the

giant up escalator, astonished by the people with full carts riding the down escalator. I couldn't even image how this would work, yet it works fine.

There's an open area at the top with a huge picture window and a panoramic view of the town. I don't even get a good look before I am greeted by the Greeter, a large, friendly older fellow named Charles Clevinger, with local ties, as evidenced by his accent and his name. Whoever picked him out knew what they were doing. His father grew up here, and he spent summers here with his grandparents. He asks me if I remember the Rexall and the dimestore. Charles Clevinger refers to Walmart complex as the "Grundy Town Center," proudly enumerating the other stores that are already open on the ground floor: Unique Nails; a sporting goods store; Subway; GameStop; and Factory Connection, a clothing store. Not a single one is local; not a single one has moved over from "old Grundy." I hadn't even noticed a smaller two-story building under construction at Walmart's base; Clevinger points it out and tells me that it will house a beauty college and salon, plus several offices, with a coal company on top. A free-standing Taco Bell will occupy a grassy plot behind. Another spot is being saved for a "sit-down, fine-dining" restaurant, such as Applebee's (though actually the town fathers just ran Applebee's off because they serve mixed drinks.)

I'm thinking I could use a mixed drink myself, or several. Maybe I'll buy some wine.

I ask where it is and then start up a brightly lit, well-stocked aisle in the grocery section, with its bins of specials in the middle — exactly like every aisle in every Walmart in the world. But before I get to the wine I run into some former Cowtown neighbors who have already got their cart all loaded up. "Oh hey, Lee," she says, "When did you get in?" and continues without missing a beat, "Isn't this Walmart just wonderful? I tell you, it has changed our lives." Her husband stands grinning behind her.

I manage to nod but turn on my heel without a word. No I can't do this, I realize. I cannot. I rush back out to the open escalator area where smiling Charles Clevinger has latched onto some other visitor, thank God, so that I have a chance to walk over to the huge wraparound picture window and get a good look at Grundy from this high vantage point: there's the flat moonscape area below us, crisscrossed by its tiny access roads with their tiny colorful cars; the busy bridges; the tame little river that started it all, improbably, running between its high ringwalls; route 460, where the old stores used to be. Across the eternal traffic jam, I can see Maple Street, the post office, the Appalachian School of Law, the Masonic Lodge — everything up to the bend of Slate Creek. The old stone courthouse with its high clock tower, once the largest and handsomest building in the county, has shrunk to insignificance. I take another picture. Later, I will blow it up. Viewed from the top floor of Walmart, the entire town looks like a toy town, like the train set Daddy always kept set up in the dimestore's basement toy section.

Suddenly I remember a long-ago spring in Grundy, one Sunday afternoon several weeks before Easter. Daddy had taken me down to the dimestore with him to help make the Easter baskets, which didn't come premade and packaged in those days. Many of the girls who worked in the store were there, too, and lots of little chocolate rabbits, and lots of candy Easter eggs. The women formed into an informal assembly line, laughing and gossiping among themselves. They were drinking coffee, wearing slacks and tennis shoes. It was almost a party atmosphere. As a "helper," I didn't last long. I stuffed myself with marshmallow chickens and then crawled into a big box of cellophane straw, where I promptly fell asleep while the straw shifted and settled around me, eventually covering me entirely, so nobody could find me when it was time to go.

"Lee!" I heard my daddy calling. "Lee!" The overhead fluorescent lights in the dime-store glowed down pink through the cellophane straw. It was the most beautiful thing I have ever seen. "Lee!" they called. I knew I'd have to answer soon, but I held that moment as long as I could, safe and secure in that bright pink world, listening to my father call my name.

Recipe Box

My mother's recipe box sits on the window-sill in our North Carolina kitchen where my eye falls on it twenty, maybe thirty times a day. I will never move it. An anachronism in my own modern kitchen, the battered box contains my mother's whole life story, in a way, with all its places and phases, all her hopes and the accommodations she made in the name of love, as I have done, as we all do. I can read it like a novel — for in fact, our recipes tell us everything about us: where we live, what we value, how we spend our time. Mama's recipe box is an odd green-gold in color. She "antiqued" it, then decoupaged it with domestic decals of the fifties: one depicts a rolling pin, a flour sifter, a vase of daisies, and a cheerful, curly-headed mom wearing a red bead necklace; another shows a skillet, a milk bottle, a syrup pitcher, three eggs, and a grinning dad in an apron.

Oh, who are these people? My father never touched a spatula in his life. My mother suffered from "bad nerves," also "nervous stomach." She lived mostly on milk toast herself, yet she never failed to produce a nutritious supper for my father and me, including all the food groups, for she had long been a home economics teacher. Our perfect supper was ready every night at six thirty, the time a family ought to eat, in Mama's opinion, though my workaholic daddy never got home from the dimestore until eight or nine at the earliest, despite his best intentions. Somewhere in that two-hour stretch, I would have been allowed to eat alone, reading a book — my favorite thing in the world. My mother would have had her milk toast. And when my father finally had his solitary supper, warmed to an unrecognizable crisp in the oven, he never failed to pronounce it "absolutely delicious — the best thing I've ever put in my mouth!" My mother never failed to believe him, to give him her beautiful, tremulous smile, wearing the Fire and Ice lipstick she'd hurriedly applied when she heard his car in the driveway. Well, they loved each other — two sweet, fragile people who carefully bore this great love like a large glass object, incredibly delicate, along life's path.

My mother's father had died when she was only three, leaving a pile of debt and six children for my grandmother to raise alone on Chincoteague Island. Grandma Annie Marshall turned their big old Victorian home into a boardinghouse, and it was here in the boardinghouse kitchen that my mother had learned to cook. Her recipe box holds sixteen different recipes for oysters, including Oyster Stew, Oyster Fritters, Oyster Pie, Scalloped Oysters, and the biblical-sounding Balaam's Oysters. Clams are prepared "every whichaway," as she would have put it. There's also Planked Shad, Cooter Pie, and Pine Bark Stew. Mr. Hop Biddle's Hush Puppies bear the notation, "tossed to the hounds around the campfire to keep them quiet." Mama notes that the favorite breakfast at the boardinghouse was fried fish, cornmeal cakes, and "plenty of hot coffee." These cornmeal cakes remained her specialty from the time she was a little girl, barely able to reach the stove, until her death eighty-four years later in the mountains so far from her island home. I imagine her as a child, biting her bottom lip in concentration and wiping perspiration off her pretty little face as she flips those cornmeal cakes on the hot griddle. Later, I see her walking miles across the ice in winter, back to college on the mainland.

Her lofty aspirations were reflected in her recipes: Lady Baltimore Cake came from Cousin Nellie, who had "married well"; the hopeful Plantation Plum Pudding and Soiree Punch had both been contributed by my Aunt Gay-Gay in Birmingham, Alabama, the very epitome of something Mama had desperately wanted to attain. She wanted me to attain it, too, sending me down to Alabama every summer for Lady Lessons. The Asparagus Souffle recipe came from my elegant Aunt Millie, who had married a Northern steel executive who actually cooked dinner for us himself, wearing an apron. He produced a roast beef that was bright red in the middle; at first I was embarrassed for him, but then it turned out he'd meant to do it that way all along; he thought red meat was good, apparently, and enjoyed wearing the apron.

Here are Mama's bridge club recipes, filed all together. My first idea of an elegant meal came from this bridge club, whose members met every Thursday at noon for lunch and bridge, rotating houses, for years and years until its members began to die or move to

Florida. I can see Mama now, greeting her friends at the door in her favorite black-and-white polka-dot dress. I sat on the top stair to watch them arrive. I loved the cut flowers, the silver, and the pink cloths on the tables, though it was clear to me even then that the way these ladies were was a way I'd never be.

The food my mama gave the bridge club was wonderful. They feasted upon molded pink salad that melted on the tongue (back then I thought all salads were Jell-O salads); something called Chicken Crunch (cut-up chicken, mushroom soup, celery, water chestnuts, Chinese noodles); and Lime Angel Cloud. All the bridge lunch recipes required mushroom soup, Jell-O, Dream Whip, or pecans.

But the recipes Mama actually used most — these soft, weathered index cards covered with thumbprints and spatters — reflect her deep involvement with her husband's family and their Appalachian community: Venison Stew, Gaynor Owens' Soup Beans, Ava McClanahan's Apple Stack Cake, my grandmother's Methodist Church Supper Salad, and my favorite, Fid's Funeral Meat Loaf. A ham was also good in case of death, glazed with brown sugar and Coca-Cola. Mama's recipe for Salvation Cake had a

Bible verse listed beside each ingredient (the almonds came from Genesis 43:11), and the only instruction given for baking was the cryptic Proverbs 23:14. Fat content was never a consideration. Biscuits called for lard, and Chocolate Velvet Cake required one cup of mayonnaise. A hearty beef and cheese casserole was named Husband's Delight.

I, too, have written out my life in recipes. As a young bride, I had eleven dessert recipes featuring Cool Whip as the main ingredient. Then came the hibachi and fondue period, then the quiche and crepes phase, then pasta, and now it's these salsa years. Just this past Christmas, I made cranberry salsa for everybody. My mother would not have touched salsa — let alone sushi! — with a ten-foot pole. One time when we all went out for bagels in Chapel Hill, she said, "This may taste good to someone who has never eaten a biscuit." Another thing she used to say is, "No matter what is wrong with you, a sausage biscuit will make you feel a whole lot better." I agree, though I have somehow ended up with a wonderful husband who eats rare meat, wears an apron himself upon occasion, and makes a terrific risotto. We share the cooking. I seldom have time to bake these days, but sometimes I still make Mama's Famous Loaf Bread upon occasion, simply because the smell of it baking takes me straight back to that warm kitchen where somebody was always visiting. I can still hear my mother's voice, punctuated by her infectious laugh, her conspiratorial "Now promise me you won't tell a soul . . ."

On impulse I reach for Mama's recipe box and take out one of the most wrinkled and smudged, Pimento Cheese, everybody's favorite, thinking as always that I really ought to get these recipes into the computer, or at least copy them before they disintegrate completely. On this card, Mama underlined Durkee's Dressing, followed by a parenthesis: "(The secret ingredient!)" Though I would never consider leaving Durkee's Dressing out, I don't really believe it is the secret ingredient. The secret ingredient is love.

KINDLY NERVOUS

"Kindly nervous" was my father's euphemistic term for the immense anguish he suffered periodically from bipolar illness, or "manic depression," as it was then called. Unfortunately for him, the manic phase was no fun — no wild sprees, no elation — instead, he just worked harder than ever at the dimestore, where he did everything, anyway. When Daddy's mania increased to the point where he could no longer sleep, sometimes I accompanied him down to the store, sleeping on a pallet under his desk while he worked all night long, then going out with him into the chilly dawn to a greasy spoon for breakfast. How I loved those breakfasts! I got to have my scrambled eggs and my own big white china cup of sweet, milky coffee alongside early-morning truckers and the miners who'd just worked the graveyard shift, their eyes rimmed with coal dust like raccoons.

But these weeks of intense activity led to scarier behavior as he became increasingly jumpy and erratic. I remember one time when Daddy had taken me to the golf course in nearby Tazewell. I tossed him a putter when he wasn't expecting it, then was terrified when he screamed and fell down flat, writhing in tears on the putting green. Before long would come the inevitable downward spiral. He'd talk less and less, stay in bed more and more, finally be unable to go to the dimestore at all.

Then my Uncle Curt or my cousin Jack or another family member would come and drive him away to the hospital — sometimes the state mental hospital over in Marion, Virginia, sometimes an out-of-state facility. My father was lucky because he was in business with several men in his family who were willing to oversee the dimestore and his other responsibilities whenever he got "kindly nervous" and had to "go off" someplace to get treatment, since there was no mental health care — none at all — available in Buchanan County.

After I moved to North Carolina, we brought him down to Duke Hospital in Durham, very near us in Chapel Hill. I remember visiting him there once, in his third-floor room of the mental hospital wing, which overlooked the famous Duke Gardens, then in full bloom. He was not looking out at the gardens, though. Instead, I found him staring at a sheet of paper with something drawn on it.

"What's that?" I asked.

He replied that his doctor had left paper and pencil for him to draw a picture of a man doing something he enjoyed.

I looked at the stick figure. The man's hands hung straight down from his tiny hunched shoulders; his legs were straight parallel lines, up and down; his round head had no face, no features at all. None.

"So what's he doing?" I asked.

"Nothing," my father said.

In the fierce grip of severe depression, this popular, active, civic man — a great story-teller, a famous yellow-dog Democrat, a man who never knew a stranger — could not imagine doing anything . . . not one thing in the entire world that he might enjoy.

But the worst part was that he was always so horribly embarrassed about this illness, never understanding that it *was* an illness, but regarding it rather as a weakness, a failure of character, which made him feel even worse. "I can't believe I've gone and done this again," he'd say. "I'm just so ashamed of myself."

I will never forget what a breakthrough it was for him when I gave him William Styron's just-published book *Darkness Visible,* a memoir of Styron's own depression. My dad respected William Styron; he had read *The Confessions of Nat Turner,* he had heard Styron speak at a literary festival at my college. Daddy read *Darkness Visible* in one sitting.

"I can't believe it!" he said. "I can't believe he would tell these things!"

Styron had laid it on the line:

Depression afflicts millions directly, and millions more who are relatives or friends of victims . . . as assertively democratic as a Norman Rockwell poster, it strikes indiscriminately at all ages, races, creeds, and classes . . . The pain of severe depression is quite unimaginable to those who have not suffered it, and it kills in many instances because its anguish can no longer be borne. The prevention of many suicides will continue to be hindered until there is a general awareness of the nature of this pain.

My mother, too, was hospitalized for depression and anxiety several times, mainly at Sheppard Pratt in Baltimore, but also at the University of Virginia Hospital in Char-lottesville. She often attributed those bouts to "living with your father" — and undoubtedly there was some truth to this — but the fact is that she came from a "kindly nervous" family herself.

Her father and a brother both committed suicide; another brother, my Uncle Tick, was a schizophrenic who lived at home with my grandmother, then in the VA Hospital. An older cousin, Katherine, had died at the state mental institution in Staunton, Virginia, where she had been hospitalized because she was "over-sexed." (I never even knew this cousin had existed until many, many years later.) But I knew that Mama's beloved niece Andre was also in and out of the hospital in Washington frequently, suffering from schizophrenia. She died alone, too young, in her own apartment.

No wonder Mama and her sisters frequently took to their beds — just lying down wherever they lived, it seemed to me — whenever life got to be too much for them. Would I just lie down, too, I worried, when the time came? I was a whirlwind of energy, to counter this possibility.

When Mama got sick, she was physically sick, too — with stomach problems, insomnia, migraine headaches, and other undiagnosed pain. She ate very little and got very thin, subsisting on things she thought she could tolerate, such as rice, oatmeal, milk toast, and cream of wheat, which were all supposed to be easy on the stomach. In my memory, my mother's food was all white. She had a special daybed downstairs next to the kitchen, where she'd stay more and more. Ava McClanahan came every day to take care of Mama and the house. Daddy did all the shopping. This could go on for a long time. Sometimes Mama and I would be taken up to stay with my Aunt Millie and Uncle Bob in Maryland for a while. Other times, she went into the hospital.

This is my story, then, but it is not a sob story. Whenever either of my parents was gone, everybody — our relatives, neighbors, and friends — pitched in to help take care of me, bringing food over, driving me to Girl Scouts or school clubs or whatever else came up. People loved my parents, and in a mountain family and a small, isolated town like ours, that's just how people were. In times of trouble, they helped each other out. Also, I had my intense reading, and my writing, and usually a dog.

All their lives, my parents were kind, well-meaning people — heartbreakingly sweet. They did not understand their problems or what caused them. It is possible that they did not even understand their problems as illnesses, but they did not blame each other for them. Nor did they involve me in any way, other than trying to make sure that I would "get out" of whatever it was that they were "in" — Grundy, it often seemed to me, and I fought against this. I loved Grundy. But they were adamant, sending me away to summer camps and then to preparatory school, where they felt I would have "more advantages." Or maybe I was just too much for them, too lively, this child who came along so late in their lives.

Only once, the year I was thirteen, did my parents' hospitalizations coincide, when my father was at Silver Hill in Connecticut while my mother was at the University of Virginia Hospital in Charlottesville, and so I was sent to live with my Aunt Millie in Maryland. She enrolled me in a nearby "progressive, experimental" private school named Glenelg Country Day, where a friend of hers taught English. With thirty or forty students at most, Glenelg was situated in a grand old house — a mansion, I thought at the time — surrounded by rolling fields. We called our teachers by their first names; meditated each morning; memorized a lot of poetry; and played a game I had never even seen before, called field hockey, with weird sticks. Everybody said I talked funny, but I thought they talked funny, too. I made some new friends and got to ride their horses, which I loved.

While I was there, I received an invitation from my mother's psychiatrist, a Dr. Stevenson, who proposed to take me out to lunch the next time I took the train down to visit my mother. In retrospect, this luncheon appears to me highly unusual, and I am surprised that my over-anxious Aunt Millie even allowed it. She customarily arranged for me to spend the night in Charlottesville with an old family friend whenever I went to visit Mama in the hospital, though neither the family friend nor my Aunt Millie had been invited to lunch. But Dr. Ian Stevenson was a well-known and respected physician, the new head of the Department of Psychiatry at the University of Virginia. He specialized in cases of psychosomatic illness — which must have included my mother.

Later, Dr. Stevenson would become famous for his interest in parapsychology, especially reincarnation. He thought that the concept of reincarnation might supplement what we know about heredity and environment in helping to understand

81

aspects of behavior and development. He was especially interested in *Children Who Remember Previous Lives,* the title of a book he would publish in 1987. But if Dr. Stevenson had any curiosity about my own past lives, he kept mum about it. Our luncheon remains one of the most memorable occasions of my youth.

He met me at the train station. He was a tall, angular man holding a pink rose, which he presented to me as he bowed. He was all dressed up in a suit and a vest and a tie. I was all dressed up, too, in my pleated plaid skirt and navy blue jacket and Add-A-Pearl necklace. Dr. Stevenson put me and my little bag into his big, shiny car and took me to a fancy restaurant up on a hill, with linen tablecloths. He told me to order anything I wanted from the largest menu I had ever seen. I chose lemonade and a club sandwich, which arrived in four fat triangles with a little flag stuck into each one, plus curly potato chips and pickles. I ate every bite.

Dr. Stevenson said that he had heard a lot about me from my mother, and he had wanted to meet me because he thought that I must be an interesting little girl. He asked me a lot of questions about my new school, and what books I liked to read, listening very carefully to my answers. I had just read *Jane Eyre* twice, cover to cover. Dr. Stevenson nodded as if this were the very thing to do. I loved poetry, I told him. Then I recited the poem we had just learned, " 'Breathes there the man, with soul so dead, Who never to himself hath said, This is my own, my native land?' " I took a deep breath and followed that one up with "Annabel Lee" in its entirety. Nobody could have stopped me. "It sounds like a wonderful school," Dr. Stevenson said, smiling.

Then Dr. Stevenson leaned forward intently and said, "Lee, since your parents are both ill, I wonder if you have ever worried about getting sick as well."

"You mean, if I am going to go crazy, too," I blurted out.

"Yes," he said, "if you are going to go crazy, too."

I stared across the table at him. How did he *know*? because that was exactly what I thought about, of course, all the time.

"Yes!" I said.

"Well, I am a very good doctor," he said, "and you seem to me to be a very nice, normal little girl, and I am here to tell you that you can stop worrying about this right now. So you can just relax, and read a lot more books, and grow up. You will be fine."

I sank back in my chair.

"Now," he said, "would you like some dessert?"

"Yes," I said.

The waitress brought the giant menus back.

I ordered Baked Alaska, which I had never heard of, and was astonished when it arrived in flames. The waitress held it out at arms' length, then set it down right in front of me. It looked like a big fiery cake. "Oh no!" I cried, scooting my chair back. Everybody in the restaurant was pointing and laughing at me. Even Dr. Stevenson was laughing.

"You're supposed to blow it out," the waitress said.

I tried, but the more I blew, the higher the flames went, and the more they jumped around. I felt like I was at some weird birthday party where everything had gone horribly wrong. "I can't," I said finally. Dr. Stevenson stood up, his expression changing to concern. Out of the corner of my eye, I could see waitresses and kitchen staff converging upon our table. I could feel the heat on my face. I blew and blew, but the Baked Alaska would not go out.

LADY LESSONS

When I was a little girl, my mother drove me all the way across the entire state of Virginia to visit my Grandmother Marshall and my Aunt Millie and Millie's best friend, Bobbie, in Baltimore. This annual trip was part of my mother's grand plan; she was raising me to be a lady. The drive took two days with my mother at the wheel. We broke our trip by staying with Mama's friend Frances at Port Republic in the Valley of Virginia. My mother always said "the Valley of Virginia" in a certain way, with a certain tilt of the head. Frances's family lived in a huge house, a plantation really, with a white-columned portico and a long view out over the golden, rolling land.

These summer journeys symbolized the difference between my parents. Mama was a real lady from the Eastern Shore of Virginia, where her father had been in the oyster business. He was a high roller and harness racer. A picture of him hung in our sitting room: a handsome man with a big mustache, dressed to the nines, standing tall and straddle-legged atop what appears to be a small mountain of oyster shells. He carries a silver-headed cane; he wears a dark broad-brimmed hat; the drooping gold chain of his watch hangs down from his pocket. A man of consequence, of style. The family lived in a substantial square white house with sidewalk and street in front, green lawn sloping down to the Chesapeake Bay behind. In the backyard stood the summer kitchen, the smokehouse, the icehouse, the cistern for catching rainwater, the little train my grandfather had constructed mostly for his children and his own amusement, which carried loads of mainland goods and groceries from dock to house. (In those days before the Bay Bridge was built, the only way to the mainland was by boat. In winter, Mama said, she had to "walk the ice" to get back to Madison Teachers College after her Christmas vacation.)

My mother was named Virginia Elizabeth Marshall, called "Gig," and she was, I have to say, an absolutely adorable young woman. Early photographs show a mop of unruly dark curls, huge blue eyes, a carefree smile, and deep, mischievous dimples. Her flapper-style looks exactly fit the prevailing beauty ideal of the day. No wonder my father fell madly in love with her at first sight and brought her home to Grundy, to those peaks and hollers where she would feel a little bit out of place forever, even though she adored him. And he adored her. In fact, as a child I was horribly embarrassed by the Technicolor-movie-style quality of my parents' passionate marriage.

I remember one bright summer Sunday when my cousins gave me a ride back from Sunday school — for some reason, my parents had stayed at home. I ran down our flagstone walk, burst into the house, and yelled, "Hello! I'm back!" but the sunlit living room seemed strangely empty. I went into the kitchen, following my nose. I smelled bacon and coffee. Sure enough, their breakfast plates were still on the table. This was not at all like Mama, the best housekeeper in the world. Maybe they had been kidnapped by aliens, I thought, which happened frequently in the pages of the *National Enquirer,* which Mama and I loved.

"Mama?" I called. "Daddy?"

Nothing.

Yet a thin blue haze of their cigarette smoke still hung in the air. "Mama?" I looked out on the back porch and into the backyard where her beloved roses bloomed. Nobody. "Daddy!" I yelled.

"Why, honey, what's the matter?" Suddenly they were there. Mama bent down to kiss me, with Daddy right behind her. Yet something was wrong with them, I could tell. Mama's pansy-sprigged blouse was buttoned up wrong, her red lipstick slapped on a little askew, while Daddy just stood there in the doorway as if in a trance, smiling at Mama, not at me — not at me, who had been so worried, so scared! The next day, at school, I told everybody I was an orphan. ("No you're not," my patient teacher said.)

A year or so later, when I was sick, I woke up suddenly in the middle of the night with my throat on fire. I headed for their bedroom, knowing that Mama would get up and give me an aspirin and put Mentholatum on my chest and a cold washcloth on my forehead, and maybe even dose me up with some of her surefire cough medicine — a spoonful of honey and bourbon. But their bedroom door stood ajar, the lamp burning on the bedside table. The chenille bedspread lay undisturbed on their carefully made bed — clearly, it had not been slept in. I checked the clock: 1:15. I padded down the hall and paused at the narrow back staircase where suddenly I heard music. I crept downstairs, with Nancy Drew–like stealth, until I could see them — dancing barefoot in the kitchen! How gross, I thought; they were old. I plopped down on the step in disgust.

My parents were jitterbugging wildly to the Louisiana rhythm of Hank Williams singing, "Jambalaya and a crawfish pie and filé gumbo . . . Son of a gun, we'll have big fun on the bayou!" Daddy would pull her to him, then swing her around. Her red skirt flew out on the turns. They were wonderful dancers. Then the record changed to that sad whippoorwill song and Daddy pulled her close and they were dancing cheek to cheek, dipping and gliding around the kitchen floor. Now he held her in a tight embrace. "The moon just went behind the clouds . . . I'm so lonesome I could cry," Hank Williams's mournful voice floated up the stairs. I started crying myself. I snuck back to bed where I lay in quivering pain and silence for a long time. Maybe I'm having a nervous breakdown, I thought, like Jane Eyre when they put her in the Red Room.

Mama was a very popular teacher at the high school; even boys signed up for her home economics classes. Years later, at her funeral, one man stood up and said that he had "gone to school to Miss Gig," and announced that she was "real nice, for a foreigner" — this despite the fact that she had been married to my father and had lived in Grundy for over fifty years.

I was not a foreigner. I was my daddy's girl through and through, a mountain girl, a born tomboy who loved Grundy and everything about it, especially in the summertime when I was part of a wild gang of neighborhood children who roamed from house to house, ran the mountains as we pleased, and generally enjoyed a degree of freedom that it is almost impossible now to imagine. Summer spread out all around us like another country, ours to plunder and explore. Aside from chores and one week of compulsory Bible School (red Kool-Aid, Lorna Doone cookies, lanyards) we were on our own. We had no day camps, no lessons, no car pools. We played roll-to-bat, kickball, Red Rover, dodge ball, Pretty Girl Station, tag, statues, hidey-go-seek. I was utterly fearless in those days; I could run like the wind, and hit like a boy.

Sometimes I wrote plays, which we'd all put on in the breezeway at Martha's house, using a quilt on a clothesline as the curtain. Some of the more fundamentalist parents got very upset, I remember, at one particular production named *The Drunken Saloon* that ended with all of us, cowboys and cowgirls alike, pretending to be passed out cold on the concrete floor.

Inspired by Nancy Drew, my cousins and I concocted an elaborate ongoing plot concerning a mystery train that ran around the tops of the mountains and an evil group of invisible beings who were inhabiting the bodies of townspeople we didn't like. We spied on these people and kept official notebooks filled with our clues and "findings," written in code.

One time my cousin Randy and I pushed an old oil drum off its rusty perch at an abandoned tipple and watched with great satisfaction as it crashed down the mountainside, gathering speed, then crossed the road and slammed into a filling station, where luckily nobody was hurt.

Sometimes my daddy took me up on Compton Mountain to ride the mine ponies, blind from their years underground. Often I'd go to town with him and work in the dimestore. But mostly summer consisted of roaming the mountains with the other kids — "like little wild animals," Mama said in disgust — building forts, waging wars, and playing make-believe games of every description. Sometimes we'd flatten out cardboard boxes and take them up to the tree line where we'd sit on them, holding the front up to form a kind of sled, and slide down the long sage-grass hillside to the road, then trudge back up again. After a few rides, the flattened grass would be really slick. We would do this all afternoon.

Despite my inclinations, my mother kept at it, trying her best to raise me to be a lady. She sent me to visit my lovely Aunt Gay-Gay in Birmingham, Alabama, every summer for two weeks of honest-to-God Lady Lessons. Here I'd learn how to wear white gloves, sit up straight, and walk in little Cuban heels. I'd learn proper table manners, which would then be tested by fancy lunches at "The Club" on top of Shades Mountain. I'd learn the rules: "A lady does not point. A lady eats before the party. A lady never lets a silence fall. A lady always wears clean underwear in case she is in a wreck. A lady does not sit *like that*!"

I didn't want to be a lady, of course; I wanted to be a boy.

Even though our visits to Baltimore were a part of Mama's grand design, I enjoyed them. I loved Baltimore itself, with its clanging streetcars, funny-looking people, lamp-lights, pigeons, and ice cream cones. I loved to sit out on the marble stoop after dinner and watch the teeming parade of street life; I always had a nickel in my pocket just in case the organ-grinder came by with his monkey. This monkey wore a little green coat with brass buttons. I loved my sweet, refined grandmother in her dim, high-ceilinged row house with lace at the windows and doilies on the tables. She always referred to my late grandfather with great respect, often making such statements as "Mr. Marshall raised trotters, you know" or "Mr. Marshall loved oysters in any form." This deference enchanted me.

Much, much later, I was astonished to learn that Mr. Marshall had, in fact, hanged himself when my mother was five years old and Millie was only three, leaving my grandmother alone with a half a dozen young children to raise. She'd turned their house into a boardinghouse; later, she'd sold it and followed Millie to Baltimore, where everybody's favorite cousin, Nellie, had made a brilliant marriage and lived in style, with — of all things — a butler! Family legend tells that I'd been instructed again and again how to behave in the presence of this butler before I was first presented to him; then I'd disgraced everyone by rolling on the floor.

In my own memory, my elegant Aunt Millie was always referred to as an "executive secretary," a phrase that fascinated me, as there was no such thing in Grundy. I loved my Aunt Mille, but I absolutely worshipped her friend Bobbie, the most glamorous woman I'd ever seen.

In hushed tones, my mother informed me that Bobbie was a divorcee; back home, there was no such thing as that, either. Bobbie was said to be a crackerjack stenographer. She was a tall woman with stylishly cut suits featuring big shoulders and tiny waists. She wore stiletto heels, stockings with black seams up the back, and red lipstick. She had the long, lovely legs of a fashion model, and — best of all — lacquered hair, which she wore up, in a jaunty French twist. It looked like patent leather.

Despite these attributes, Bobbie was reputed to be "unlucky in love," an expression that never failed to send a great dark thrill shooting through me. During our visits, Mama and Millie and Bobbie always sat up late and giggled and blew smoke rings and drank Black Russians, and talked about men. I'd fall asleep to the muffled sound of their squeals and laughter.

My grandmother died when I was about ten. This time, our long trip was a sad one. My father drove, my mother cried. They both smoked cigarettes all the way, filling our fishtailed car with a blue haze indistinguishable from the constant rain outside. I was asleep when we got there, waking at noon to hear myself deemed "too young to go to the funeral." Bobbie would stay with me.

I will never forget that long afternoon, which I spent sitting on the horsehair sofa looking out at the rain and the row houses opposite us while Bobbie drank red wine and railed against the latest "jerk" who had betrayed her. She wore black silk pants and a lime green sleeveless angora sweater.

"Listen," she said, stabbing out a cigarette. "Never, ever, trust a man who says, 'Trust me.' "

Then her mood changed abruptly. "Well," she said, "we've got all afternoon. You might as well learn to dance." She got up and crossed the room to the record player.

"Come here," she said, and I did. "Now stand like this. Put your hand on my waist. Good. Now put your other hand on my shoulder, like this." I did. "Okay," she said. "Follow me."

We glided off into the dramatic opening of "Begin the Beguine." It was easy, easy. I imitated Bobbie's proud carriage, the reckless set of her crimson mouth, and my legs moved of their own accord across the flowered, threadbare carpet. Round and round we went, now to "Deep Purple": "when the deep purple falls over sleepy garden walls, and the stars begin to twinkle in the sky . . ."

I remembered my parents, dancing in our kitchen. I could imagine my grandmother dancing with the doomed and dashing Mr. Marshall. And suddenly, for the first time, I could imagine myself, dancing with a man whose face I could not yet see. For despite Bobbie's warning, I would grow up to love several men, some of them trustworthy and some of them not — though perhaps I would never love anybody else in quite the same way I loved Bobbie herself that afternoon of my grandmother's funeral, as we swept back and forth across the darkening apartment to those old sweet strains . . . "Through the mist of a memory, you wander back to me, breathing my name with a sigh . . ." while her angora sweater brushed my cheek like angels' wings.

Marble Cake and Moonshine

Although I don't usually write autobiographical fiction, the main character in one of my short stories sounds suspiciously like the girl I used to be: "More than anything else in the world, I wanted to be a writer. I didn't want to learn to write, of course. I just wanted to be a writer, and I often pictured myself poised at the foggy edge of a cliff someplace in the south of France, wearing a cape, drawing furiously on a long cigarette, hollow-cheeked and haunted. I had been romantically dedicated to the grand idea of 'being a writer' ever since I could remember."

I had started telling stories as soon as I could talk — true stories, and made-up stories, too. My father was fond of saying that I would climb a tree to tell a lie rather than stand on the ground to tell the truth. In fact, a lie was often called a "story" in southwest Virginia, and well do I remember being shaken until my teeth rattled with the stern admonition, "Don't you tell me no story, now!"

But I couldn't help it. I got hooked on stories early, and as soon as I could write, I started writing them down, first on my mother's Crane stationery when I was about nine, later in little books with covers I carefully made for them, pasting on pictures I'd cut out of magazines or catalogs, or illustrating them myself. I wrote my way through school, fueled by my voracious reading. I'd read anything: mysteries, romances, true crime, science fiction, all the books that came to our house from the Book of the Month Club. Finally at St. Catherine's School in Richmond, during my last two years of high school, I was gently but firmly guided into the classics, though my own fiction remained relentlessly sensational.

At Hollins College, I wrote about stewardesses living in Hawaii (where I had never been), about orphans, evil twins, fashion models, and alternative universes, receiving Bs and Cs and cryptic little comments from my professors Lex Allen and Richard Dillard that said, basically, "Write what you know." I thought this was terrible advice. I didn't know what they meant. I didn't know what I knew. All I knew was that I was not going to write anything about Grundy, Virginia, ever, that was for sure. My last glimpse of home had been my mother and two of her friends sitting on the porch drinking iced tea and talking (endlessly) about whether one of them ought to have a hysterectomy or not. Well! I was outta there!

But I was still drunk on words and books, just as I had been as a child, when I used to read under the covers with a flashlight all night long. My favorite professor at Hollins was Louis D. Rubin, Jr., who introduced us to Southern literature; I hadn't even known it existed when we started out. I had already gotten drunk on Faulkner a couple of times, then had to go to the infirmary for a whole day when we read William Styron's *Lie Down in Darkness* — I got too "wrought up," as my mother used to say. The nurse gave me a tranquilizer, and made me lie down.

Even so, I considered cutting class on the day that this woman with a funny name, from Mississippi, was coming to visit us. She was on campus, I believe, to receive the Hollins Medal, an honor undoubtedly engineered by Mr. Rubin, one of her earliest and greatest champions. But I had never heard of her, and it was so pretty outside, a great day to cut class and go up to Carvins

Cove and drink some beer or just stomp moodily around campus smoking cigarettes and acting like a writer. This was my plan until I ran into Mr. Rubin in the campus post office, and then I had to go to class.

There were a lot more people in that old high-ceilinged classroom than we had ever had before, and some of them were male, a rarity at Hollins in those days. The seats in the back of the room were filling up fast with faculty from our own college and from other area colleges, too, (beards, leather patches on the elbows of their ratty sports jackets: not your dad) as well as graduate students from UVA and W&L. The graduate students needed haircuts, and looked intense. In fact they looked exactly like the fabled sixties, reputed to be happening somewhere outside our fairytale Blue Ridge campus at that very time.

A ripple of anticipation ran through the crowd. Mr. Rubin was ushering Eudora Welty into the room.

I was deeply disappointed. Why, she certainly didn't look like a writer! She didn't have a cape, or boots, or anything. What she wore was one of those nice-lady linen dresses that buttoned up the front, just like all the other nice ladies I had known in my life, just like my mother and all her friends.

In fact, she looked a little bit like Miss Nellie Hart, my eighth-grade English teacher. (My favorite English teacher ever, but still . . .) I lost interest immediately.

I can't remember what Mr. Rubin said when he introduced her; I was probably too busy stealing glances at the back of the room while appearing not to.

Then Eudora Welty began to read "A Worn Path" out loud in her fast light voice that seemed to sing along with the words of the story. And I was suddenly right there — in Mississippi with Phoenix Jackson as she sets out to get the medicine for her grandson, encountering the thorny bush, the scarecrow, and the black dog, the young hunter and the lady along the way. I could see that "pearly cloud of mistletoe" near the beginning and then Phoenix's little grandson near the end: "He got a sweet look. He going to last. He wear a little patch quilt and peep out holding his mouth open like a little bird." I sat stunned when it was over.

Miss Welty had seemed perfectly composed as she was reading; her face was luminous, lit from within. Now, having finished, she looked nearly shy, though her huge blue eyes were shining. "Well," she said, looking all around, "any questions?" Hands waved everywhere.

She chose the young man who seemed the most impassioned. Knowing what I know now, I'll bet anything his dissertation was riding on his question. He leapt to his feet to ask it.

"I wonder," he said, his dark curly hair going everywhere, "if you could comment upon your choice of marble cake as a symbol of the fusion between dream and reality, between the temporal and the eternal, the male and the female, the union of yin and yang . . ." He made yin-yang motions with his hands.

Miss Welty smiled sweetly at him. "Well," she said slowly, considering, "it's a lovely cake, and it's a recipe that has been in my family for years."

Marble cake! My own mother made the best marble cake in town.

It would be years before I would understand that exchange, and what really took place in our classroom that day. Later, in the final section of *One Writer's Beginnings*, Miss Welty would put it best when she wrote that "the outside world is the vital component of my inner life. My work, in the terms in which I can see it, is as dearly matched to the world as its secret sharer. My imagination takes its strength and guides its direction from what I see and hear and learn and feel and remember of my living world."

Immediately after Miss Welty's visit, I read everything she had ever written. And it was like that proverbial lightbulb clicked on in my head — suddenly, I knew what I knew! With the awful arrogance of the nineteen-year-old, I decided that Eudora Welty hadn't been anywhere much either, and yet she wrote the best stories I had ever read. Plain stories about country people and small towns — my own "living world." I sat down and wrote a little story myself, about three women sitting on a porch drinking iced tea and talking endlessly about whether one of them does or does not need a hysterectomy. I got an *A* on it.

Based on Eudora Welty's influence upon my own beginnings, I have always felt that one of the most important functions of any good writing teacher is to serve as a sort of matchmaker — "fixing up" a new writer with the fiction of a successful published author whose work comes out of a similar background, place, sensibility, or life experience. A certain resonance, or recognition, occurs. This can be an important step in finding a voice. Especially when we are just starting out, we encounter other writers who are like lighthouses for us.

For instance, when I introduced young Kentucky writer Silas House to the work of Larry Brown. Silas recalls, "*Father and Son* had a profound impact on me. The way his characters were so intertwined with place — they couldn't be separated. I recall shortly after reading the book that a major reviewer said Brown wrote 'about the characters with whom you'd never want to have supper.' I thought: 'Those are the folks I've been eating with my whole life!' And so Larry's work really gave me permission to write about my people in all of their gritty glory, a grit formed by the rough land where we lived."

But even though my reading of Eudora Welty had led me to abandon my stewardesses, setting my feet on more familiar ground, telling simpler stories about small-town Southern life, I was never able, somehow, to set my first stories in those deep mountains I came from, or to write in my first language, the beautiful and precise Appalachian dialect I had grown up hearing as a child.

This did not happen until I encountered James Still — all by myself, actually, perusing the *S*s in the Hollins College library.

Here I found the beautiful and heartbreaking novel *River of Earth,* a kind of Appalachian *The Grapes of Wrath* chronicling the Baldridge family's desperate struggle to survive when the mines close and the crops fail, familiar occurrences in Appalachian life. Theirs is a constant odyssey, always looking for something better someplace else — a better job, a better place to live, a promised land. As the mother says, "Forever moving, yon and back, setting down nowhere for good and all, searching for God knows what. Where are we expecting to draw up to?"

At the end of the novel, I was astonished to read that the family was heading for — of all places! — *Grundy.*

"I was born to dig coal," Father said. "Somewhere they's a mine working. I been hearing of a new mine farther than the head of Kentucky River, on yon side Pound Gap. Grundy, its name is . . ."

I read this passage over and over. I simply could not believe that Grundy was in a novel! In print! Published! Then I finished reading *River of Earth* and burst into tears. Never had I been so moved by a book. In fact it didn't seem like a book at all. That novel was as real to me as the chair I sat on, as the hollers I'd grown up among, as the voices of my kinfolk.

Suddenly, lots of the things of my own life occurred to me for the first time as stories: my great-granddaddy's "other family" in West Virginia; Hardware Breeding, who married his wife, Beulah, four times; how my Uncle Vern taught my daddy to drink good liquor in a Richmond hotel; how I got saved at the tent revival; John Hardin's hanging in the courthouse square; how Petey Chaney rode the flood; the time Mike Holland and I went to the serpent-handling church in Jolo; the murder Daddy saw when he was a boy, out riding his little pony — and never told . . .

I started to write these stories down. Many years later, I'm still at it. And it's a funny thing: Though I have spent most of my working life in universities, though I live in piedmont North Carolina now and eat pasta and drive a Subaru, the stories that present themselves to me as worth the telling are often those somehow connected to that place and those people. The mountains that used to imprison me have become my chosen stalking ground.

This is the place where James Still lived most of his life, in an old log house built in the 1800s between Wolfpen Creek and Dead

Mare Branch near Wolfpen, accessible only by eight miles of dirt road and two miles of creek bed. Still was born into a farm family of five sisters and four brothers in Alabama in 1906; went to Lincoln Memorial University near Cumberland Gap, Tennessee, where he worked as a janitor in the library to earn his scholarship and discovered *The Atlantic* magazine, which he read cover to cover, every issue. Later he would publish ten stories and several poems in the very magazine that he had read so carefully. He earned another bachelor's degree in library science at the University of Illinois at Urbana–Champaign and a master's in English at Vanderbilt, but was still unable to get a job in the midst of the great Depression. After picking cotton and riding the rails, he came to Knott County, Kentucky, in 1932, where he finally found employment at the Hindman Settlement School, an association that would last for the rest of his long life. As the librarian, he carried books to people all over remote Knott County, working for room and board only. Eventually the school paid him $15 a month, and he began to sell his poems and stories to magazines nationwide. He also worked for the Federal Emergency Relief Administration, traveling the county on foot, talking to everybody, writing their stories down in his ever-present notebook.

After six years, as he liked to tell it, he "retired" and turned to reading and writing full-time. As one of his neighbors said, "He's quit a good job and come over in here and sot down." Another called him "the man in the bushes," and yet another suspected him of "devilish writing." But he was a gardener and a beekeeper as well, soon becoming almost like a family member of his dulcimer-making neighbors, the Amburgeys. Though not locally read, he was locally accepted. He talked to everybody, at every opportunity — at country stores, pie suppers, and the like. "You may talk smart, but you've got hillbilly wrote all over you," one man told him. His neighbors' writings and sayings appeared in *The Wolfpen Notebooks*, published in 1991.

When the nearby Hindman Settlement School started its now-famous Appalachian Writers' Workshop, I had the immense pleasure of getting to know Mr. Still and becoming his friend, from my first visit there in the seventies until his death in 2001, when we buried him up on the mountain above the school. We always called him "Mr. Still," all of us — even Mike Mullins, who ran the Settlement School and knew

Mr. Still better and longer than anybody. The continuing Appalachian Writers Workshop gave me (and many others) an Appalachian community of the heart, just as Mr. Still gave us all the example of a real writer, not in it for money or fame but for the love of the language and the telling of the truth as he saw it. Deeply erudite, he once told me he had read an average of three hours a day, every day, for over seventy years. He was a world traveller who had visited twenty-six countries, yet he was as interested in the sayings and doing of his neighbors as he was in the Mayan culture of Central America, where he returned time after time. Though *River of Earth* (1940) remained his masterpiece, his short stories and poetry were widely and justly praised as well, appearing not only in *The Atlantic* but also in *The Yale Review, Saturday Review, The Saturday Evening Post, Esquire,* and many other publications, textbooks, and anthologies. He loved children and also wrote for them — *Sporty Creek, Jack and the Wonder Beans* — and in his later years I had the honor of helping him get together a collection of his Appalachian Mother Goose poems.

Mr. Still never married, but loved women, even at ninety. I will always treasure a note he wrote to me then in his firm, inimitable handwriting: "Dear Lee, When are you getting here? Let's ride around. Love, Jim." We liked to sip a little moonshine or bourbon in paper cups while driving his big old Lincoln over the mountain to Hazard for a restaurant steak. Just before his death, Mr. Still wrote, asking me to come and "pick up a little old leather suitcase I've got up here someplace"; the suitcase turned out to contain the handwritten, jumbled manuscript of *Chinaberry,* a novel he had written years before, a mysterious story he had often repeated to all of us there on the porch after dinner, about being taken to Texas as a child to pick cotton. Now it has been beautifully edited by Silas House and published by the University of Kentucky Press.

What is it about Appalachia that so captures the mind, echoes in the ear, and lodges in the heart? An old woman once told me, "Well, there's just more *there* there." In the preface to his *The Wolfpen Notebooks,* Mr. Still wrote:

Appalachia is that somewhat mythical region with no known borders. If such an area exists in terms of geography, such a domain as has shaped the lives and endeavors of men and women from pioneer days to the present and given them an independence and an outlook and a vision such as is often attributed to them, I trust to be understood for imagining the heart of it to be in the hills of eastern Kentucky where I have lived and feel at home and where I have exercised as much freedom and peace as the world allows.

This is an enviable life, to live in the terrain of one's heart. Most writers don't — can't — do this. Most of us are always searching, through our work and in our lives: for meaning, for love, for home.

Writing is about these things. And as writers, we cannot choose our truest material. But sometimes we are lucky enough to find it.

HERITAGE

I shall not leave these prisoning hills
Though they topple their barren heads to
    level earth
And the forests slide uprooted out of the
    sky.
Though the waters of Troublesome, of
    Trace Fork,
Of Sand Lick rise in a single body to glean

the valleys,
To drown lush pennyroyal, to unravel rail
  fences;
Though the sun-ball breaks the ridges into
  dust
And burns its strength into the blistered
  rock
I cannot leave. I cannot go away.

Being of these hills, being one with the fox
Stealing into the shadows, one with the
  new-born foal,
The lumbering ox drawing green beech
  logs to mill,
One with the destined feet of man climbing
  and descending,
And one with death rising to bloom again,
  I cannot go.
Being of these hills I cannot pass beyond.
                                — James Still

Big River

Sometimes life is more like a river
than a book.
— Cort Conley

In my novel *The Last Girls,* the trip starts like this (imagine a winter afternoon on the historic campus of a women's college in Virginia; imagine a group of girls discussing *Hucklebery Finn* around a table in their American Literature seminar) . . .

Another day, Mr. Gaines read from the section where Huck and Jim are living on the river:

Sometimes we'd have that whole river to ourselves for the longest time. Yonder was the banks and the islands, across the water, and maybe a spark — which was a candle in a cabin window . . . and maybe you could hear

113

a fiddle or a song coming over from one of them crafts. It's lovely to live on a raft.

His words had rung out singly, like bells, in the old classroom. Harriet could hear each one in her head. It was a cold pale day in February. Out the window, bare trees stood blackly amid the gray tatters of snow.

Then Baby had said, "I'd love to do that. Go down the Mississippi River on a raft, I mean." It was a typical response from Baby, who personalized everything, who was famous for saying, "Well, I'd never do that!" at the end of *The Awakening* when Edna Pontellier walks into the ocean. Baby was not capable of abstract thought. She had too much imagination. Everything was real for her, close up and personal.

"We could do it, you know," Suzanne St. John spoke up. "My uncle owns a plantation right on the river, my mother was raised there. She'd know who to talk to. I'll bet we could do it if we wanted to." Next to Courtney, Suzanne St. John was the most organized girl in school, an angular, forthright girl with a businesslike grownup hairdo who ran a mail-order stationery business out of her dorm room.

"Girls, girls," Mr. Gaines had said disapprovingly. He wanted to get back to the book, he wanted to be the star. But the girls were all looking at each other. Baby's eyes were shining. *"Yes!"* she wrote on a piece of paper, handing it to Harriet, who passed it along to Suzanne. Yes. This was Baby's response to everything.

That's an excerpt from the novel. But this is the truth.

The summer after my junior year at Hollins, I actually did go down the Mississippi River on a raft with fifteen other girls, inspired by reading *Huckleberry Finn* in Louis Rubin's American literature class. This trip was organized by the indomitable senior Patricia Neild from Shreveport, but might not have happened without the help of a sophomore named Vicki Derby, whose old New Orleans family had invaluable ties up and down the river. Underlying the entire project was the subliminal message that Hollins had been giving us all along: that we could do anything, if we worked hard enough for it. Girls could do anything. We browbeat all our families for cash, then raised more any way we could think of, including loans and endorsements for various products. We made actual commercials for Chicken of the Sea tuna, Rayovac batteries, and Wrangler jeans.

On June 9th, 1966, we launched the *Rosebud Hobson* at Paducah, Kentucky, and headed 950 miles down the Ohio and Mississippi Rivers to New Orleans. The *Rosebud Hobson* was a forty-by-sixteen-foot wooden platform built on fifty-two oil drums and powered by two forty-horsepower motors. It cost us eighteen hundred dollars to build. We had a superstructure of two-by-fours with a tarpaulin top that we could pull over it, mosquito netting that we could hang up, and a shower consisting of a bucket overhead with a long rope attached to it. The raft was named for an early Hollins College alumna from Paducah, a pianist whose European career had involved some mysterious "tragedy," according to her sister, Miss Lillian Hobson, who entertained us before the launch.

Our captain was a retired riverboat pilot named Gordon S. Cooper. We painted rosebuds all over the raft and sang, "Goodbye, Paducah" to the tune of "Hello, Dolly" as we left. In fact, we sang relentlessly all the time, all the way down the Mississippi.

We sang in spite of all our mishaps and travails: the tail of a hurricane that hit us before we even got to Cairo, sending the temperature down below forty degrees and driving us onto the rocks; a diet consisting almost entirely of tuna and doughnuts; the captain's severe sunburn, requiring medical care; mosquito bites beyond belief and rainstorms that soaked everything we owned despite the useless tarp. If anything really bad happened to us, we figured we could call up our parents collect, and they would come and fix things. We expected to be taken care of. Nobody had ever suggested to us that we might ever have to make a living, or that somebody wouldn't marry us and then look after us for the rest of our lives. We all smoked cigarettes. We were all cute. We headed down that river with absolute confidence that we would get where we were going.

We worked and fished and played cards and talked and talked and talked. It was wonderful. In between stints as cook and keeper of the ship log, I was writing my own first novel. I had it all outlined, and every day I sat down crosslegged on deck and wrote five or six pages of it, on a yellow legal pad. I followed my outline absolutely. In creative writing class, I had learned how plot works: beginning, middle, and end; conflict, complication, and resolution.

Huck, our inspiration, was an American

Odysseus off on an archetypal journey —
the oldest plot of all. According to the
archetype, the traveler learns something
about himself (not herself) along the way.
What was I learning? Not much. Only that
if you are cute and sing a lot of songs,
people will come out whenever you dock
and bring you pound cake and ham and
beer and keys to the city, and when you get
to New Orleans you will be met by the band
from Preservation Hall on a tugboat, and
showered by red roses dropped from a
helicopter, paid for by somebody's daddy.

In all my yellowed newspaper clippings,
the press refers to us as "girls"; today, of
course, they'd call us "women." We were
the last girls. In 1966, a lot of things were
changing for good, though we didn't know
it yet. More possibilities and opportunities
for women would bring greater expectations
and responsibilities — along with a lack of
both illusions and stability. Whatever happened to romance, for instance? or the
sacred Fifties Family?

Over the years, many people asked when I
was going to write about the raft trip — it
seemed like such a natural. Why, we'd been
famous at the time, appearing nationally on
Huntley-Brinkley, covered by every TV station up and down the river and by every

newspaper in the South. A three-column closeup photograph of me had appeared on the front page of the Memphis *Commercial Appeal,* wearing a bandana on my head, cut-off jeans, my Rosebud Hobson T-shirt and a big grin, smoking a cigarette. (When somebody sent this clipping to my mother, she went to bed immediately.)

In that picture, I was clearly having the time of my life. We all were. But this was the problem, this was why the raft trip was not a natural for fiction, even though the journey is, of course, the archetypal plot for a novel or a story. Somebody once said that there are only two plots in fiction. The first is, somebody takes a trip (*The Iliad, The Odyssey, Don Quixote, Huckleberry Finn, Heart of Darkness*). The second one is, a stranger comes to town (*Absalom, Absalom; The Great Gatsby; The Glass Menagerie*). If you think about it, this is absolutely true.

But a trip — or a plot, let us say — is merely a series of events, and even the most interesting events do not add up to a story. We have to know who these events are happening to, and the better we know this person, the more we will care about what happens to him, the more we will want to read his story. There is a big difference between a plot and a story. A story requires not only events, but character, theme, meaning — and above all, conflict. Conflict is the essential difference between fiction and all other types of prose narrative. For fiction is a structured imitation of life, not life itself. Fiction organizes and reforms the raw material of fact to emphasize and clarify what is most significant in life for its characters. What do they want? What do they love? — hope for? — fear? What is up for grabs in the world of this story? What do these events mean to these characters? Because frequently, their lives will be forever changed by the events of the story. In any case, the possibility of change must arise: that's conflict, and without conflict, fiction does not exist.

The story happens at the point where event and character converge — or, more frequently, collide. The story tells how events affect and change the character(s), and how the character(s) affect and change events. The events of the story must mean something to the characters — or at the very least, to the reader, who is sometimes able to discern a pattern in these events that the character himself cannot see or understand.

So . . . taking a trip, even the best trip in the world, with the best companions, is not enough. Fact is, we had a great time on the raft. Period. And that was not a story. But years passed, and then many years passed. I attended my thirtieth Hollins reunion, where I was stunned by all our lives. We were divorced; we were gay; we were running large companies; we were living alone on an island; we were dealing with cancer, mental illness, aging parents, children who had not grown up as we'd expected. Some of us had already died, including Mimsy Spieden, who had been on the raft with us. Another woman had simply disappeared. There was a big difference between our youthful expectations and the reality of our lives, between the girls we were then and the women we had become. Suddenly I had plenty of conflict, brought to us by the simple passage of life itself.

Not long after the reunion, a tipsy book club member about my age buttonholed me at a literary festival someplace in the South: "Why do you keep writing about old mountain women?" she demanded. "Why don't you write about us?" Her question hit me with the force of revelation. Okay, I thought, okay. Time to get back on that raft.

Since it's always easier for me to tell the truth in fiction, *The Last Girls* is a novel. Many of its events are real — luckily I had saved that ship's log, so I knew exactly where and when we had docked all the way down the river, and what happened there. The time the photographer fell in the river trying to take our picture in Arkansas, for instance, or the time that sheriff in Mississippi insisted upon bringing "trusties" from the jail to guard us as we camped — we were all terrified of the trusties, and kept a watch on them ourselves. But we are not the characters of the novel. I made the characters up from scratch, to exemplify various aspects of women's lives that I wanted to talk about. The most important one was Baby — the wild one, the unpredictable one, the catalyst for everything. We have all known somebody like Baby. Conflict follows her around like a puppy dog.

In the novel, a tragedy has brought four of the original "girls," now middle-aged — plus one husband — back together for a repeat voyage under very different circumstances, on the luxurious steamboat *Belle of Natchez*. These women are all carrying a lot of psychological baggage from the past, while dealing with unresolved conflicts in their present lives. In *The Last Girls,* I'm trying to examine the idea of romance, the relevance of past to present, the themes of memory and desire.

For me — and for most of us on the real raft, I suspect — it was the only journey I ever made that ended as it was supposed to. Subsequent trips have been harder, scarier. We have been shipwrecked, we have foundered on hidden shoals, we have lost our running lights. The captain is dead. I can't stick to a traditional plot anymore. I've got plenty of conflict, plenty of complication, but no resolutions in sight. Such a plot (the heroic quest and conquer) may have been more suited to boys' books anyway. Certainly, the linear, beginning-middle-end form doesn't fit the lives of any women I know. For life has turned out to be wild and various, full of the unexpected, and it's a monstrous big river out here.

ON LOU'S PORCH

It was the hot, muggy summer of 1980; I was in Abingdon, Virginia, for a week to teach the creative writing class that always preceded "literary day" at the Virginia Highlands Festival. I got hotter and hotter each step I took up the long staircase to the room where the class would meet, above the sanctuary in the old United Methodist Church right on Main Street. Finally I made it, and surveyed the group seated around a big oak table. It was about what you'd expect — eight or ten people, mostly high school English teachers, some librarians, some retirees. We had already gone around the table and introduced ourselves when here came this old woman in a man's hat and fuzzy bedroom shoes, gray head shaking a little with palsy, huffing and puffing up the stairs, dropping notebooks and pencils all over the place, greeting everybody with a smile and a joke. She was a real commotion all by herself.

"Hello there, young lady," she said to me. "My name is Lou Crabtree, and I just love to write!" My heart sank like a stone. Here was every creative writing teacher's nightmare: the nutty old lady who will invariably write sentimental drivel and monopolize the class as well.

"Pleased to meet you," I lied. The week stretched out before me, hot and intolerable, an eternity. But I had to pull myself together. Looking around at all those sweaty, expectant faces, I began, "Okay, now I know you've brought a story with you to read to the group, so let's start out by thinking about beginnings, about how we start a story . . . let's go around the room, and I want you to read the first line of your story aloud."

So we began. Nice lines, nice people. A bee hummed at the open window; a square of golden sunlight fell on the old oak table; somebody somewhere was mowing grass. We got to Lou, who cleared her throat and read this line: "Old Rellar had thirteen miscarriages and she named every one of them."

I sat up. "Would you read that line again?" I asked.

"Old Rellar had thirteen miscarriages and

she named every one of them," Lou read.

I took a deep breath. "Keep going," I said.

"Only of late, she got mixed up and missed some. This bothered her. She looked toward the iron bed. It had always been exactly the same. First came the prayer, then the act with Old Man gratifying himself . . ."

She read the whole thing. It ended with the lines: "You live all your life and work things up to come to nothing. The bull calf bawled somewhere."

I had never heard anything like it.

"Lou," I asked her after class, "have you written anything else? I'd like to see it."

The next day, she brought a battered suitcase. And there it all was, poems and stories written on every conceivable kind of notebook and paper, even old posters and shirtbacks.

Lou grinned at me. "This ain't all, either," she said. The next day, she brought more.

All that week, I read these poems and stories, immersing myself in Lou's magic, primal world of river hills and deep forest, of men and women and children as elemental as nature itself, of talking animals and ghosts, witchcraft and holiness. For Lou Crabtree was that rarity — a writer of perfect pitch and singular knowledge, a real artist. And most amazing of all (to me, anyway, simultaneously revising a mediocre novel of my own), she had written all this with no thought of publication. Writing was how she lived, I realized. It was what she lived by.

"I just write for my own enjoyment," Lou told me. "It pleases me very much to sit down with pencil and paper, and something will come out that looks pretty good, and sounds pretty good, and it gives me pleasure in my soul. I think the best writing time is in the night time. And it is a wonderful time between twelve o'clock and maybe four . . . It is a very strange feeling when all the world is asleep but you. You feel like you're in touch with something special. And then as I write, I don't know what time it is, what day it is. It is that thing of getting out of yourself, of getting out of the world, going out of the world. You feel good, real good. You have none of these problems or hurts or anything. It is something I wish everybody could discover in their work. If they really are doing the thing they like to do, they are able to get out of their self. And it is wonderful. Very wonderful."

I asked her then what she'd do if somebody came along and told her that she couldn't write anymore. "Well, you know, I would just have to sneak!" she said.

For the first time, I began to understand the therapeutic power of language, the importance of the writing process itself. Years later, I would write a novel named *Fair and Tender Ladies* in which my main character writes letters in order to make sense of her life, in much the same way Lou had always written her poems and stories.

But that summer, I put aside the lackluster novel I was working on, and took Lou up on her offer to guide me and my little boys out "adventuring." We climbed down into a cave where Lou swore that Daniel Boone himself had "hid out." We went walking in the woods. She showed them how to make frog houses and pokeberry ink; we all took off our shoes to wade in the creek, then made little plates and cups for fairies from the red clay mud.

"Here, honey," she said, leaning over to pick up a buckeye as we walked back beneath the sunset sky. "Put this in your pocket. It's good luck. And get your head out of them clouds, honey. Pay attention." We went back to sit on her porch, talking to everybody that came by. We had potato chips and Moon Pies for dinner.

I've been trying to pay attention ever since, realizing that writing is not about fame, or even publication. It is not about exalted language, abstract themes, or the escapades of glamorous people. It is about our own real world and our own real lives and understanding what happens to us day by day, it is about playing with children and listening to old people.

The passage of time added a special poignancy to Lou's work. In her poem "Smith Creek No. 1," for instance, she told how she "loathed the likes of Smith Creek where I followed my husband to . . . those years of borning five young ones by myself with no doctor and washing for five on a board until four o'clock, until the sun dropped behind Gumm's Hill." Hard times. Yet after the passage of many years, this period took on a beautiful elegaic glow. In " 'Smith Creek No. 2 (feeling bad about writing Smith Creek No. 1),' " she is "calling back those years of planting harvesting / Breathing touching among our meanderings / In and out of lives where we pursued / All strange and wonderful things / Down deep into the mysterious dark / Where the roots wind about the heart" as "The seasons change and go. The fire eyes of an opossum glow." The final image was one of peaceful beauty, life come gloriously full circle at last: "In

Smith Creek, a scarlet leaf floats round and round."

"You know how the mist comes up and covers the land, lots of times?" Lou asked me. "Some of these people that I write about are from a long time ago, they're not anymore, they're just kind of like the mist that covers my mountains. Sometimes I think they may still be there in those mountains. My people may still be right there."

Lou was born on the North Fork of the Holston River, one of ten children in the Price family. "We ran all over the hills and watched from behind trees and played Indians, and I knew more flowers and animals than I did people." She went to the Radford Normal School at sixteen, graduating cum laude in three years, then returned home to teach. Lou married Homer Crabtree in 1942 and moved to the Smith Creek area, near where she was born. She had five children in seven years, taking a ten-year leave from teaching to "raise cattle, tobacco, and young'uns. Oh, money is scarce on a mountain." Lou characterized her husband as a "very soft-spoken man . . . a very calm and kind man . . . a man that people would come and sit down and talk to." Later she returned to the classroom, teaching just about every subject at every level, from a one-room school to elementary and high schools.

After Homer's death, Lou bought her home at 313 Valley Street for $4,000, money she'd "saved up" from teaching, and moved into town in 1960 as a widow with five teenagers. In reminiscing about the "early widow phase," Lou winks at me: "Oh, you'll have lots of opportunities as a young widow. They say, 'When you're old, I'll take care of you' . . . like hell they will! I was through and done with all that." Her son George "who raises those old Charolais cattle" shared her Valley Street home for a long time. Even after her official retirement, Lou continued to teach all manner of classes, especially enjoying the GED and English as a Second Language groups, "getting to know some gorgeous people, from Viet Nam, and Japan, and Venezuela . . . well, everyplace!"

She was also the leader of the Rock of Ages Band of senior citizens, which performed all over the area. "We have three pianists in case one gets sick, we can fall back on another one. We have a mandolin player and a guitar player and an autoharp. Mr. Harold Clark on the mandolin, he is eighty-some years old, and he can play that 'Somewhere My Love.' His wife is one of our chaperones. You wouldn't think we need chaperones, but we do! We have got the best banjo player in town, her name is Love Craig, and she is eighty-five years old. Oh, can she play that banjo! Now that is really something, to hear Love Craig play the banjo."

I agree, having served as "roadie" on several tours with the Rock of Ages Band.

But always, Lou was writing, her life a testament to the sustaining and revitalizing power of language. She often stuck her brother into a story. "He died at the age of thirty, after coming back from the war one year, and he was an alcoholic, so that was a great grief to me. Oh yes, we were close. Now once in a while when I put in this character Bud, that's my brother. It makes me feel good, you know, that though he died, I can keep him going." Her writing was widely published; Louisiana State University Press brought out her collection of stories, *Sweet Hollow,* in 1984. (The publisher was startled when he first called her house and George answered, as he invariably did, "Hello! Poorhouse!" — "Hoping they'd think it was something else, and sometimes they did!" Lou laughed.) Her book of poems, *The River Hills and Beyond,* came out from Sow's Ear Press in

1998. Lou won the Virginia Cultural Laureate in Literature Award, the Governor's Award for Arts in Virginia, as well as a special award from the Virginia Highlands Festival. *Calling on Lou,* a one-woman stage play celebrating her life and work, premiered at the Barter Theater in Abingdon and then toured Virginia; she even appeared on the *Today Show.*

But none of this meant much to Lou. She called the later phase of her life "the porch years" and what she liked to do most was sit out on that porch where I visited her so many times amid the jumble of old furniture and plants and knickknacks, just talking and reading and watching the traffic pass by. Sometimes we sang a little. "Oh darling, you can't love but one. Oh darling, you can't love but one. You can't love but one and have any fun . . . You can't love ten and love me again — Oh boy, I'm leaving on that midnight train!" or "Cindy got religion, she danced around and 'round, she got so full of glory, she knocked the preacher down!" We laughed a lot.

In winter, we'd sit inside by the heater near her sturdy bed layered with quilts, books, and manuscripts piled everyplace. Everything in that room was precious to her. "Now, take these cabinets. My husband's people were cabinetmakers. Fine old cabinetmakers. They could join up two pieces of wood so it looked like it growed together. That's my mother's blue vase up there. It is a cobalt blue and they don't make that cobalt anymore. They use all that cobalt in cancer treatment." Lou herself never took so much as an aspirin. She lived entirely in the front room by then, with kitchen and bathroom at hand and a good view of Valley Street out the bay window. She had a steady stream of visitors, pilgrims like myself.

"Why, there've been people here from the Arctic regions, just dying to talk. A man was in here the other day that had climbed Mt. Everest, and a woman came who was going on the Trans-Siberian Railroad. I've always wanted to go on that myself," Lou told me.

"Why not?" I asked. "A lot of people take up traveling when they retire."

"Why, I don't have to!" she laughed. "I have traveled all over the world right here on this porch. People talk to me, they take me to all these places that they've been to. We are in a changing time, but people do like to talk. They will come and sit down here and talk — especially if they can laugh!"

"These porch years are very creative for

me," Lou said. She also called them her "spiritual years." She became interested in space, even taking a course from the University of Virginia. She wrote more than fifty "space poems."

When I asked why she had gotten so fascinated with space, Lou answered, "Because it's out there! Our universe is like a great big clock, run by God's laws of chemistry, math, biology, and science . . . Now you know He doesn't do things mish-mash! And there'll come a day when the spirit will take leave of this old body. It's going to rise up to Paradise, and I wanted to know where Paradise was! So I've found out by science how it's going to happen. When you go faster than the speed of light, then you get younger and younger. Science and scripture agree! You're going to live forever in paradise, and you'll be young. I can't wait!"

Lou's new interest seemed to be an expansion — not a contradiction — of traditional religion. "I went to churches all my life," she told me, mentioning the old Centenary Methodist Church in particular. "I never went to a church in my life that I wasn't helped. And now," she said, "I'm open! I'm open to everything!"

I told Lou that I believed I finally understand something she told me so long ago:

135

" 'You have to travel a lonely road. It is you yourself traveling along, and if you are able along the road to meet a friend, to meet a love . . . you're very, very lucky. But it is a lonely road even though you have sons and daughters that you love better than your own life — that you'd give your own life for. One day you have to let them go, you let them all go. Oh, all right, it's a lonely road.' "

Now I know what she meant.

"Do you ever have times you can't sleep?" she asked me. "You probably don't, but you will, honey, you will. Well, things will rise out of the night, some way or other. All our people back of us can rise and come out in the night time awful good, and talk to us, and comfort us. Why I saw your mother one time, Lee, sitting in a rocking chair on the porch of the Martha Washington Inn! I saw your pa driving that fancy car right up to heaven.

"Death should be thought of as a beautiful part of life," Lou said. "I'm not a bit afraid of dying. I want to die right here in this old bed with a pencil in my hand." But not anytime soon — "I want to make it to 2000. I'd like to see what they do and say about it!"

Actually she made it to April 10, 2006,

dying in her sleep at ninety-three. I had promised Lou I would "preach at her funeral" and I did — one of several speakers at the same Abingdon United Methodist Church where we had first met in the creative writing class, all those years ago. I read her poem "Salvation" aloud at the service. Afterward I walked over to Valley Street and stood for a long time looking at Lou's house, which had been sold and spruced up. The porch looked like anybody's porch now. I remembered her words, "We are all going in a circle, and death is not the end of our circle. It is just a word that some people have." I fingered the buckeye in my pocket.

Lou's poem "Salvation" was printed in the program for her funeral on April 14, 2006.

SALVATION

jesus jesus jesus i got something
  this old body aint so important
in this old body i feel holiness i got
  holiness
  i got jesus flirtin with death

ever day in the coal mines flirtin with death
my daddy flirted and my brothers flirted
  and my uncles and cousins

and my daddy got his back broken
  flirtin with death

brother flirtin with death motorcycles, race
  cars
  not my way flirtin with death
sister flirted i danced around her coffin
  high in my hand same snake caused her
  death
laid her three weeks baby in her dead arms
sister got holiness flirtin with death

i feel holiness jesus i got something
washing the feet laying on hands dancing
  the fire dance
  glory glory glory
praying for the sign the wounded blood of
  jesus
  on the feet on the hands on the head
praying three years for the jesus sign
  glory hallelujah

in the church house old snake washed
  clean
i put him to my shoulder flirtin with death
i touch him to my lips flirtin with death
flirtin with death i raise him to my breast
old velvet lips with his singing tail and
  lightning breath

i offer old velvet lips my snowy white
   breast

jesus jesus this old body aint so important
i got holiness flirtin with death
                        — Lou V. Price Crabtree
               (March 13, 1913–April 10, 2006)

LIGHTNING STORM

When I was a child, books brought my deepest pleasure, my greatest excitement. Reading, I often felt exactly the way I felt during summer thunderstorms: I just had to run out of the house and up the mountain into the very storm to whirl in the thunder and rain on the rocky top while lightning cracked all around me.

Since the next best thing to reading books was writing them and talking about them, I ended up becoming a writer and a professor. But then there came a time when I realized that I was hearing entirely too much about agents and advances, about "revising the canon" and "privileging the text" and "writing across the curriculum." I became depressed about writing, which no longer seemed relevant to anything real. I had lost the lightning.

So when a Lila Wallace–Readers' Digest Writers' Award in 1992 offered me the chance to get out of my college classroom and affiliate with a nonprofit group of my choice for some community involvement, I jumped at the chance to get back to the coal fields.

I chose to work with the Hindman Settlement School in Hindman, Kentucky. I had often been a visiting writer for their summer creative writing workshop. The school's adult learning center, a no-nonsense brick building overhanging a muddy creek, offered a year-round literacy program, adult education classes, and tutoring services for the high school equivalency exam. The need for these programs is great. Half the county's population hasn't made it through high school; most dropouts leave before the ninth grade. Unemployment is high, and incomes are low.

I had the privilege of visiting this ongoing program each fall and spring for three years. At the Settlement School, I lived in a log house, gave readings and talks at area schools and community colleges, and conducted several daily workshops with students in the programs at the Adult Learning Center. We usually had ten to eighteen people per group; I also worked one-on-one with several people who really had a lot to say — some began writing their own life stories.

Since I can't actually remember the time when I couldn't read and write, I didn't understand the enormous sense of empowerment that comes with mastering written language. It was a revelation for me to meet red-headed, good-looking Connel Polly of Vicco, Kentucky, a successful grading contractor who had kept his illiteracy secret from everybody but his wife for fifty years. In *It's Like Coming Out of a Deep Hole,* his booklet of memories printed by the Hindman School, he recounts this incident:

One time, the mining company sent me to Canton, Ohio, going after mine parts in a pickup truck. They had told me which roads to take and what the exit was, and I was supposed to find this company that was on Fifth Street. So I drove all around looking for a five, and I couldn't find it. That's when I realized "Fifth" was a word, and I couldn't read it. I couldn't find it. That's the only time I ever cried in my life. I just pulled off the road and sat there and cried. I was eight hours away from home and it was getting dark. That was pitiful. Finally I had to ask somebody, and it turned out I was sitting right at it. I could see it. I felt so bad I didn't even stay the night. After I did my business I drove on back, and I was down all the way home. I was so blue. I felt the worst I've ever felt. There I was — a grown man — trying to make a living in that shape!

Now, he writes:

I didn't know learning to read would change my life so much. It has made me have more confidence in myself. Before, I even had a fear of going into a public rest-room. I had fear of being embarrassed by someone handing me something to read. I stayed away from places such as banks, post offices, and doctors' offices. The first visit to a new doctor was hardest because you had to fill out forms. I always had my wife with me. Now, I'll go anywhere. Also, me and my wife leave notes for each other. Now that's something!

Lively Florida Slone, a well-known local ballad singer, did not enroll until the death of her husband. She writes:

I always thought of myself as a bean planted in a garden, and then someone put a big rock on top of me so that I could not get out of the ground. Now . . . I have gotten my driver's license, and I can write my own checks. I can read my Bible and my songbooks. I have always liked to make up songs and stories, but I never could write them down before. Now I can. I am beginning to grow. Maybe one of these days I'll be like Jack's beanstalk!

Mrs. Slone became a participant in many activities at the Adult Learning Center, where her outgoing personality brought her many friends.

The school put together a collection of Mrs. Slone's writing entitled *A Garden of Songs,* which range from love songs to hymns ("Voice of Angels"); to funny party tunes like "Chew Tobacco" and "Big Fat Dog." There are also story songs such as "Red Hot Election" and "School Bus Wreck in Floyd County" that chronicle local events.

She tells the circumstances that occasioned the writing of each song. "One time I was asked to leave a church because my husband had been married before — they called him 'a old double-married thing.' I went home and wrote this song. I wrote it to give me comfort. I wanted the world to know that Jesus was the pastor in my church, not somebody else." That song is

144

entitled "To All the People Looking Down Their Nose at Me."

Some of Mrs. Slone's songs are pure poetry. About the composition of "Last Night," she tells us, "It was rainy one night, and the clouds were passing by, and I could hear the whippoor-wills calling — it's been years ago."

> Last night I sat and watched the clouds go
>   by
> I heard whippoorwills call from the
>   mountains so high
> I heard the water as it dropped soft and low
> Seems like death is a secret nobody
>   knows.

Other writers also took the opportunity to express deep feelings. Pretty young Promise Sandling wrote about her childhood:

> I used to feel like no one loved me cause
> My family was always falling apart
> All my dads always left
> But now I feel wonderful-N-I am happy
> Because guess what?
> I think I am smart!

Most of my writing students were women. Some had been unable go to school when they were girls because of early pregnancies; local churches and general opinion were against abortion, so this had not been an option. Married or not, these women had raised their children, often in difficult circumstances. Other girls had needed to stay home from school to help out with younger children or sick family members. Many enrolled upon discovering, after divorce or widowhood, what they could do for themselves.

Glenda Johnson, who eventually had to drop out of the program to tend ailing relatives, first found the time to write about her son:

This is a poem about Roy Glen Johnson.

He lives in a wooden house
At Mallie, KY 41836
He has blue eyes
and blond looking hair and
he likes to ride his bike.
He likes to play outside all the time.
He is afraid of my father.
He would like to have
His family whole again.

When I first visited the high school equivalency program, black-haired, statuesque Ollie Wallen had just enrolled. She looked down all the time, and didn't say much. Two years later, Ollie was wearing nail polish and joining vigorously in every discussion. She wrote to her congressman with a complaint and was pleased when he called her at home to advise her how to take action on getting benefits she was due. Here is a poem by Ollie:

I used to be married
But now I am divorced.
I used to do things for my husband
But now I do things for myself.
I used to feel bad about myself,
But now I feel great about myself,
Like a rope was wrapped around me
But now it is loose.

It's a long, winding road from where I am living now to the mountains of eastern Kentucky. But it brought me home. My involvement with this program made me remember what reading and writing were all about in the first place, before book tours and disputes about deconstructionism. Helping people express themselves in writing for the first time is like watching them fall in love. For me, it brought back the old thrill, the lightning storm.

DRIVING MISS DAISY CRAZY; OR, LOSING THE MIND OF THE SOUTH

Carrboro, N.C. — April 12, 2000.

I want to start by introducing you to Miss Daisy. Chances are, you already know her. She may be your mother. She may be your aunt. Or you may have your own private Miss Daisy, as I do: a prim, well-educated maiden lady of a certain age who has taken up permanent residence in a neat little room in the frontal lobe of my brain. I wish she'd move, but as she points out to me constantly, she's just no trouble at all. She lives on angel food cake and she-crab soup, which she heats up on a little ring right there in her room.

Miss Daisy was an English teacher at a private girls' school for forty-three years, back in the days when English was English — before it became Language Arts. She was famous for her ability to diagram sentences, any sentence at all, even sentences so complex that their diagrams on the board looked like blueprints for a cathedral. Her favorite poet is Sidney Lanier. She likes to be elevated. She is still in a book club, but it is not Oprah's book club. In fact, Miss Daisy is not quite sure who Oprah is, believing that her name is Okra Winfrey, and asking me repeatedly what all the fuss is about. Miss Daisy's book club can find scarcely a thing to elevate them these days, so they have taken to reading *Gone With the Wind* over and over again.

Miss Daisy's favorite word is *ought,* as in "You ought to go to church this morning." She often punctuates her sentences with "you know," as in, "Lee Marshall, you know you don't believe that!" or, "Lee Marshall, you know you don't mean it!" She believes it is true about the two ladies who got kicked out of the Nashville Junior League: one for having an orgasm, and the other for having a job.

In fact, Miss Daisy reminds me of another lady I encountered many years ago, when I moved down to Alabama to become a reporter for *The Tuscaloosa News.* The former editor of the ladies page of the paper had just retired. "Thank God!" everybody said, since for many years she had ceased to write up events in the paper the way they actually happened, preferring instead to write them up the way she thought they should have happened.

The South runs on denial. We learn denial in the cradle and carry it to the grave. It is absolutely essential to being a lady, for instance. My Aunt Gay-Gay's two specialties were Rising to the Occasion and Rising Above It All, whatever "it" happened to be. Aunt Gay-Gay believed that if you can't say something nice, say nothing at all. If you don't discuss something, it doesn't exist. She drank a lot of gin and tonics and sometimes she'd start in on them early, winking at my Uncle Bob and saying, "Pour me one, honey, it's already dark underneath the house." Until she died, I never knew that another of my aunts had had a previous marriage. It had been edited right out of the family, in the same way all pictures of that husband had been removed from the family albums.

Denial affects not only our personal lives, but also our political lives, our culture, and our literature. In her book *Playing in the Dark: Whiteness and the Literary Imagination,* Toni Morrison talks about a kind of denial she sees operating in American literature and criticism; she chides liberal critics for what she calls their "neglect of darkness." She says that "the habit of ignoring race is understood to be a graceful, even generous, liberal gesture . . . but excising the political from the life of the mind is a sacrifice that has proven costly. . . . A criticism that needs to insist that literature is not only 'universal' but also 'race-free' risks lobotomizing that literature, and diminishes both the art and the artist." Morrison suggests that black characters in classic American novels have been as marginalized as their real-life counterparts.

But back to Miss Daisy. I'm taking her out to lunch today. Miss Daisy claims she "just eats like a bird," not deigning to confess to anything as base as hunger or even appetite, but she does like to go out to lunch. And while she's making her final preparations — that is, clean underwear in case we are in a wreck, gloves, money safely tucked in her bra in case her purse is stolen — let me tell you about this restaurant we're going to.

You may be surprised to learn that I actually own this restaurant, and that it is actually a sushi bar. But, hey! It's the New South, remember? And actually, our sushi bar (named Akai Hana and located in Carrboro, North Carolina) presents a little case study in the New South.

The land Akai Hana stands on today, at

206 W. Main St, was farmland not so very long ago, when Carrboro was a dusty, sleepy little farm village on the old road from Chapel Hill to Greensboro. This was an open field, with a tenant house at the end of it. Then Carr Mill came in, and mill houses sprouted up in neat little rows, like beans, to house the families that worked at Carr Mill. As the university grew, Chapel Hill grew, too, spreading outward toward Carrboro, which gradually became a service adjunct of Chapel Hill. This was the place you came to buy your grass seed or to get your tires fixed at the Chapel Hill Tire Company, right across the street from us. Carrboro was mostly black then, and all poor. Miss Daisy never came here except to pick up her cook. Every business in Carrboro closed at noon on Wednesday, because everybody went to church on Wednesday night. And nothing was open on Sunday.

Our brick building, constructed in the early fifties, was first occupied by a popular, locally owned café named the Elite Lunch, which featured Southern cooking and lots of it. It had two dining rooms, one for white and one for colored. In the early sixties it was superseded by Pizza Villa, whose name alone testifies to Chapel Hill's — and Carrboro's — increasing sophistication. By now, plenty of graduate students and even some professors lived in Carrboro. The mill had closed, and those mill houses were affordable.

By the mid-seventies, when an outrageously colorful chef took over and turned it into Avanti, Carrboro was coming of age. The mill became Carr Mill Mall, filled with trendy boutiques. In the eighties, a cooperative health-food grocery named Weaver Street Market opened up. Artists moved in. Carrboro started calling itself the Paris of the Piedmont.

Avanti's chef hung paintings by his artist friends. He stuck candles in wine bottles on each of his artfully mismatched tables. He opened the patio for outdoor dining. He made soup with forty cloves of garlic. Then, even Avanti was superseded by the truly gourmet Martini's. The owner's wife's mother came from Italy to run the kitchen, while her homemade pasta dried on broomsticks upstairs. My first husband and I had some memorable meals there, and my present husband remembers that he was eating polenta in this very gazebo when a former girlfriend gave him the gate. Ah, what sweet revenge it is now to own that gazebo, which we have (of course) transformed into a pagoda.

But back to our narrative. The owner died in a wreck, Martini's closed, and the restaurant underwent a total transformation before opening again, for breakfast and lunch only, as a bakery and café, very French, with a marble floor and lace curtains at the windows. Pre-Starbucks, the two ladies who now owned it served muffins accompanied by the first good coffee in Carrboro.

We bought the place from the muffin ladies. Why? You might well ask. Have I always had a burning desire to go into the sushi business? No, actually, my own attitude toward raw fish is closer to Roy Blount's poem about oysters:

I prefer my oyster fried.
Then I'm sure my oyster's died.

It was my husband's idea. He always called my son Josh the "samurai stepson," and their favorite thing to do together was to go out for sushi. The closing of the only sushi bar in town coincided with Josh's improvement from schizophrenia. New medications made it possible for him to have a more regular life, and what better job could a samurai stepson get than in a sushi bar? (I can hear Miss Daisy saying in my ear, "Now

154

Lee Marshall, you know you shouldn't have told that!" But I am telling it anyway.) We held long conferences with Bob, the sushi chef. We met with the muffin ladies and the bank. We hired a designer and a construction firm. We were under way, even though nobody except us thought this was a good idea. Our accountant was horrified. The guys from the tire shop across the street kept coming over to ask, "How's the bait shop coming along?"

We opened in 1997. Let me introduce you around.

Bob, manager and head chef, hails from the coastal North Carolina town of Swansboro. At college in Chapel Hill, he wrote poetry and played guitar until his wanderlust led him to California, where he eventually became an ardent convert of the Reverend Moon and joined the Unification Church. He married his Japanese wife, Ryoko, in a ceremony of twenty-five thousand couples in Madison Square Garden. They are still happily married, with six beautiful children.

Under Bob's direction, Akai Hana employs people from diverse backgrounds, including Hispanic, Burmese, Thai, Japanese, Filipino, Chinese, Korean, African-American, and African. Meet Rick, for instance, who heads the kitchen in back (yes, we do have cooked food, for people like Miss Daisy, who is enjoying some grilled teriyaki chicken right now). Anyway, both Rick and his wife, a beautician, are Chinese Filipinos who have been in this country for eighteen years, sending for their siblings one by one. Their son, a physician, is now completing his residency in Seattle. Their daughter, who recently earned her doctorate in public health, works for a world health organization in L.A. Rick's nephew Brian, one of the wait staff, plays saxophone in the UNC jazz band.

Ye-tun, a cook and a former Burmese freedom fighter whose nickname is "Yel," proudly showed me a picture of himself coming through the jungle dressed in camo, carrying an AK-47. Now my husband calls him the "Rebel Yell," but nobody gets it.

Okay: Bob, Ryoko, Brian, Helen Choi, Ye-tun, Miguel, Jose, Genita, Mister Chiba, and Mister Choi — these people are Southerners. We are all Southerners. Akai Hana is a Southern restaurant, just like Pittypat's Porch or Hardee's.

Judging merely from our lunch at Akai Hana, we are going to have to seriously overhaul our image of the South, and of Southerners, for this millennium.

My little piece of land in Carrboro is typical. The South was two-thirds rural in the 1930s. Now it is over two-thirds urban. One half of all Southerners were farmworkers in the thirties; now that statistic is at 2 percent. And out of those farmworkers in the thirties, one half were tenant farmers. Now we have no tenant farmers, but migrant workers instead.

Our Southern birthrate, which used to be famously above the national average, is now below it. This means that immigration — and in-migration — are defining the South's population. Soon Texas and Florida will both have nonwhite majorities.

Well, this very idea has given Miss Daisy a headache. She just doesn't have a head for figures, anyway. She'd like some dessert, but Akai Hana serves only green tea ice cream, which is too weird to even think about, in Miss Daisy's opinion. So we pay up and drive a few blocks down to Mama Dip's Country Kitchen, where Mildred "Dip" Council, Miss Daisy's former cook, has opened her big, fancy new restaurant. She's published a cookbook, too. She's been written up by Calvin Trillin and Craig Claiborne; she's been on TV. She's an entrepreneur now. Miss Daisy orders the

157

lemon chess pie. I go for the peach cobbler myself.

Some things never change. Some Southern food will never go out of style, no matter how much it may get nouveau'ed. And large parts of the South still look a lot like they used to — the Appalachian coal country where I'm from, for instance, and the old Cotton Belt. A layer of cultural conservatism still covers Dixie like the dew. As a whole, we Southerners are still religious, and we are still violent. We'll bring you a casserole, but we'll kill you, too. Southern women, both black and white, have always been more likely than Northern women to work outside the home, despite the image projected by such country lyrics as "Get your biscuits in the oven and your buns in the bed, this women's liberation is a-going to your head." It was not because we were so liberated; it's because we were so poor. This, too, is changing: now our per capita income is at 92 percent of the national average.

With all these changes, what should I tell my student, one of my very favorite students, who burst into tears after we attended a reading together at which Elizabeth Spencer read her fine short story "The Cousins." "I'll never be a Southern writer!"

my student wailed. "I don't even know my cousins!" Raised in a military household, relocated many times, she had absolutely no sense of place, no sense of the past, no sense of family. How did she spend her childhood? I asked. In the mall in Fayetteville, North Carolina, she tearfully confessed, sneaking cigarettes and drinking Cokes.

I told her she was lucky.

But she was also right. For a writer cannot pick her material any more than she can pick her parents; her material is given to her by circumstances of her birth, by how she first hears language. And if she happens to be Southern, these factors may already be trite, even before she sits down at her computer to begin. Her neurasthenic, fragile Aunt Lena is already trite, her mean, scary cousin Bobby Lee is already trite, her columned, shuttered house in Natchez is already trite. Far better to start out from the mall in Fayetteville, illicit cigarette in hand, with no cousins to hold her back, and venture forth fearlessly into the New South.

I once heard the novelist George Garrett say that the House of Fiction has many rooms. Well, the House of Southern Fiction is in the process of remodeling. It needs so many more rooms that we've got brand-new wings shooting out from the main house in every direction. It looks like one of those pictures of the sun as drawn by a second-grader. In fact, that's the name of it — the House of the Rising Sun — which is right over here by the interstate. I'll run you by it as we drive Miss Daisy home.

Look — there's my student right now, knocking on the door, suitcase in hand. She doesn't know yet that once she takes a room in there, she can never come out again. She doesn't understand that she's giving up her family and her home forever, that as soon as she writes about those things she will lose them, in a way, though she will mythologize them in her work, the way we all do, with all our little hometowns of the heart.

Allan Gurganus has called ours "the literature of nostalgia," pointing out that many of the great anthems of the South are written from a position of exile such as "Way down upon the Swanee River"; "I wish I was in the land of cotton"; James Taylor's "going to Carolina in my mind"; or "Country roads, take me home."

The writer puts herself in exile by the very act of writing. She will feel guilty about leaving, and for the rest of her life, she will write, in part, to expunge this guilt. Back home, they will be embarrassed by what she's become, wishing that she'd married well and joined the country club instead. Mostly, they just won't mention it, sticking to safer subjects.

Miss Daisy and I sit in the car watching my student, who keeps banging on the door, trying to get in there. "Honey, don't do it!" Miss Daisy rolls down her window and cries across the grass. "Go back home! It's not too late to stop!" But of course it is. Now my student is trying to peer in a window, shading her eyes with her hand.

Oh, I remember when I was that age myself, desperate for a room in the House of the Rising Sun. You think you'll pay for it out of your day job, and maybe you will for a while, but you'll whore out, too, eventually. We all do. The House of the Rising Sun is full of desperate characters. Some of us are drinking ourselves to death quietly, in our rooms, or loudly, at MLA. A lot of us are involved in secret affairs and unseemly couplings — we'd be real embarrassed if everybody knew who we're sleeping with. Some of us just can't do it anymore, but we put on our makeup anyway, and sit at the window all dressed up, and talk about doing it.

Look! The door is opening, just a crack. It's the Madam herself, but she stands just far enough back in the shadows so you can't really see who she is — maybe it's Shannon Ravenel, or maybe it's Okra.

My student slips inside. She does not look back.

"Well, I never!" Miss Daisy announces before falling over into a dead faint on the seat beside me.

But I know she'll be all right. I know she'll be herself again by the time I get her back to her room, and she'll be talking about what's happened to my student, and she'll make a big story out of it, and she will never, ever, shut up.

This is the main thing that has not changed about the South, in my opinion — that will never change. We Southerners love a story, and we will tell you anything.

Just look at Miss Daisy now. She's already sitting back up on the seat fanning herself and going on and on about what happened to that poor girl, which reminds her of another awful thing that happened to her niece Margaret's daughter, not the Margaret I know that lives in Atlanta, but the other one that lives in middle Tennessee who was never quite right in the head after that terrible automobile accident that happened when she was not but six when Cousin Dan

was driving in that open car, you know he
was such an alcoholic . . .

Good-bye to
the Sunset Man

Key West, Florida — January 29, 2004
Once again my husband and I line up for
sunset cruise tickets on the tall vintage
schooner *Western Union,* which sways in its
dock here at the end of William Street, here
at the end of America.

"How many?" The handsome blonde in
the ticket booth looks like she used to be a
man.

"Three," I say.

"Two," Hal says, turning around to look
at me.

"So how many is it?" She drums her long
nails on the wooden counter.

"Two," Hal says. He gives her his credit
card.

She slides over two tickets for the sunset
cruise and two coupons for free drinks,
which we order on the roof of the Schooner
Wharf Bar where we wait until time to
board. This year we are here without my

son, Josh, who died in his sleep this past October 26. The cause of his death was an "acute myocardiopathy," the collapse of an enlarged heart brought about, in part, I believe, by all the weight he had gained while taking an antipsychotic drug. He was thirty-three; he had been sick for half his life, doing daily heroic battle with the brain disorder that first struck while he was in a program for gifted teen musicians at the Berklee College of Music in Boston, the summer between his junior and senior years in high school.

Back in Chapel Hill, we'd started getting wilder and wilder phone calls from him about "birds flying too close to the sun," reports of all-night practice sessions on the piano, strange encounters in the park, and no sleep — no sleep, ever. He flew home in a straitjacket.

Then the hospitalizations began — first a lengthy stay at Holly Hill in Raleigh, followed by a short, heartbreaking try at returning home to normalcy and Chapel Hill High; then long-term care at Highland Hospital in Asheville, where he lived for the next four years, sometimes in the hospital itself, sometimes in their group home, sometimes in an apartment with participation in their day program. For a while he was better, then not. All kinds of fantasies and scenarios rolled through his head. He moved, talked, and dressed bizarrely; he couldn't remember anything; he couldn't even read. We brought him back to the University of North Carolina's Neurosciences Hospital. They referred him to Dorothea Dix's test program for the recently approved "wonder drug" clozapine.

Up on that beautiful, windy hill looking out over the city of Raleigh, Josh started getting truly better for the first time. He could participate in a real conversation; he could make a joke. It was literally a miracle.

He was able to leave the hospital and enter Caramore Community in Chapel Hill, which offered vocational rehabilitation, a group home, and then a supervised apartment — as well as a lot of camaraderie. He came by with some great stories as he worked with the Caramore lawn and housecleaning business. Once, the housecleaning crew dared one of the gang to jump into the baptismal pool at a local church they were cleaning — and then they all "baptized" him on the spot. Before long, Josh graduated into a real job, at Carolina Cleaners. Against all odds, Josh had become a "working man," as he always referred to himself; his pride in this was enormous.

Though other hospitalizations ("tune-ups," he called them) would be required from time to time, Josh was on his way. He lived in his own apartment, drove a car, managed his weekly doctor visits, blood tests, pharmacy trips and medication. But as the most important part of his own "treatment team," he steadfastly refused his doctor's eventual urging to switch to one of the newer drugs, such as olanzapine, risperidone, or geodon, in hopes of jump-starting his metabolism. Clozapine had given him back his life, and he didn't want to give it up. And in spite of his weight and smoking, he seemed healthy enough; physical examinations didn't ring any warning bells.

Josh became a familiar figure in Chapel Hill and Carrboro, with friends and acquaintances all over town — especially his regular haunts such as Weaver Street Market and Caffé Driade, where he went every day. Josh worked at Akai Hana for the last seven years of his life, doing everything from washing dishes to prep work to lunchtime sushi chef. He was the first one there every morning — he opened up and started preparing the rice. It was his favorite time of the day, as he often said. He played piano there every Saturday night: a mix of jazz, blues, and his own compositions. He put together a tape that he named *Five Not So Easy Pieces.*

The live music produced by the Wharf Bar's Jimmy Buffett wannabe band is way too loud, and our drinks, when they come, are a startling shade of red, with umbrellas in them. Hal raises his plastic glass high. "Here's to the big guy," he says. We drain them.

Josh considered the schooner trip a requisite for his annual Key West experience. He loved the ritual of it all, beginning when the crew invited the evening's passengers to participate in raising the mainsail. He always went over to line up and pull, passing the halyard hand over hand to the next guy. He loved to stand at the rail as we passed the town dock and Mallory Square, where all the weird pageantry of the sunset was already in full swing: the tourists, the guy with the trained housecats, the flame swallower, the escape artist tied up in chains, the oddly menacing cookie lady. The aging hippie musician on board invariably cranked up "Sloop John B" as we headed out to sea while the sun sank lower on the starboard side. I remember on our last trip together, the sun was so bright that I couldn't even face it without sunglasses, but

Josh didn't wear them. He just sat there perfectly still, staring straight into the sun, a little smile playing around his lips.

What thoughts went through his head on that last voyage?

Perhaps more to the point, what thoughts did not go through his head, in this later stage of schizophrenia characterized by "blank mind" and "lack of affect"? Gone were the voices, gone the visions, gone the colored lights, to be replaced by . . . what? Maybe nothing, like the bodhisattva, a person who has achieved the final apotheosis, beyond desire and self. Here he sat, an immense man in a black T-shirt and blue jeans, silent, calm, apparently at peace. He no longer seemed to know what he had lost. Some call this a "blessing," and some days I am among them; but most days I am not, remembering instead that wild boy of seventeen who wanted the world — all the music; all the friends, BMX bikes and skateboards; all the poetry; all the girls — all the life there ever was.

Now the captain is blowing the conch shell from the deck of the *Western Union*. We stand. The sun slants into our eyes. A breeze is coming up. I pull on my windbreaker, fingering the little bronze vial of ashes in my pocket.

It's time.

The previous January Josh and I had flown into Key West together, arriving around 9 p.m. on a cool and blustery Tuesday night. Wind rattled the palm fronds as we walked out onto the brightly lit but somehow lonely-looking Duval Street. Only a few people scurried past, their shoulders hunched against the wind. We passed the Chicken Store, a "safe house" for the much-maligned chickens that have overrun Key West. We passed the Scrub Club, an "adult" bathhouse that usually featured its scantily clad ladies blowing bubbles over the balcony rail, calling out, "Hi there! Feeling dirty? Need a bath?" to the amused passersby. But it was too cool for bubbles that night, and the girls were all inside behind their red door. The wind whipped paper trash along the street.

We crossed Duval and went into the friendly-looking Original Coffee and Tea House. Big trees overhung the old bungalow, its porch and yard filled with comfortable, mismatched furniture. Josh was very tired. He had that blank look he sometimes got, almost vegetative, like a big sweet potato. We walked up the concrete steps and into the bar, with its comforting, helpful smell of coffee brewing. People clustered at little tables, on sofas, in armchairs in adjacent rooms, talking and reading the newspapers strewn everyplace.

The bartender's long, gray hair was pulled back into a ponytail. He came over to Josh and said, "What can I get for you, sir?"

"Well, I'll tell you," Josh said in a surprisingly loud voice (maybe it even surprised him), shaking his head like a dog coming up from under the water. "I'll tell you, buddy, I don't know what the hell it is I want, and I don't know where the hell it is I am, and I don't know what the hell it is I'm doing!"

Heads along the bar swiveled, and the bartender burst out laughing. "In that case, sir, you've come to the right island!" he announced, as everybody applauded.

Josh had found his Key West home for the next week. At bars or beaches, he talked to everybody; you never knew what he was going to say next.

He told a great version of the Christmas story, too, conflating the Bible with O. Henry: "Once upon a time there was a young girl who was very sick, and somehow she got the idea that she would die when all the leaves fell off the tree that grew just outside her bedroom window. One by one they dropped. She got sicker and sicker.

Finally there was only one red leaf left on the tree; she was just about to die. That night while she was asleep, Jesus flew up to her window. Jesus was a French artist. He wore a red beret. So he brought his box of oil paints with him and painted red leaves all over the window, finishing just as the sun came up and the last red leaf fluttered down to the ground. Then he flew away. Then she woke up, and she was well, and it was Christmas."

I asked him whether or not he believed in Jesus. "Well, I don't know," he said. "Every time I'm in the hospital, there are at least three people in there who think they're Jesus. So sometimes I think, well, maybe Jesus wasn't Jesus at all — maybe he was just the first schizophrenic."

Josh's eventual diagnosis was schizoaffective disorder, meaning partly schizophrenic (his mind did not work logically, his senses were often unreliable, his grip on reality sometimes tenuous) and partly bipolar — actually a blessing, since the characteristic "ups and downs" allowed him more expression and empathy. But psychiatric diagnosis is tricky at best. The sudden onset of these major brain disorders usually occurs in the late teens or early twenties, and it's usually severe. However all psychosis looks alike at first. There's no way to distinguish between the "highs" of bipolar illness, for instance, and the florid stage of schizophrenia — or even a garden-variety LSD psychosis. Reality has fled in every case. The best doctors make no claims; "Wait and see," they say.

As far as prognosis goes, medical folklore holds to a "rule of three": About a third of all people with major psychotic episodes will actually get well, such as Kurt Vonnegut's son, Mark, now a physician, who wrote the memoir *The Eden Express.* The next, larger group will be in and out of hospitals and programs for the rest of their lives, with wildly varying degrees of success in work and life situations; the final group will have recalcitrant, persistent illnesses that may require lifelong care or hospitalization — though now, I suspect, the new drugs and community care models have shrunk this group considerably.

But here's the bottom line: All mental illnesses are treatable. Often, brain chemistry has to be adjusted with medication. If symptoms occur, go to the doctor. Don't downplay it, don't hide it — seek treatment immediately. Mental illness is no more embarrassing than diabetes. And the earlier we get treatment, the more effective it will be. I myself could never have made it through this past year of grief and depression without counseling and medication. As Josh proved, very real, valid and full lives can be lived within these illnesses.

Now my husband and I sit discreetly at the very back of the *Western Union,* right behind the captain at the wheel. He has given the order; the crew has cried "fire in the hole" and shot off the cannon. We have covered our ears. We have gotten our complimentary wine, our conch chowder. We have listened to our shipmates talk about how much snow they left behind in Cleveland, how many grandchildren they have, and how one guy played hockey for Hopkins on that great team in 1965. Then we duck as, with a great whoosh of the jib, we come about. We sit quietly, holding hands, hard. Now there's a lot of wind. All around us, people are putting on their jackets.

Independent of any of this, the sky puts on its big show, gearing up for sunset. The sun speeds up as it sinks lower and lower. The water turns into a sheet of silver, like a mirror.

Like Hal, Josh was a major sunset man, always looking for that legendary green flash right after the sunset, which nobody I know has ever actually seen, though everybody claims to have known somebody who has seen it. Here where sunset is a religion, we never miss the moment. In Key West the sun grows huge and spreads out when it touches the water, so that it's no longer round at all but a glowing red beehive shape that plunges down abruptly to the thunderous applause of the revelers back at Mallory Square.

"Get ready," Hal says in my ear. "But look, there's a cloud bank, it's not going to go all the way."

I twist the top of the vial in my windbreaker pocket.

The sun glows neon red, cut off at the bottom by clouds.

A hush falls over the whole crowd on board the *Western Union.* Everybody faces west. Cameras are raised. It is happening.

"Bon voyage," Hal says. Suddenly, the sun is gone. The crowd cheers. I throw the ashes out on the water behind us; like a puff of smoke, they disappear immediately into the wake. I say, "Good-bye, baby." Nobody notices. The water turns into mother of pearl, shining pink all the way from our schooner to the horizon. The scalloped edge of the puffy clouds goes from pink to gold. The crowd goes "aah." Good-bye baby. But no green flash. The crowd stretches, they move, they mill around on deck. The light fades and stars come out.

There is a theory that mental illness conveys certain gifts. Even if this sometimes seems to be the case, as in bipolar disorder's frequent association with creativity, those gifts are not worth the pain and devastating losses the illness also brings with it. Yet sometimes there are moments. . . .

I am remembering one starry summer night back in North Carolina, the kind of breathtakingly beautiful summer night of all our dreams, when Josh and I took a long walk around our town. He'd been staying with us for several days because he was too sick to stay in his own apartment. He'd been deteriorating for months, and his doctor had arranged his admission to UNC's Neurosciences Hospital for the next morning. Josh didn't know this yet. But he was always "compliant," as they call it. We were very lucky in this. My friend's son wouldn't take his medicine and chose to live on the street; she never knew where he was. Schizophrenia is like an umbrella diagnosis covering a whole crowd of very different illnesses; but very few people with brain disorders actually become violent, despite the stereotype.

Josh liked the hospital. It was safe, and the world he'd been in that week was not safe, not at all, a world where strangers were talking about him and people he used to know inhabited other people's bodies and tables turned into spiders and all the familiar landmarks disappeared so that he couldn't find his way anywhere. He couldn't sleep, he couldn't drive, he couldn't think.

Yet on that summer night in Hillsborough, a wonderful thing happened. We were walking through the alley between the old Confederate cemetery and our backyard when we ran into our neighbor Allan.

"Hi there, Josh," Allan said.

Instead of replying, Josh sang out a single note of music.

"A flat," he said. It hung in the hot honeysuckle air.

"Nice," Allan said, passing on.

The alley ended at Tryon Street, where we stepped onto the sidewalk. A young girl hurried past.

"C sharp," Josh said, then sang it out.

The girl looked at him before she disappeared into the Presbyterian Church.

We crossed the street and walked past the young policemen getting out of his car in front of the police station.

"Middle C," Josh said, humming.

Since it was one of Hillsborough's "Last Friday" street fairs, we ran into more and more people as we headed toward the center of town. For each one, Josh had a musical note — or a chord, for a pair or a group.

"What's up?" I finally asked.

"Well, you know I have perfect pitch," he said — I nodded, though he did not — "and everybody we see has a special musical note, and I can hear every one." He broke off to sing a high chord for a couple of young teen girls, then dropped into a lower register for a retired couple eating ice-cream cones.

"Hello," another neighbor said, smiling when Josh hummed back at him.

So it went, all over town. Even some of the buildings had notes, apparently: the old Masonic Hall, the courthouse, the corner bar. Josh was singing his heart out. And almost — almost — it was a song, the symphony of Hillsborough. We were both exhilarated. We walked and walked. By the time we got back home, he was exhausted. Finally he slept. The next day, he went into the hospital.

Josh loved James Taylor, especially his song "Fire and Rain." But we were too conservative, or chickenshit, or something, to put it on his tombstone, the same way we were "not cool enough," as Josh put it, to walk down the aisle to "Purple Rain" (his idea) while he played the piano on the day we got married in 1985.

But now I say the words to Hal as the light fades slowly on the water behind us.

I've seen fire and I've seen rain
I've seen sunny days that I thought would
    never end
I've seen lonely times when I could not find
    a friend
But I always thought that I'd see you again.

Well, I won't. I know this. But what a privilege it was to live on this earth with him, what a privilege it was to be his mother. There will be a lessening of pain, there will be consolations, I can tell. But as C. S. Lewis wrote in *A Grief Observed:* "Reality never repeats. . . . that is what we should all like. The happy past restored" . . . as it can never be, and maybe never was. Who's got perfect pitch, anyway? Yet to have children — or simply to experience great love for any person at all — is to throw yourself wide open to the possibility of pain at any moment. But I would not choose otherwise. Not now, not ever. Like every parent with a disabled child, my greatest fear used to be that I would die first. "I can't die," I always said whenever any risky undertaking was proposed. So now I can die. But I don't want to. Instead, I want to live as hard as I can, burning up the days in honor of his sweet, hard life.

Night falls on the schooner ride back to Key West. I clutch the bronze vial that held some of Josh's ashes, tracing its engraved design with my finger. The wind blows my hair. The young couple in front of us are making out.

"Let's get some oysters at Alonzo's," Hal says, and suddenly I realize that I'm starving.

"Look," the captain says, pointing up. "Venus."

Sure enough. Then we see the Big Dipper, Orion, Mars. Where's that French artist with the red beret? No sign of him, and no green flash, either — but stars. A whole sky full of them by the time we slide into the dock at the end of William Street.

BLUE HEAVEN

May 1965

We leave Hollins at 10 a.m., six of us girls crammed into the car, Mary Withers driving. "My Girl" is on the radio. Some of us know the dates we'll meet in Chapel Hill; some don't. I don't. He is an SAE frat brother, but I can't remember his name. I am already tired. I have been up for hours, ironing my clothes, ironing my hair. At Martinsville, we stop for gas and road beer. We sing along with the radio. Now it's "Help Me, Rhonda," by the Beach Boys. We are getting hot in the car because it doesn't have any air-conditioning, but we can't open the windows much because we would mess up our hair. I keep trying to remember my date's name. We stop in Danville for more road beer. "Ticket to Ride" is on the radio. In Chapel Hill, we pull up in front of the fraternity house; all these boys stand up and walk out to the car. Oh no. What is his name? Oh no.

Later that night, much later, we walk right up the middle of Franklin Street in formal clothes, giggling and singing. Doug Clark and the Hot Nuts played at the party. My date passed out, but now I have another date. He is from Scotland Neck, which I find hysterically funny. The sun is coming up. I'm carrying my shoes. It was some party.

June 1966

Summer School. I sit on the grass near the Davie Poplar, books thrown down beside me. A soft wind blows my hair. I stretch out my legs. The boy puts his head on my lap. He wears a pastel knit shirt, pastel slacks, loafers. He looks like an Easter egg. But he is a golfer. I sigh languidly. I am in love.

August 1966

It is a hot, smoky café, the smoke barely stirred by the sluggish overhead fan. The backs of my legs stick to the sticky wooden booth. This conversation is the most intense conversation I have ever had, and also the most beer I have ever drunk. It is very, very late. This is a great conversation, I can't believe how significant it is. He leans across the table toward me. He pounds on the table to make a point. With his other hand, he touches my knee under the table. He is a member of the Student Democratic Society. We light more cigarettes. I am in love.

August 1967
It is raining, and we have been walking for hours, in a light, fine drizzle that jewels the edges of everything. We are soaked through. We stop to sit on one of the gray stone walls that are everywhere in Chapel Hill. We kiss. I run my finger along the jeweled stone. This time I am really in love. Later, much later, this guy will move to Chicago, taking my life-size painting of the Supremes and breaking my heart. Eventually I will recover. He was from Connecticut and talked funny.

June 1973
Finally, I move to Chapel Hill with my husband, James Seay, a poet who has gotten a job teaching at UNC. I have always wanted to live here. So has everybody else who ever went to school here, and once school is over, many of them can't stand to leave. So everybody who comes to work on our house has a Ph.D. in something: the plumber's degree is in philosophy; the painter is a historian. I am embarrassed to have all these educated people doing manual

labor on my house. I offer them coffee and cake. The carpenter listens to opera while he builds bookshelves. I have second thoughts — are we cool enough to live in Chapel Hill? I won't let the children play with toy guns while the workmen are here, so they won't think we are rednecks.

September 1973

It is the first day of my new job teaching language arts at Carolina Friends School. I got this job by telephone from Nashville, where I'd been teaching seventh grade at Harpeth Hall, a prestigious girls' school. There the girls wore green and gold uniforms, the school colors, and the faculty dressed up. So I'm all ready for my first day at Carolina Friends, wearing a red linen suit with a straight skirt, pearls, patent leather heels, and stockings.

Only, I can't find the school. I drive out into the countryside as directed, on narrow roads past fields and cows and split rail fences, and then finally turn onto an unpaved road that disappears ahead of me into the forest. This can't be right! Gradually I perceive a number of ramshackle buildings here and there in the trees, then a large log house, apparently built by hand, up the hill, with a sizable deck running all around it.

Built by hand? Where's the school? Harpeth Hall had a stone wall around its landscaped grounds, with paved walkways running everywhere.

Finally I spot an old man in a baseball cap and overalls, trudging up the road carrying a toolbox. I pull beside him and announce, "I'm looking for Carolina Friends School."

"Well, you've found us." He gives me a big smile and sticks his hand in the window for me to shake. I had him pegged as a janitor, but maybe not.

"But where are the students?" I still haven't seen one.

He points up the hill at the log house.

"They're settling in," he says.

I stare at him.

"We start every day with meditation," he says. "Quiet time."

Really? I'm still thinking as I park in a cluster of old pickups and vans with peace signs on them. I have never known any middle school students to be capable of quiet time, much less meditation. It's pretty hard walking up the pebbly dirt road in these patent leather heels, covered by dust when I finally make it.

Nobody seems to be around, so I go on in the open door, mortified to find myself sud-

185

denly in the midst of about seventy people, young and old, all of them down on the polished wood floor, where they form a huge, ragged circle in every posture imaginable, heads mostly bowed, eyes mostly closed. Everybody's wearing blue jeans, cut-offs, or shorts, with sneakers, flip-flops — or simply bare feet. There's a giant, colorful handwoven mandala on the wall above them. Across the big room I spot a guy I somehow know to be Don Wells, the head of the school, the guy who hired me on the phone. He's got long, blondish hair, he's sitting crosslegged, grinning at me. He does not get up. Out of some wrong-headed perversity I pick my way through the meditating students, across the open part of the circle, my heels clicking on the wood floor. Nobody says a word. But when I have almost made it, here comes a long, single, expert wolf whistle, and then a rising chorus of other wolf whistles. Oh no. I feel myself turning as red as this smart little red suit, which I will never, ever, wear again. The guy Don gets up and hugs me, laughing. Now everybody is laughing, scrambling to their feet, heading outdoors. Another teacher brings me some sandals so I can participate in the ropes course and the relay races and the trust-building exercises. Well, some of them, anyway.

I'm getting the drill — or the lack of the drill, I should say. They have no uniforms and no school colors and no sports except for Ultimate Frisbee, whatever that is. I stand out on the deck looking down at the hilly, wooded landscape covered with kids and grownups in all kinds of activities that are, I realize suddenly, much less random than they seem. This will turn out to be true of everything.

I am surprised and horrified to hear my first assignment, which is to plan and buy the food for a hundred people for one day of our upcoming weekend retreat at Quaker Lake.

"I don't know anything about feeding that many people. I just can't do that," I tell Don.

"Oh, sure you can," Don says.

At my first faculty meeting that afternoon, I have to settle in, too. Then Don welcomes me and asks, "What individual courses do you want to teach?"

"Well, what are the requirements?" I ask. "I mean, the curriculum."

"We're in the process of figuring that out," Don says. "You tell me."

Everybody speaks up. They all listen to each other. They all have great ideas. I have no ideas. In fact, I'm having a panic attack, but then after a while something else starts happening. Somewhere, way down inside, it's like a dam gives way and I start getting excited. I love plays, I have always wanted kids to write plays and then put them on. I have always wanted to teach a class that mixes up art and writing, or photography and writing, I have always wanted to teach ghost stories, and Greek mythology, and poetry out loud, really loud. Also I've got this recipe for taco pie casserole that might work great for that retreat.

Summer, mid-1970s

A party on Stinson Street, probably Anne Jones's house. Everybody I know has lived on Stinson Street at one time or another. Stinson Street has constant parties, constant yard sales. Anyway, at some point during one of these parties, I go outside to get some air and wander across the street to Leonard Rogoff's yard sale, where I stand transfixed before a chest of drawers with a mirror attached to the top of it. I stand before the chest and look into the mirror for a long time. The mirror is tilted so that I can see a tree, the moon, my face. Oh no, I think. This is really my life, and I am really living it. I remember thinking that then, on

Stinson Street.

I sit on the edge of the Rainbow Soccer
Field, where my kids are playing Rainbow
Soccer, which is noncompetitive. You can't
yell anything like "Kill 'em!" or "Stomp
'em!" This is hard for some parents. My son
Josh is playing center forward. I am writing
a novel.

I sit at the Chapel Hill Tennis Club, waiting for my son's match to start. This is my
son Page. He's real good. I am writing a
novel.

I sit on a wing chair before the fire in the
Chapel Hill Public Library on Franklin
Street . . . in a booth at Breadmen's . . . at
a picnic table at University Lake . . . on a
quilt at Umstead Park . . . in a wicker chair
on my own back porch on Burlage Circle. I
am writing a novel. I am always writing a
novel in this town. Nobody cares. Nobody
bugs me. Nobody thinks a thing about it.
Everybody else is writing a novel, too.

"In Chapel Hill, throw a rock and you'll
hit a writer," someone once said. This has
always been true. For Chapel Hill is pri-
marily a town of the mind, a town of trees
and visions. Thomas Wolfe praised the "rare
romantic quality of the atmosphere." Maybe

189

the quiet, leafy streets themselves are still informed by his giant spirit, that wild young man from the mountains who raged through them in his archetypal search for identity.

The much-loved UNC English professor Hugh Holman wrote, "The primary thing that Chapel Hill gives those who come to be a part of it is the freedom to be themselves. It is an unorganized town. It is easy to persuade its citizens, along with the students of the university, to join briefly in a cause, to march for a little while beneath a banner . . . but to remain permanently organized is something else indeed, for Chapel Hill does not organize very well. Those who come to this town can find in it just about the quantity of freedom to be themselves which they wish to have."

Circa 1980

I am with my children, and we run into some of their friends from their former community church preschool, along with the friends' mother.

"Hello, Naomi," I say. "Hi, Johnny."

"We have changed our names," their mother says. "This is Trumpet Vine," she indicates Naomi, "and this is Golden Sun. I myself am Flamingo."

Oh my, I think. Oh no. My kids do not

think that Trumpet Vine is a very good name. But then my younger son, Page, changes his own name (briefly) to Rick. He has always hated Page, a family name; he gets teased because it is too girly. Soon after this, Trumpet Vine, Golden Sun, and Flamingo moved away from Chapel Hill with some kind of sect, I think they were called the Orange People.

I never changed my name, but I have thought about it ever since. I would go with three syllables, too: Biloxi, Chardonnay, Sunflower . . .

Surprises, Spring 1981

In retrospect, it seems inevitable. Both people of good will, my husband and I have been kept together by children and family and friends and common interests, but we are very different. When he suddenly moves out, I am traumatized. I am thirty-seven, old as the hills, old as dirt. And now I am getting a divorce. My mother bursts into tears. "Nobody in our family has *evah* gotten a divorce," she weeps, though later she will admit that a numbah of them should have. My mountain father weighs in with his mountain advice: "Change the locks and get a handgun." I don't do that. I do lose twenty pounds, almost overnight. In fact I lose everything, leaving jackets and purses all over town. I let my boys ride their skateboards through our empty house and eat exclusively from the Red Food Group so beloved by boys (SpaghettiOs, Hawaiian Punch, bacon, barbecued potato chips). I take them skiing in Colorado with my cousins for spring break.

I desperately need a real job instead of the part-time position I've got. Suddenly one comes up at North Carolina State University, full-time. Only I don't have the nerve to apply for it, I don't have the academic credentials. "Don't give me that crap," my friend and fellow writer Doris Betts says. "Just go for it." She pushes me into it, and to my surprise I get the job, which I will keep for nineteen years.

On Valentine's Day I get myself together, as my mother used to say, and go out for an afternoon Valentine party thrown by Marilyn Hartman, who directs the Evening College at Duke University, where I teach creative writing once a week. Here I meet another writer, a journalist named Hal Crowther, a recent transplant from Buffalo who is teaching critical writing in this same program. I know who he is, I have been admiring his columns in the new *Spectator* magazine. We start talking and it turns out that we have both stashed our children in video parlors so we can come to this party. Then we start talking about Robert Stone's recent novel, *A Flag for Sunrise,* which we have both just read. Hal keeps rattling his tiny cup in his tiny saucer and looking for wine. But there's only tea. "Would you like to go out for a drink sometime?" he asks.

A man is the last thing I'm looking for, but I'm not a fool, either. "Sure," I hear myself saying from a great distance as I levitate over the Valentine party, something I have been doing a lot lately.

Soon after that I have to go to a meeting at N.C. State, so I meet Hal for lunch at a restaurant in Raleigh. But I am so nervous, I lean forward right in the middle of this lunch and say, "Well, how do you think this is going? Because I'm so nervous I would just as soon bag it if we're not having fun." Hal says he is having fun, so I keep on seeing him.

"Cut it out," my friends say. "This is supposed to be your interim man."

I write a country song named "Interim Man." I keep on seeing Hal.

Summer 1981
Hal's daughter, Amity, is ten and very beautiful, all legs and big blue eyes, very

feminine and very sophisticated. An only child, she has spent lots of time with adults, especially her adoring father. This is the first entire summer day she has spent alone at my house, while my boys are at a tennis day camp and her father is in Raleigh at work.

"Well, Amity, what would you like for lunch?" I ask her. "Would you rather have a grilled cheese sandwich or a peanut butter and jelly sandwich?"

She hesitates. "How about French bread and brie?" she says, used to little gourmet picnics with her dad.

All I have is Velveeta and Wonder.

But we bridge the yawning culture gap between us as the summer goes on. For one thing, Amity actually likes to go to the grocery store with me, a thing my boys can't stand. And we both like to cook, especially cakes. We bake cake after cake for the ravenous boys while my visiting mother, a former home economics teacher, calls out measurements from her reclining position on the sofa.

All three of us — me, my mother, and Amity — read the *National Enquirer* and *The Midnight Sun* from cover to cover as soon as we get them home from the grocery store. We especially love UFO abductions and multiple births and anything at all about Elvis. (This *National Enquirer* habit is Amity's own mother's only complaint about my parenting skills . . . though, Lord knows, she has plenty of other things to choose from as well.) But I claim that I am doing research for a novel named *Lives of the Stars,* which turns out to be sort of true anyway.

One day Hal and I are reading the newspaper and I read that genius woman's column and say, "Guess what? There is no other word in the English language that rhymes with 'orange.' "

Hal thinks for a minute. "What about Warren G. Harding?" he says.

Okay. I am in love.

Spring 1982

Hal and I are walking in the woods, following one of the green-space trails that run all over town, when suddenly we come upon a life-size concrete hippo, climbing out of Bolin Creek as if emerging from the Blue Nile. Oh no, I think stupidly, a hippo! Anything can happen in Chapel Hill. I realize that we'll probably get married.

January 1983

A Snapshot of the End of My Youth. Chapel Hill Community Center. A recreation-department basketball game is in progress.

My son's team, the Tigers, is ahead by two points, but it's nip and tuck all the way. "Shoot, Monty, shoot!" yells somebody's father, sitting next to me. For some reason, I turn around and look at this father. He's an attractive black man wearing a leather hat and a diamond ring. For some reason, he looks familiar. Then it hits me. Oh no! It's Doug Clark! of Doug Clark and the Hot Nuts! He's got a kid, Monty, on the opposing team . . . oh no. I am really old.

Summer 1983. The Beehive
I drive from my house on Burlage Circle over toward the university on Franklin Street along those old stone walls on a hot, green summer day, which reminds me of that first time I ever came to Chapel Hill for summer school so long ago. Now I am going to visit Dr. Louis Rubin, who has retired from teaching English (and Southern Literature, which he invented) in order to start a publishing company, of all things. It is located in the garage behind his old stone house on Gimghoul Road. A sign on the fence reads: ALGONQUIN BOOKS OF CHAPEL HILL, EDITORIAL OFFICES. PLEASE KEEP GATE CLOSED AGAINST DOG.

Louis Rubin was my creative writing teacher at Hollins for four years, which is why I still call him Mr. Rubin. I couldn't call him Louis if my life depended upon it. Mr. Rubin was a great, great teacher who changed my life, as he has changed so many others. In fact it is probable that I would never have become a writer at all if I had not encountered him when I did, because I was a wild girl, and I'm not sure what would have happened to me. But I do know for sure that if I am ever able to write anything real, or beautiful, or honest — anything that ever speaks truly about the human condition — it will be due to this man.

I enter carefully through the gate and go into the garage.

It's like a beehive in here. I say hello to Mimi Fountain, also from Hollins, Ann Moss, and Garrett Epps. Shannon Ravenel, Mr. Rubin's partner in this enterprise, works from St. Louis. Mr. Rubin has just written her a letter about their new venture: "This is going to be fun, I think." In the newspaper he has said, "Editing is just like teaching, but publishing is something else. I don't want to just put new people into print; I want to launch them." Right now Mr. Rubin is making a peanut butter sandwich on top of an old filing cabinet in the back, where he will eat it, standing up. He does this every day. All around him, manuscripts rise to his knees.

The FedEx man comes in and the dog runs out, then we all run out after the dog. The postman comes. Eva Rubin drives back from her job teaching political science at N.C. State. She waves and goes into the house, followed by the miscreant dog. Now Mr. Rubin feeds the birds, which means throwing several handfuls of seed straight up into the air. The sky goes black with birds and beating wings. I start squealing and batting at them. Mr. Rubin is laughing. Finally the birds fly away and he looks at me. "Whatcha got?" he asks and I hand him the pages I've brought, all wrinkled up and sweaty from me holding them.

I follow him inside the house to his office where he sticks a cigar in his mouth and sits down and starts reading immediately. Mr. Rubin never does anything later. "I know it's got too many voices in it," I say when he gets done, but he grins and hands it back.

"Keep on going," he says, which is all he needs to say and all I need to hear, because I am already thinking what comes next, and I can't even remember driving home.

June 29, 1985
Amity, age thirteen and very grown up, has specified a church wedding for her father

198

and me, and so here we are at the Chapel of the Cross, rehearsing hurriedly for our tiny 10 a.m. ceremony, which will take place in less than an hour. Radiant in her white dress, Amity walks endlessly up and down the aisle carrying her bouquet, carrying herself just so. She looks beautiful. But the ladies arranging the flowers at the altar scowl at her, whispering among themselves, casting dark looks at the middle-aged groom.

Finally one of the ladies says acidly to me, "Just how old is she, anyway?" and I realize that they think she's the bride, not me in my green linen dress. Oh no. This is what I get for fancying myself a bride at my age! I ought to know better. I ought to stay single and write novels out in the woods.

But then, forty minutes later, I am the bride, and I am the happiest bride ever, as the organ plays and the bells ring and we step out into the bright June day married, of all things, and my boys wave at some other boys who are skating on skateboards down Franklin Street.

Thanksgiving 1985, '86, '87, '88 . . .
For many years we hold the Wild Turkey Classic every Thanksgiving. Originally it was Hal's idea to go out and play a couple in-

nings of softball before the big traditional dinner in the afternoon. I jumped right on it. Genius! A morning softball game gives the kids and the visiting relatives and friends something to do (and keeps us all from drinking too much) during those long hours while the turkey roasts and those floats roll interminably down Fifth Avenue on TV. The baseball diamond at Phillips Junior High is right up the street. Hal makes some calls, especially to other diehard Durham Bulls fans like himself. I tell friends and neighbors. I make the dressing and mash the potatoes ahead of time.

Thanksgiving Day dawns clear and cold with a brilliant Carolina blue sky. Hal heads for the field early, taking bats and bases and gloves and his brother Jeff, who is reputed to have been scouted by the Yankees but right now is hung over. Hal pushes him out the door, not easy. I've already got the turkey in the oven, covered with tons of butter and several old kitchen towels and tin foil — my substitute for basting. I corral the wild boys and fill up the station wagon with dogs, kids, juice, store-bought doughnuts and coffeecake and a folding table to put it all out on. We turn right off Estes and head up to the raised grassy baseball field, which looms like some kind of Indian mound or ancient fort. Coming up over the hill I stop amazed at the scene before me, like a Brueghel painting. Who are all these people? I guess the word spread. People are everywhere, doing knee bends, running, tossing the ball back and forth, talking, hugging, hugging. Lots of hugging. I set up my table and talk intensely with friends I haven't seen for years. People spread quilts on the sidelines. Somebody has brought a brand new baby in a little yellow suit, and he is passed around and admired. Laughter rings out like bells. Our breath makes white puffs in the chilly blue air, cartoon conversation. Kids and dogs cover the outfield. Now whistles are blowing. They're already choosing sides. It's Michael McFee vs. Jay Bryan . . . two poets! Whoever thought the poets would be competitive? But they're cool, choosing wimpy kids like my own as well as grownups. Each side has got about thirty players. Bill Leuchtenburg, in his seventies, is playing second. Jimmy Mills, very slightly younger, is at third. A huge scream goes up when a yellow lab snatches the ball and runs off into the trees with it.

"PLAY BALL!" somebody hollers, and then we do, for the next twenty years or so, as the Massengale boys and the Ludingtons grow up before our very eyes and other kids go away and get married and then come back with their own kids, first in strollers and then on the field, another generation. Some people divorce and return with other people. Some people go to graduate school in Iowa, or to rehab, or New York or Asheville or Austin, places too far to come back from. Every year, more girls are playing, not only our perennial Elva, a ringer. Bill Leuchtenburg is still playing second. Jim Watson still bikes to the game wearing that Duke hat, his hair flying out behind him. All of Amity's boyfriends have to come and play ball, this is a requirement. On and on it goes, year after year, on sunny Thursdays and cloudy Thursdays and freezing Thursdays, in fog, in sleet, the sweet taste of doughnuts, the crack of the bat, the screams and yells and laughter of the crowd, old friends and new, all these dear and changing faces, these lovers of the game.

June 2012
Hal and I have lived in Hillsborough for sixteen years now, so it's not often I find myself driving alone through Chapel Hill this late at night, windows down, after a concert with friends. I glimpse a little sliver of moon above the moving treetops. Maybe because it's that precious time at the end of

the semester, before summer school has started, but it's quiet as quiet can be tonight on Franklin Street, no people and no other cars, only a little breeze rustling the thick leaves on all these big trees and bringing me the unbearably sweet and somehow sad scent of honeysuckle. This reminds me of eating dinner one June night at Crook's Corner when Bill Smith had just invented his famous honeysuckle sorbet, which he brought out to our table, and it was true, I could taste it, all the inexpressible longing of honeysuckle as it melted on my tongue. Now the breeze brings laughter, and music from far away. All those years, all that music . . . starting with Bland Simpson and Jim Wann's early seventies performance of *Diamond Studs* at the old Ranch House restaurant on Airport Road, everybody dancing on the tables to "Cakewalk in Kansas City," I had never seen anything like it, "musicians' theater" they called it, and they would take it straight to Broadway. . . . And always, Jim Watson's annual Christmas show at the Cave . . . and Callie Warner singing the title song of our own show *Good Ol' Girls* in its first production at Swain Hall right here on campus. I remember Tommy Thompson of the Red Clay Ramblers singing his "Hot Buttered Rum," one of the most beautiful songs in the world, at the old Cat's Cradle in the dead of winter. Most of all I remember my son Josh sitting down at the piano in our Akai Hana sushi restaurant to play his own signature jazz set, "Five Not So Easy Pieces" he used to call it, which always included "Pachelbel," those running purely joyous notes, a celebration. The music of this night comes closer now, and the laughter, and then I see them, barefooted girls four abreast walking down the middle of the street, long hair swinging, singing. That blonde, second from the left, looks somehow familiar to me as she doubles over in laughter and almost falls, oh she's got no idea what's going to happen to her in the years to come, she doesn't care, either. All she wants is now, and she wants it bad, and I want her to have it all. But then the van ahead of me stops to let some people out and when I can see again, they're gone, those girls, she's gone, my girl, if she ever was there at all.

A Life in Books

I was a reader long before I was a writer. In fact, I started writing in the first place because I couldn't stand for my favorite books to be over, so I started adding more and more chapters onto the ends of them, often including myself as a character. Thus the Bobbsey twins became the Bobbsey triplets, and Nancy Drew's best friends, Bess Marvin and George Fayne, were joined by another character named Lee Smith — who actually ended up with Ned Nickerson! The additional chapters grew longer and more complicated as my favorite books became more complicated — *Heidi, Anne of Green Gables,* and *Pippi Longstocking,* for instance.

Mama was indefatigable in reading aloud to me when I was little, and I'm sure that the musical cadence of her soft Southern voice is one reason I took to reading the way I did, for the activity itself was so pleasurable. Later, we pored over the huge pages of the *National Enquirer* together, marveling at the lives of the stars, the psychic who could bend spoons with the power of his mind alone, and that Indiana couple who got kidnapped and taken away in a space ship where they were given physical examinations by aliens before being dropped back down into their own cornfield, none the worse for wear. Mama and I loved this stuff. My father read a lot of newspapers, magazines, and sometimes history or politics. Though neither of my parents read novels, they received the *Reader's Digest* Condensed Books, which I devoured, and they also encouraged me to go to our fledgling library.

This soon got out of hand. I became a voracious, then an obsessive reader; recurrent bouts of pneumonia and tonsillitis gave me plenty of time to indulge my passion. After I was pronounced "sickly," I got to stay home a lot, slathered with a vile salve named Mentholatum, spirit lamp hissing in the corner of my room, reading to my heart's content. I remained an inveterate reader of the sort who hides underneath the covers with a flashlight and reads all night long. But I did not read casually, or for mere information. What I wanted was to feel all wild and trembly inside, an effect first produced by *The Secret Garden,* which I'd read maybe twenty times.

The only man I had ever loved as much as Colin of *The Secret Garden* was Johnny Tremain, from Esther Forbes's book of that title. I used to wish it was *me* — not Johnny Tremain — who'd had the hot silver spilled on my hand. I would have suffered anything (everything!) for Johnny Tremain.

Other books had affected me strongly: *Little Women,* especially the part where Beth dies, and *Gone With the Wind,* especially the part where Melanie dies. I had long hoped for a wasting disease, such as leukemia, to test my mettle. I also loved *Marjorie Morningstar, A Tree Grows in Brooklyn,* and books like *Dear and Glorious Physician, The Shoes of the Fisherman, Christy,* and anything at all about horses and saints. I had read all the Black Stallion books, of course, as well as all the Marguerite Henry books. But my all-time favorite was a book about Joan of Arc, especially the frontispiece illustration depicting Joan as she knelt and "prayed without ceasing for guidance from God," whose face was depicted overhead in a thunderstorm. Not only did I love Joan of Arc, I wanted to *be* her.

I was crazy for horses and saints.

"By the way," my mother mentioned to me one day almost casually while I was home being sick in bed and she was straightening my covers, "You know, Marguerite Henry stayed at your grandmother's boarding house on Chincoteague Island while she was writing that book."

"What book?" I sat right up.

"*Misty*," Mama said. "Then she came back to write *Sea Star,* and I think the illustrator, Wesley Dennis, stayed there, too. Cousin Jack used to take him out on a boat."

I couldn't believe it! A real writer, a horse writer, had walked up the crushed oyster shell road where I had gone barefoot, had sat at the big dinner table where I'd eaten fish and corncakes for breakfast; had maybe even swung in the same wicker porch swing I loved.

I wrote a novel on the spot, on eight sheets of my mother's Crane stationery. It featured as main characters my two favorite people at that time: Adlai Stevenson and Jane Russell. In my novel, they fell in love and then went West together in a covered wagon. Once there they got married and became — inexplicably! — Mormons. I am not sure how I knew about Mormons. But even at that age, I was fixed upon romance, flight, and religion, themes I would return to again and again.

What did my parents think of this strange little girl who had come to them so late in life, after they had become resigned to never having children? Well, they spoiled me rotten and were simply delighted by everything I did, everything I showed any interest in. I believe if I had told my mother that I wanted to be, say, an ax murderer, she would have said, without blinking an eye, "Well, that's nice, dear, what do you think you might want to major in?" My daddy would have gone out to buy me the ax.

Though my parents might feel — as Mama certainly said, later — that they wished I would just stop all that writing stuff and marry a lawyer or a doctor, which is what a daughter really ought to do, of course, the fact is that they were so loving that they gave me the confidence, and the permission, early on, to do just about anything I wanted to do. Decades later, I would realize how unusual this was, and how privileged I have been because of it. Now I see this issue — permission to write — as the key issue for many women I have worked with in my classes, especially women who have begun writing later in their lives.

But my childhood was not entirely a happy one. No writer's childhood ever is.

There was my father's inexplicable sadness and my mother's "nerves"; there was my strange Uncle Tick; there was a scary little neighborhood "club" we formed, which did bad things. There was a lot of drinking. There were hospitalizations and long absences and periods of being sent away to live with other relatives. Life was often confusing and mysterious, which inspired Martha Sue and my cousin Randy and me to start our own espionage firm, which I would describe much later in a short story named "Tongues of Fire":

We lived to spy, and this is mainly what we did on our bike trips around town. We'd seen some really neat stuff, too. For instance we had seen Roger Ainsley, the coolest guy in our school, squeezing pimples in his bathroom mirror. We had seen Mister Bondurant whip his son Earl with a belt, and later, when Earl suddenly dropped out of school and enlisted in the Army, we alone knew why. We had seen our fourth-grade teacher, prissy Miss Emily Horn, necking on a couch with her boyfriend, and smoking cigarettes. Best of all, we had seen Mrs. Cecil Hertz come running past a picture window wearing nothing but an apron, followed shortly by

Mr. Cecil Hertz himself, wearing nothing at all and carrying a spatula.

It was amazing how careless people were about drawing their drapes and pulling their shades down. It was amazing what you could see, especially if you were an athletic and enterprising girl such as myself. I wrote my observations down in a Davy Crockett spiral notebook I'd bought for this purpose. I wrote down everything: date, time, weather, physical descriptions, my reaction. I would use all this stuff later, in my novels.

This is true. And though it's also true that we actually did spy on people, that first paragraph is mostly made up. When you write fiction, you up the ante, generally speaking, since real life rarely affords enough excitement or conflict to spice up a page sufficiently. This passage also illustrates another technique that has saved my neck — maybe even my life — many times: the use of humor to allow us to talk or write about the scariest things, things we couldn't articulate and deal with otherwise. It is another way of whistling past the graveyard.

My first actual novel was named *The Last Day the Dogbushes Bloomed* (1969), and its main character was a weird little nine-year-old girl named Susan, much like this very same nine-year-old girl we have been talking about. She was often a solitary child, though her imaginary friends and pursuits were legion. In this excerpt, she describes a favorite hideout, her "wading house."

The way to the wading house was hard. That's what was so good about it. After I got there, no scouts could track me down. First I went out from under the other side of the dogbushes, then I went by a secret path through the blackberry bushes, which tried to grab me as I went by. They reached out their hands at me but I got away. When I came to the riverbank, I walked on the rocks to the wading house. That way, if anybody chased me with dogs, they would lose the trail.

The wading house was not a real house. It was a soft, light green tree, a willow that grew by the bank. The way the branches came down, they made a little house inside them. The land and the tiny river were both inside the house, and it was the only wading house in the world, and I was the only one that knew about it. It was a very special place. There were a lot of other people that lived there too and they were my good friends. There was a young lizard named Jerry, because I didn't know if it was a boy or a girl, and Jerrys can go either way. Jerry had a long, shiny tail and he stayed mostly in the weeds but he would come out to say hello to me every time I came. A very wise old grandfather turtle lived there too. He blinked his eyes slow at me, and I could tell that he knew everything there was to know. Grandfather Turtle had three silly daughters, but I liked them because they were so cute. Their shells were like the rug in the Trivettes' living room, brown and green by turns. The big rock by the side of the river was not a rock at all, it was a secret apartment house. A baby blacksnake sat on the top. He was so black and fast that it hurt you to look at him. On the second floor, the sides of the rock, there lived a family of little brown bugs. They were always busy and never had much time to play. The worms did, though. They lived on the ground floor under the rock, and I liked them almost best of all. I never knew a family that had so much fun. All they ever did was wiggle and laugh.

After I said hi to everybody in the wading house I liked to sit under the big tree on the bank and think about a lot of things.

There were a lot of things to think about then, and there was nothing to keep from thinking about like there is now. Or sometimes I would sit, like that day, and look at everything very hard so it would stay in my head for always.

What this little narrator is trying very hard not to think about is that her family is breaking up because the mother has run off with a man. This was an entirely fictional plot, of course, but a novel must have conflict; conflict is the single absolutely necessary ingredient of fiction.

As soon as my book was accepted, I was really excited, of course, and sent a copy to my parents. I waited anxiously for their reply, but I heard nothing. Nothing. Finally I called them up on the "long-distance telephone," as we used to say then.

My mother answered.

"Have you read my book?" I asked.

"Yes, I have," she said.

"Well, how did you like it?" I asked.

"Not much," my mother said. "In fact, I have thrown it in the river."

"*What?*" I said. "What's wrong with it?"

"Everybody in this town is going to think I ran off with a man," my mother said.

"Mama, that's just crazy," I said. "Look,

you're still there. You and Daddy have been married for thirty years."

"It doesn't matter," my mother said. "That's what they'll think anyway. So I am taking steps to make sure that they are not going to read it, any of them."

"Wait a minute," I said. "What steps?"

"I have told your father that he cannot order the book," she said — my father's Ben Franklin dimestore being naturally the only place in town where you could possibly buy a book — "And I have told Lillian Elgin that she cannot order the book either." Mama's friend, Lillian Elgin, was the town librarian.

So, that was it! Total censorship! Nobody in town ever read that first book, or the second book either. My mother banned that one because it had sex in it. But that was just as well, I guess, because it was also just awful, as second novels sometimes are if we write them too soon, having used up our entire life so far, all the great traumas and dramas of our youth, in the first one. My second was all about a sensitive English major who keeps having disastrous yet generic romances; luckily, publishing it was exactly like throwing it in the river.

But now I was in big trouble, as a writer. I

had used up my childhood, I had used up my adolescence, and I had nothing more to say. I had used up my whole life! Furthermore I was happily married to the poet James Seay, my first husband, so there was also no conflict, that necessary cauldron of creativity.

But luckily, by then I was a reporter working at *The Tuscaloosa News* in Tuscaloosa, Alabama, where my editor assigned me to cover the all-south majorette contest taking place on the campus of the University of Alabama. This was an enormous contest with categories you might expect — such as "Fire Baton" and "Best Personality" — but also a lot of categories you might not expect, such as "Improvisation to a Previously Unheard Tune," which I thought was a riot. The winner of the whole thing would be called Miss Fancy Strut. The girls were really sweet, because they were all trying to get Miss Personality, which would give them a lot of extra points, but their mothers were just bitches from hell, very competitive. Anyway, it lasted for days, and then finally all the points from all the categories were tallied up, and the winner turned out to be a beautiful little blonde girl from Opp, Alabama, whom I had to interview.

So I asked, of course, "How does it feel to

be Miss Fancy Strut?"

And she said, with tears streaming down her face, "This is the happiest moment of my life!"

I was completely stunned, because I could tell this was true, and I was thinking, Oh honey, it's going to be a long downhill slide from here. You are so young to peak out like this.

You will not be surprised to learn that my next novel was named *Fancy Strut,* and it was all about majorettes and their mamas. It was a real breakthrough for me, because nobody in it was anything like me at all. Finally I had made that necessary imaginative leap — which is a real necessity, since most of us writers can't be out there living like crazy all the time. These days, very few are the writers whose book jackets list things like bush pilot, big game hunter, or exotic dancer.

No, more often we are English teachers. We have children, we have mortgages, we have bills to pay. So we have to stop writing strictly about what we know, which is what they always told us to do in creative writing classes. Instead, we have to write about what we can learn, and what we can imagine, and thus we come to experience that great pleasure Anne Tyler noted when somebody asked her why she writes, and she answered, "I write because I want more than one life." Let me repeat that: "I write because I want more than one life."

And let me tell you, this is the greatest privilege, and the greatest pleasure, in the world. Over the years I have moved away from autobiography to write about housewives and whores, serpent handlers and beauticians, country music singers and evangelists and nineteenth-century schoolteachers — lots of people I will never be, living in times and places I have never been. But somewhere along the way, I have also come to realize that the correspondences between real life and fiction are infinitely more complicated than I would have ever guessed as a younger woman.

Peter Taylor once said, "I write in order to find out what I think." This is certainly true for me, too, and often I don't even know what I think until I go back and read what I've written. My belief is that we have only one life, that this is all there is. And I refuse to lead an unexamined life. No matter how painful it may be, I want to know what's going on. So I write fiction the way other people write in their journals.

My husband, Hal, has been heard to bemoan my lack of self-knowledge. He envisions our respective psyches like this: his is a big room in a factory, brightly lit. He's got uniformed guys in there carrying clipboards and constantly working on all his problems, checking gauges and levels, in day and night shifts. He's always monitoring their work, reading their reports. He sees my mind, by contrast, as a dark forest with no path, where huge beasts loom up at you suddenly out of the night and then disappear, only to return again and again.

Maybe so. But when I read what I've written, I know what they are.

In 1980, for instance, I wrote a novel named *Black Mountain Breakdown,* about a girl named Crystal Spangler who is so busy fitting herself into others' images of her (first fulfilling her mother's beauty-queen dreams, then altering her image to please the various men in her life) that she loses her own true self and finally ends up paralyzed: "Crystal just lies up there in that room every day, with her bed turned catty-corner so she could look out the window and see Lorene's climbing rambler rose in full bloom on the trellis if she would turn her head. But she won't. She won't lift a finger. She just lies there. Everybody in town takes a fancy to it" . . . feeding her jello, brushing her hair, reading *The Read-*

er's Digest out loud to her. The most terrifying aspect of her condition is that "Crystal is happy . . . as outside her window the seasons come and go and the colors change on the mountain." When I wrote that, my first marriage should have ended years earlier, something I'd been unable to face or even admit; later, reading those words over, I finally understood how I'd felt during the last part of that marriage. I was able then to deal with its inevitable ending, and move on with my life.

No matter what I may think I am writing about at any given time — majorettes in Alabama, or a gruesome, long-ago murder, or the history of country music — I have come to realize that it is all, finally, about me, often in some complicated way I won't come to understand until years later. But then it will be there for me to read, and I will understand it, and even if I don't know who I am now, I will surely have a record of who I was then.

Writing is also my addiction, for the moment when I am writing fiction is that moment when I am most intensely alive. This "aliveness" does not seem to be mental, or not exactly. I am certainly not thinking while I write. Whatever I'm doing is almost the opposite of thinking. Especially during the pre-writing phase, when I am simply making up the story and imagining its characters, and during those first drafts, I feel a dangerous, exhilarating sense that anything can happen.

It reminds me of a woman in eastern Kentucky I interviewed years ago when I was writing about serpent-handling believers. I had seen her lift a double handful of copperheads high in the air during a religious service. Now we faced each other across a little Formica table in a fast-food restaurant, drinking Cokes and eating fries. I asked the obvious: "Why do you do this, when it's so dangerous? You could die any time." She merely smiled at me, a beautiful, generous smile without a trace of irony.

"Honey," she began, "I do it out of an intense desire for holiness." She smiled at me again, while that sank in. "And I'll tell you something else, too. When you've held the serpent in your hands, the whole world kind of takes on an edge for you."

I could see that. Chill bumps arose on my arms as she spoke. For I was once the girl who had embarrassed her mother so much by rededicating my life over and over at various revivals, coming home dripping wet from total immersion in those standup pools from Sears that they set up in the little tents behind the big revival tents, or simply in the fast-flowing creeks that rushed down the mountainsides.

And the feeling I get when I'm writing intensely is much the same.

For me, writing is a physical joy. It is almost sexual — not the moment of fulfillment, but the moment when you open the door to the room where your lover is waiting, and everything else falls away.

It does fall away, too. For the time of the writing, I am nobody. Nobody at all. I am a conduit, nothing but a way for the story to come to the page. Oh, but I am terribly alive then, too, though I say I am no one at all; my every sense is keen and quivering. I can smell the bacon cooking downstairs in my grandmother's kitchen that winter morning in 1952, I can feel the flowered carpet under my bare feet as I run down the hall, I can see the bright blue squares of the kitchen wallpaper, bunches of cherries alternating with little floral bouquets. Sun shines through the frost on the windowpanes, almost blinding me; my grandaddy's Lucky Strike cigarette smoke still hangs in the air, lazy blue, though he is already up and gone, he has walked the bridge across the river to the old stone courthouse where he will work all day long as the county treasurer. I love my granddaddy, who always wears a hat and a dark blue suit. I do not love my grandmother so much, who tells me not to be a tomboy and keeps moistening her lips with her tongue in a way I hate. I wish my mother would get out of the hospital so I could go home. I don't see why I can't stay with Daddy, anyway. I could make us peanut butter sandwiches for dinner, and cut the crusts off.

See what I mean? I am there now, and I want to stay there. I hate to leave that kitchen and come back to this essay.

All my senses are involved when I am writing fiction, but it is hearing that is most acute. This has always been true. I can see everything in the story, of course — I have to see that kitchen in order to walk through it; the icy river, in order to get my grandfather across the bridge. I make a lot of maps before I start writing, Scotch-taping them to the wall. But I am not a visual person in real life. I never know how high to hang pictures, for instance, or where the furniture should go. None of my clothes match. It was words I loved first, words and sentences and music and stories, the voice that comes out of the dark when you're almost asleep, sitting in somebody's lap on a porch, trying to keep your eyes open long enough to hear the end of the story.

So a story always comes to me in a human voice, speaking not exactly into my ear but somewhere deep inside me. If I am writing from a first-person point of view, it is always the voice of the person who is telling the story. If I am writing from a third-person point of view, it is simply the voice of the story itself. Sometimes this voice is slow and pondering, or tentative and unsure. Sometimes it is flat and reportorial: just the facts, ma'am. Sometimes it's gossipy, intimate — a tale told over a Coke and a cigarette during a work break at Food City. Sometimes it's sad, a long, wailing lament, telling and retelling again and again how he done me wrong. It can be furious or vengeful: "I hated him from the moment I first laid eyes on him, hated him instinctively, as if I knew somehow what he would do to our family . . ." It can be a reliable narrator — or an unreliable narrator, sometimes even more interesting. It can be a meditative, authoritative voice, told as if from the distant past or from a great and somehow definitive distance (I confess that ever since we moved into this old house where I work in an upstairs office looking out over the town, this has happened more frequently!)

The most thrilling, of course, is when it is a first-person voice telling a story of real urgency. At these times, all I have to do is keep up; I become a stenographer, a court secretary, a tape recorder. My biggest job is making sure that I have several uninter-rupted hours whenever I sit down to write, so this can happen. Whenever a story like this is in progress, it is so exciting that I will do almost anything to get those hours — break appointments, call in sick, tell lies. I become a person on drugs, somebody in the throes of a passionate affair. I'll do anything to get there, to make it happen again. I know I can't ignore the voice, or waste it. I may be a fool, but I'm not that kind of a fool.

Since the writing of fiction is such a physi-cal and personal process for me, I have to write in longhand, still. I have to write with a pen or pencil on a legal pad. I can't have anything mechanical between my body and the page. Later, I'll type it on a computer in order to revise. I can compose nonfiction directly on the computer, but not fiction. Perhaps it's because fiction is so messy, like life. Often I jot down three or four words before I hit upon the right one — or I hope it's the right one. So I mark all the others out, and go on writing, but I want to keep them all, all those words I thought about first and then discarded. I also want to keep that paragraph of description I marked out, and that earlier section about how Ray drowned the dog when he was eleven, and that chapter from the point of view of the mother, because I might change my mind later on and include them. The novel, at this point, is organic, living, changing; anything can still happen, and probably will. This is true up until the very moment when I print the whole thing out and put it into its little coffin, usually an old paper box. Then I hit that SEND button and it's gone to the publisher. Then it's dead, they're all dead, all those people who have been my familiars, who have lived under my skin for weeks and months or years, and I am no longer a writer, but a murderer and mourner, infinitely more alone in the world.

Writing can also give us the chance to express what is present but mute, or unvoiced, in our own personalities . . . because we are all much more complicated and various people than our lives allow.

During the early eighties, the mountains where I came from began to change rapidly. The fast food restaurants went in around the bend of the Levisa River near my parents' house, for instance, and those satellite TV dishes sprouted like weird mushrooms on every hillside — meaning that the children growing up there wouldn't sound like I do, or like their grandmothers did, but like Walter Cronkite instead. That's when I began to tape my relatives and elderly mountain friends, collecting the old stories, songs, and histories in earnest, with the aim of preserving the type of speech — Appalachian English — and the ways of life of a bygone era. But then a very strange thing happened to me. In *Oral History,* the first novel I wrote using this material exclusively, a voice began speaking who was truly me, in a way in which all these other, more contemporary, and ostensibly autobiographical characters were not — although she (Granny Younger, an old mountain midwife) was certainly more removed from me in time, and place, and circumstance, than any other character I'd ever come up with.

Here is what she says in the first chapter of my novel *Oral History:*

. . . I'll tell it all directly.

I'll tell it all, but don't you forget it is Almarine's story. Almarine's, and Pricey Jane's, and Lord yes, it's that red-headed

Emmy's. Mought be it's her story moren the rest. Iffen twas my story, I never would tell it at all. There's tales I'll tell, and tales I won't. And iffen twas my story, why I'd be all hemmed in by the facts of it like Hoot Owl Holler is hemmed in by them three mountains. I couldn't move no way but forward. And often in my traveling over these hills I have seed that what you want the most, you find offen the beaten path. I never find nothing I need on the trace, for an instance. I never find ary a thing. But I am an old, old woman, and I have traveled a lot in these parts. I have seed folks come and I have seed them go. I have cotched more babies than I can name you; I have put the burying quilts around many a soul. I said I know moren you know and mought be I'll tell you moren you want to hear. I'll tell you a story that's truer than true, and nothing so true is so pretty. It's blood on the moon, as I said. The way I tell a story is the way I want to, and iffen you mislike it, you don't have to hear.

Granny Younger is expressing that part of me that is the writer part, that knows things I don't know, and that does not find its expression in any other role I perform — as mother, wife, or teacher, for instance.

228

Writing has become a source of strength for me, too. I had barely begun a novel named *Fair and Tender Ladies* — intended as an honest account and a justification, really, of the lives of so many resourceful mountain women I'd grown up among, women whose plain and home-centered lives are not much valued in the world at large — when my beloved mother went into her last illness, a long and drawn-out sequence of falls, emphysema, and finally heart failure. This period coincided with the onset of Josh's schizophrenia; I spent two years visiting hospitals, sitting by hospital beds, often reading students' work as I tried to hold on to my teaching job. I don't know what I would have done if I hadn't been writing that novel. I worked on it a bit every day; it was like an open door to another world, another place for me to be for a little while.

Its heroine, Ivy Rowe, grew stronger and stronger, the more I needed her. Every terrible thing in the world happened to her — extreme poverty, too many children, heartbreak, illness, the death of a child — but she could take it. She hung in there, so I did, too. Ivy made sense of her life through writing a constant stream of letters: to her children, to her friends, to her sisters —

especially to her favorite sister, Silvaney, even though Silvaney had died young and would never read most of them. Near the novel's end, Ivy burns all her letters, and it is finally my own voice as well as hers that concludes:

. . . The smoke from the burning letters rose and was lost in the clouds. . . . With every one I burned, my soul grew lighter, lighter, as if it rose too with the smoke. And I was not even cold, long as I'd been out there. For I came to understand something in that moment . . . which I had never understood in all these years.

The letters didn't mean anything.

Not to the dead girl Silvaney, of course — *nor to me.*

Nor had they ever.

It was the *writing* of them, that signified.

In 2003 I had done a lot of historical research but had barely begun a novel named *On Agate Hill* when Josh died. My grief — and rage — were indescribable: "oceanic," to use one doctor's terminology. He told me that there are basically two physiological reactions to grief. Some people sleep a lot, gain weight, become depressed and lethargic.

I had the other reaction — I felt like I was standing with my finger stuck into an electrical outlet, all the time. I couldn't sleep. I couldn't read, I couldn't eat, I couldn't remember anything, anything at all. I forgot how to drive to the grocery store. I couldn't find the school where I had taught for twenty years. In group situations, I was apt to blurt out wildly inappropriate remarks, like a person with Tourette's syndrome. I cried all the time. I lost thirty pounds.

Weeks passed, then months. I was wearing out my husband and my friends. But I couldn't calm down. It was almost as if I had become addicted to these days on fire, to this intensity. I felt that if I lost it, I'd lose him even more.

Finally I started going to a psychiatrist, a kind, rumpled man who formed his hands into a little tent and listened to me scream and cry and rave for several weeks.

Then came the day when he held up his hand and said, "Enough."

"What?" I stared at him.

"I am going to give you a new prescription," my psychiatrist said, taking out his pad and pen. He began to write.

"Oh good," I said, wanting more drugs, anything.

He ripped the prescription out and handed it to me.

"Write fiction every day," it said in his crabbed little hand.

I just looked at him.

"I have been listening to you for some time," he said, "and it has occurred to me that you are an extremely lucky person, since you are a writer, because it is possible for you to enter into a narrative not your own, for extended periods of time. To live in someone else's story, as it were. I want you to do this every day for two hours. I believe that it will be good for you."

"I can't," I said. "I haven't written a word since Josh died."

"Do it," he said.

"I can't think straight, I can't concentrate," I said.

"Then just sit in the chair," he said. "Show up for work."

Vocational rehabilitation, I thought. Like Josh. So I did it. For three days. The fourth day, I started to write.

And my novel, which I'd planned as the diary of a young girl orphaned by the Civil War, just took off and wrote itself. "I know I am a spitfire and a burden," Molly Petree begins on May 20, 1874. "I do not care. My family is a dead family, and this is not my home, for I am a refugee girl . . . but evil or good I intend to write it all down every true thing in black and white upon the page, for evil or good it is my own true life and I WILL have it. I will."

Molly's spitfire grit strengthened me as she proceeded to "give all her heart," no matter what, during a passionate life journey that included love, betrayal, motherhood, and grief (of course, grief). But by the time we were done with it, Molly and I, two years later, she had finally found a real home, and I could find my way to the grocery store. I could laugh. And yes, through the mysterious alchemy of fiction, my sweet Josh had managed to find his own way into the final pages of the novel after all, as a mystical bluesman and healer living wild and free at last in the deep piney woods he used to play in as a child.

When Joan Didion published *My Year of Magical Thinking,* with its close observation of her life during the painful year following her husband's death, a friend wondered, "How can she do that — write at such a time?"

"The right question is, how could she *not* do that?" I answered. Writing is what Joan Didion does, it's what she has always done. It's how she has lived her life.

In a different way, I realized, this is how I have lived my life, too. Of course writing is an escape, but it is a source of nourishment and strength, too. My psychiatrist's prescription may benefit us all. Whether we are writing fiction or nonfiction, journaling or writing for publication, writing itself is an inherently therapeutic activity. Simply to line up words one after another upon a page is to create some order where it did not exist, to give a recognizable shape to the chaos of our lives. Writing cannot bring our loved ones back, but it can sometimes fix them in our fleeting memories as they were in life, and it can always help us make it through the night.

ANGELS PASSING

Do we ever get beyond the images of childhood? The way we first hear language, for instance (old women on a porch, talking on and on as it gets dark) or how Mama smells (loose powder, cigarettes, Chanel No5). Or in particular, Christmas: my Aunt Bess's quivery soprano on "O Holy Night" in the chilly stone church. The sharp strange smell of grapefruit, shipped from Florida in a wooden crate. The guns of Christmas morning, echoing around and around the ring of frosty mountains. How the air smells right before it snows, and how the sky looks, like the underside of a quilt. Oranges studded with cloves, in a bowl on a coffee table. The blazing fires in the oil drums as we go screaming down Hoot Owl Holler on our sleds ("sleigh-riding," we call it), then get hauled back up the mountain in the back of somebody's truck to do it all over again. My daddy in his dimestore wearing a red bow tie. All my images of the holiday season cluster around the dimestore, the Methodist Church, and my mama's winter kitchen, which was always filled with people and food.

It seemed like everybody in the whole world dropped by to sit a spell and see what she was up to. And sure enough there she was, wearing a pretty apron over a pretty dress (Mama was the kind of woman who dressed up every day), turning out batch after batch of her famous fudge. She'd already made the fruitcakes, of course, and now they sat in the "cold corner," drenched in rum. (Does anybody really like fruitcake? I doubt it. But fruitcake at Christmas was the law.) Sherry pound cakes, sugar cookies, and pecan pies got wrapped in tin foil, then tied up in bows. If the back doorbell rang, it would be a man named George or a man named Arnold, drunk and wanting money, which I got to give them if my Mama had her hands in some kind of dough, which she usually did.

My parents gave lots of presents; Daddy was always worried about giving everybody "enough." Besides their many friends, we were surrounded by relatives — they lived on either side of us and up the road from our house in the Levisa River bottom, and all over town. Delivering the gifts took three days, because of course Mama and I had to sit and talk for a while at every house we went to. Daddy used to order oysters at Christmastime, especially for Mama. The wooden barrel of oysters, packed in ice, came all the way across Virginia from Chincoteague Island. We went down to the station for days on end, meeting every Norfolk and Western train, looking for them. When they finally arrived, it took several men to carry them to our house. A mining engineer who'd been born in South Carolina came over to open them. A couple of women were waiting to help Mama cook. They worked on the oysters for two days, and on the evening of the second day, just about everybody in town showed up to help eat them. We had oysters in the shell, fried in cracker meal, in fritters, in stew, and scalloped. Everyone was fascinated; most of the townspeople had never even heard of oysters before "Miss Gig" moved to town. As old Dr. Burkes said, arranging a red bandana over his fancy three-piece suit, "I'd like to know who was the first man that ever thought to eat such a monstrosity as this!" Like the fruitcakes, the oysters were mainly something to put up with, in my opinion. What I liked was the ambrosia and the floating island for dessert.

We ate holiday dinners at the big round table in the dining room at my grandparents' house, with Grandmother presiding blue-haired and ethereal above the snowy linen. I used to drop my napkin on purpose just to lean down and look at the huge dark claws on the pedestal base of the table — cruel, strong, and evil, evil. I'd come up flushed and thrilled.

Christmas was a time for cousins, who'd arrive next door from southside Virginia with such long names that it'd take their mother forever to call them in out of the snow — "Martha Fletcher Bruce! Anne Vicars Bruce!" My relationship with my pretty redheaded first cousins Randy and Melissa was more complicated. I liked them, but mainly I wanted to *be* them . . . to belt out "I Enjoy Being a Girl" the way Melissa did in the Rotary Talent Show, to be as smart and exemplary as Randy. It was clear that Jesus liked her better than me.

I aspired to sainthood in those days. I might have settled for a little miracle, or a vision, or at least a sign. I remember one Christmas Eve staring fixedly at Missy, my Pekingese, for hours, because a grannywoman had told me that God speaks through animals on Christmas Eve. He didn't say a word through Missy. But never mind, I was all eaten up with holiness anyway, excited by the holly in the church, the candles, the carols, and the Christmas pageant, which we acted out at the altar year after year, wearing our bathrobes, until we were too old to be in it. There were not enough boys in that little church, so I usually had to be a Wise Man, while Randy and Melissa and Frances Williams got to be the angels. I wanted to be an angel so bad. But would I ever fit through the eye of the needle? Didn't I have too much stuff?

At school we drew names and I gave gifts to kids from up in the hollers, saving my allowance to buy them the nicest things — Evening in Paris perfume, Avon dusting powder, a pen and pencil set in a clear plastic case. In return I got a hooked potholder once, and a red plastic barrette, and a terrific homemade slingshot. On snowy nights around Christmas I used to sit out by myself for hours, hearing the wild dogs bark way up in the mountains, listening hard for the high, sweet song of angels. I never heard it, either. When my daddy came home from the dimestore, I'd finally go in the house.

He never left on Christmas Eve until the store was closed, cash counted and put in

the safe, the last layaway doll picked up —
and if somebody couldn't pay, which happened often enough when the mines weren't
working, he'd give it away. In early October,
I'd go with him to the Ben Franklin Toy
Fair in Baltimore, where we'd order presents for Christmas. I was the doll consultant.

In those days, in that town, it was a sin to
sell on the Sabbath; but from Thanksgiving
until Christmas, every Sunday, I got to go
downtown to "work" in the dimestore, helping Daddy and the "girls" fix things up for
the week ahead. As doll consultant, I'd dust
the dolls and fluff up their dresses and stand
them up just so . . . I particularly liked to
raise their arms a bit, so they'd be ready to
hug any little girl they got on Christmas
morning.

Weren't these Christmases idyllic? Wasn't
my childhood wonderful? Yes and no. It's
like those awful claws beneath the festive
table at my grandmother's house. For there
were terrible resentments and quarrels
about money and old unhealed wounds
right beneath the surface in that family, as
in all families. Somebody was always going
off to "take the cure," while others were
"kindly nervous." In the parlance of today,

our family was dysfunctional (is any family not?)

I would never become an angel, or even a saint. Instead I would grow up wild, marry young, and settle down. We'd have two boys, forming our own dysfunctional family. We'd do the best we could. Then we'd divorce, and I'd feel "kindly nervous" myself. I'd remarry. I'd try like crazy. (We all do, don't we? We try like crazy.) My new husband and I would form our own new, blended dysfunctional family. And even now that we've been married for thirty years, I realize how hard divorce always is for kids, no matter what those self-help books say. Though the kids are all grown up now, they lost some big bright pieces out of their childhoods, out of their lives.

For I could never give them what I had: my father in a red bowtie standing forever in front of his dimestore; my mother forever in her kitchen wearing Fire and Ice lipstick and high heels; the cousins next door and across the street; Jesus right up the road in the little stone Methodist Church.

The church is a parking lot now. The dimestore is gone. Walmart looms over the river. I'm seventy, an age that has brought no wisdom. When I was young, I always thought the geezers knew some things I didn't; the sad little secret is, we don't. I don't understand anything anymore, though I'm still in there, still trying like crazy.

We do what we can, don't we? Before Christmas, I still make fudge, party mix, sherry pound cakes, and sugar cookies. With four small grandchildren, our holiday plans vary now. We go where the children are. I always make a trip to Nashville to visit Lucy and Spencer Seay right around Christmastime. Last year, our granddaughter Ellery Ferguson was chosen to play Mary in an Episcopal church pageant in Raleigh. Her younger sister Baker was First Donkey. On Christmas Eve, I still make scalloped oyster casserole. But sometime on Christmas Day — around the tree or at the table — there will come a moment when the conversation spontaneously ceases while we pause, and remember. One of those little silences that sometimes fall upon us all — angels passing.

THE LITTLE LOCKSMITH

Castine, Maine

I wake early here, in our corner bedroom already flooded with light. Beyond the window, light winks on the shining water of Penobscot Bay and glows through the mist that still shrouds Islesboro and Belfast and the Camden Hills beyond; light rolls golden down the sloping yard to the water. I'm instantly wide awake, so wide awake it's scary. I get up immediately, pull on some jeans and sneakers, go downstairs, feed Betty the dog, and together we walk out through the tall, dewy grass and down the wooden steps to the rocky shore, which changes with every high tide. The birch trees rustle in their papery, conspiratorial way. Birds cry out. Little white waves break on the shore. But this water is cold, not like the Myrtle Beach or Wrightsville Beach of my youth, where you could jump the waves all day and they would pick you up and hold you in their warm, salty embrace. No, this water would kill you; you have to enter and exit quickly, shivering. There's no boardwalk, no dance pavilion, no Krispy Kreme doughnut place. It's beautiful here, but it's a severe, rigorous beauty. A loon calls across the water. Light leaps off the little waves like a thousand arrows aimed at me; I fish my sunglasses out of my pocket and put them on, though it isn't even 7 a.m. yet. I breathe deeply in this chilly air, which seems strangely effervescent, like breathing champagne.

And actually I'm feeling a little intoxicated, the way I often feel here, the way I always feel when I'm starting a new novel, which I am — or will, as soon as I get up my nerve. It's that old disorientation, that scary lightness of being, that moment before you spring off the diving board straight out into the shining air, head first. You could kill yourself, and you know it, and you've got to get to the point where you don't care.

I'm not quite there yet.

But by fortunate chance, I'm here in Castine, a place I associate with taking risks and writing. Nobody's home but me and an old dog and an accommodating husband who doesn't care how crazy I act when I'm starting a novel. So I don't even leave him a note when I take Betty back inside and grab up my windbreaker and gulp down two Advils because I have a long hill to climb now and I've got a bad knee which is par for the course when you're old, which I am. This is a true thing I have only recently discovered and it is like an ugly scab someplace on my body I never noticed before but now I can't quit picking at it. Finally I open my book bag and take out my current copy of *The Little Locksmith,* by Katharine Butler Hathaway. I've given away at least a dozen copies of this book since it was republished by the Feminist Press, after Maine writer Alix Kates Shulman found it in a secondhand bookstore and brought it to their attention. It first came to me here, years back, when I really needed it — as books so often do. Since then it has become my talisman, my Bible, my lucky charm.

I give it mostly to my sister writers (because it is one of the best books ever written about writing) but also to anyone suffering adversity of any sort, especially any kind of illness or disability, for it is truly a story of transformation, one of the finest spiritual autobiographies ever written. Basically I give it to people I love, trusting that it will mean as much to them as it has to me. As Katharine herself says (I'm going to call her Katharine in this essay since I consider her my true friend), hers was "a lonely voyage of discovery" that began when she decided that she "couldn't let fear decide things" for her, when she decided "to follow the single, fresh living voice" of her "own destiny." Indeed this is a fearless book, as well as an entirely original one. It is not at all like anything else I have ever read. Though she was very frail, Katharine was tough as nails, intellectually; wielding her pen with a jeweler's precision, she crafted this book like an exquisitely cut jewel — a topaz, I think, rather than a diamond (maybe I think this since it's my own birthstone, but everybody who reads this books wants to claim it as her own). Each facet reveals a new insight or an indelible image. Hold it up to the window, turn it this way and that, and it will cast off rays of light in every direction, piercing even the oddest, most secret depths of the reader's psyche. *The Little Locksmith* tells the story of how Katharine overcame her severe physical and psychological handicaps (her "predicament," she calls it) and came to this tiny, out-of-the-way village on Maine's stern rocky coast where, against her family's wishes and all advice, she bought a house on Court Street, overlooking the harbor.

I'm headed there now. I give Betty a biscuit, close the front door softly, and walk out our leafy lane, turning right onto the main road. I walk through swirling ground mist across the old British Canal, then climb up the long, steep curve into town. Katharine's book fits easily in the pocket of my windbreaker; it's a small book, like its author.

Born in 1890 into a loving, prosperous family in Salem, Massachusetts, Katharine Butler Hathaway was stricken with spinal tuberculosis at age five and "changed from a rushing, laughing child into a bedridden, meditative one." The most advanced medical theories of the day dictated her new "horizontal life," which would last for ten years. "For the doctor's treatment consisted in my being strapped down very tight on a stretcher, on a very hard sloping bed, with my shoulders pressed against a hard pad. My head was kept from sinking down on my chest . . . by means of a leather halter attached to a rope which went through a pulley at the head of the bed. On the end of the rope hung a five-pound iron weight. This mechanism held me a prisoner for twenty-four hours a day, without the freedom to turn or twist my body or let my chin move out of its up-tilted position in the leather halter, except to go from side to side. My back was supposed to be kept absolutely still." However, Katharine's "hands and arms and mind were free. . . . I held my pencil and pad of paper up in the air above my face, and I wrote microscopic letters and poems, and made little books of stories, and very tiny pictures" along with paper dolls, dollhouse furniture, and doll clothes. In these Brontë-like pursuits she was accompanied always by her loving brothers and sister, who "took it for granted that no other amusement was really interesting compared with drawing or writing or making something" and made her bedroom "the natural center of the house for the others."

Yet her natural "happy, sparkling" sense of herself was challenged by the "ghoulish pleasure" of visiting children who stared at her halter and strap, and by their parents' overt pity. Worst of all was the occasional appearance of the hunchback who came to the house to fix locks. Katharine had been told that without the treatment she would have grown up to be like him. Yet she felt the "truth was that I really belonged with him, even if it was never going to show. I was secretly linked with him, and I felt a strong, childish, amorous pity and desire toward him, so that there was even a queer erotic charm for me about his gray shabby clothes, the strange awful peak in his back, and his cross, unapproachable sadness which made him not look at other people, not even me lying on my bed and staring sideways at him."

When Katharine was finally released from her board at fifteen, this suspicion was, alas, confirmed: "That person in the mirror couldn't be me! I felt inside like a healthy, ordinary lucky person. . . . A hideous disguise had been cast over me." Katharine's refusal to accept her limitations — including her desire for sexual love, which shocked many readers when this book was first published in 1943 — strikes me as an act of great courage. She always "believed passionately that every human being could be happy," including herself.

She was admitted to Radcliffe College, where she spent three blissful years as a special student and made several good friends for life: smart, artistic, bohemian girls among whom she flourished in her "perfect imitation of a grown-up person, one who was noted for a sort of peaceful wise detachment," whose "curious, impersonal life gave her an enviable agelessness and liberty." But this self fell apart when she returned home after college. She fell into deep depression and "toxic fear" (ago-raphobia), a complete disintegration from which she finally emerged through her old childhood pastime, writing.

"A block of paper and a pencil had saved me. They had not only saved me by satisfying my hunger and canceling the over-whelming terror of the universe, but they gave me also an inexhaustible form of entertainment because they gave me, or seemed to give me, the equivalent of all sorts of human experience. There was no end and no limit to this kind of living." Her writing restored "the greatest visible world" to her as "an object of love, full of mystery and meaning." Thus she "got hold of a most extraordinary joy."

Katharine's transformation was further accomplished by buying the house I'm standing in front of right now, atop this windy hill. When an unexpected legacy allowed her to conceive her grand plan of living independently, she first thought she'd buy "a thimble . . . something *mignonne* and doll-like," just like herself: "a very small childish spinster . . . a little oddity, deformed and ashamed and shy." Instead, she found herself "awestruck by the force of destiny" when she came upon this "very large high square house on Penobscot Bay overlooking the Bagaduce River and the islands and the Cape Rosier Hills. . . . I knew that whether I liked it or not this at last was my house."

Somebody else lives in Katharine's house now, of course, and yet it's all here, just as she described it: the bright sun, the endless wind, the flower-studded fields dropping down to the harbor. It's easy to imagine her sitting on this wide stone doorsill, "rapturously at home," as she often sat that first summer while workmen hammered and painted and restored the chimneys, the twelve-paned windows, the "old heavy original door" whose "panels, set with narrow, handmade moldings, made a great serene sign of the cross — two short panels at the top and two tall ones below." Indeed it is still the "sober, grand, romantic house" that was to be her "rebellion against cuteness. . . . I wanted room to find out what I really was, and room to be whatever I really was." *The Little Locksmith* is the story of how Katharine grew to fit her house, shedding her self-identity as a cripple and assuming her true identity as artist.

Katharine's transformation, her "new world," is described in terms of light: "I had never seen a world so gilded and so richly bathed and blessed by such a benign sun as that world was by that sun. The sun seemed to pour down a lavish, golden, invulnerable contentment on everything, on people, houses, animals, fields — and a sweetness like the sweetness of passion." Which would come to her, too, against all odds, in "that graceful sitting room, full of sunshine, on the southwest corner, the room destined to become the one most used and most loved of the entire house. Wonderful, strange things happened to me and were said to me there, which I never could have believed were possible at the time when I was so eagerly preparing it."

Eventually, Katharine left this house and found her way to Paris, where she became part of a vibrant circle of friends, writers, and artists. "Everything is different since Castine. Yet it all began there. For there and then I first began in utter ignorance and naïveté and to heed the little voice which spoke to me and told me which way to turn." Eventually Katharine came to believe that this was in fact the voice of God; she wrote that *The Little Locksmith* was "going to be my bread-and-butter letter to God, for a lovely visit on the earth." Her happiness was complete when she fell in love with Dan Hathaway of Marblehead, Massachusetts, marrying him in 1932. Though the Depression forced them to sell Katharine's beloved house, perhaps it had already served its purpose; the couple ended up blissfully happy in a "smaller and cozier" house in Blue Hill, Maine — just up the peninsula from Castine.

Chapters of *The Little Locksmith* were being serially published in *The Atlantic Monthly* magazine in the fall of 1942 — to great acclaim and national interest — when Katharine's precarious health "went haywire." "At present," she wrote from the Blue Hill Hospital in early December, "my only comfortable posture is on the knees with head bent down in front of me, like a snail or an unborn child. Only then can I breathe." She died on Christmas Eve. *The Little Locksmith* was published posthumously the following year. Writing it meant everything to her ("I love this book and I can hardly bear to leave it now" she wrote at the end); its publication seemed almost irrelevant.

And yet it's still here. This book is in my pocket. This house is still here on its hill, everything just as Katharine described it: the fanlight over the heavy door; the twelve-paneled windows; the brick path, lovingly uncovered; the swaying willows; and most of all, the light. The entire "great visible world" is here before us, our own real world, where amazing things are possible. It's all still here for us all, if we can overcome our fears and summon the courage to trust ourselves, to listen to whatever voice speaks within us, to trust Katharine's "magic of transformation." I check my watch: seven forty-five. There's still time to walk back down the hill, make some coffee for my husband, if he hasn't done it already, and maybe — who knows? start a novel.

ACKNOWLEDGMENTS

Since these essays are drawn from every part of my life, there's no end to the people I'd like to thank — so many that I'm scared to make a big list for fear of leaving anyone out. So here I will try to acknowledge those who have contributed most to the actual writing of *Dimestore*. First comes my old friend Debbie Raines, senior English teacher at Grundy High School, whose insights and on-the-scene commentary have been invaluable to me, as was the time I spent working with her students to publish our oral history of downtown Grundy, *Sitting on the Courthouse Bench,* in 2000 (Tryon Publishing Co., Inc., Chapel Hill). My longtime editor Shannon Ravenel (recently retired) offered initial enthusiasm and some shrewd judgments at the outset of this project; my present editor Kathy Pories brought close editing and a much needed sense of order and shape to this collection. I also want to thank Mona Sinquefield, friend and secretary, who suffered through version after version, draft after draft; Chris Stamey, the best copy editor in the world; Brunson Hoole, whose sleight of hand somehow turns all this stuff into an actual book; art designer Anne Winslow; and too many other people at Algonquin to name, starting with publisher Elisabeth Scharlatt, Ina Stern, Craig Popelars, and the whole wonderful publicity team. It's such a pleasure to work with you all. I'm indebted to sister writers and early readers Frances Mayes and Marianne Gingher, who came up with great ideas and suggestions. Big thanks go out to my special support group of "Good Ol' Girls" — Jill McCorkle, Marshall Chapman, and Matraca Berg. To my beloved friend Elizabeth Spencer, always an inspiration, and to the wonderful and steadfast Liz Darhansoff, who has been my agent practically since we were girls. Special thanks to the Hindman Settlement School in Hindman, Kentucky, where I have spent so much valuable time over the past thirty years. My essay "Lightning Storm" honors the people I was privileged to know during my three years working in the literacy programs at Hindman's adult learning center. I also want to thank all my Grundy and southwest Virginia relatives, especially my father's business partner and best friend, Curtis E. Smith, his son Jack Smith, and Steve Smith, now CEO of the Food City stores, which have benefited so many in southwest Virginia, for their constant support always and especially their loving care of my parents during their later years. Thanks to Ava McClanahan for this as well as being a constant source of lore and stories all my life. Love and apologies for general ditziness during the writing of this book go to my children Page Seay and Amity Crowther, and always, always, to Hal.

The employees of Thorndike Press hope you have enjoyed this Large Print book. All our Thorndike, Wheeler, and Kennebec Large Print titles are designed for easy reading, and all our books are made to last. Other Thorndike Press Large Print books are available at your library, through selected bookstores, or directly from us.

For information about titles, please call:
  (800) 223-1244

or visit our Web site at:
  http://gale.cengage.com/thorndike

To share your comments, please write:
  Publisher
  Thorndike Press
  10 Water St., Suite 310
  Waterville, ME 04901

73

W9-COT-006

TOBY TYLER
or Ten Weeks with a Circus

BY JAMES OTIS

ILLUSTRATED BY LOUIS S. GLANZMAN

INTRODUCTION BY MAY LAMBERTON BECKER

J

THE WORLD PUBLISHING COMPANY

Cleveland and New York

Rainbow Classics

are published by THE WORLD PUBLISHING COMPANY

2231 West 110th Street · *Cleveland 2* · *Ohio*

Contents

Contents

Introduction

HOW THIS BOOK CAME TO BE WRITTEN

by May Lamberton Becker

JAMES OTIS KALER (1848-1912), who wrote under the pen name of James Otis, produced almost a hundred books for boys. Most of them have faded with time, but the first one he wrote is still as bright as when it started. This was a long while ago, in the pages of a magazine called *Harper's Young People*. The children on our block that year read all the children's magazines, for each of us subscribed to one and borrowed those of his friends. We read them from cover to cover, including advertisements: the first money I earned by hard labor was a dollar my father promised me when I could play "The Shepherd Boy" on the piano without one wrong note—and if you don't call that hard labor, remember that I was seven years old at the time and this piece has a tricky bit through which I had been accustomed to slide with my foot on the loud pedal. But I needed the money to buy a toy theater advertised on the cover of *Harper's Young People*, a magazine about the size of a modern tabloid but otherwise entirely different—on beautiful

7

paper with excellent reading matter and really delightful illustrations. So of course had *St. Nicholas*,
which had more pages and came once a month, but
the special charm of *Harper's Young People* was that
it came every week so you did not have to wait so long
for the serial. In the first year my parents gave me
Harper's Young People, I don't see how I could have
waited a month to find out what happened next to
Toby in that year's serial, *Toby Tyler; or, Ten Weeks
with a Circus.*

Any circus is wonderful, but in those days there
was something about a one-ring country circus that
made it a regular magnet for small boys. Excitement
began a long time ahead, with posters stuck up on
people's barns for miles around telling the place where
the circus was coming and the day when it was due.
When that great day arrived, it opened with a parade,
led by a steam-calliope playing at the top of its lungs,
and followed by solemn elephants, beautifully dressed
ladies riding on white horses, and lions and tigers pac-
ing in painted cages. Of course the parade was trailed
by every small boy in town who had a ticket, or hoped
to earn a pass by watering the elephants, or intended
to creep under the tent if the guard took his eye away.
This street parade was grand, but if you should ask a
man who as a boy lived in a small town or on a farm
what he liked most about the circus, I think he would
tell you that the most marvelous, mysterious part was
when it arrived—usually before sunrise, with the great
elephants helping to unload closed cages of wild ani-

mals, beautiful blanketed horses tossing their heads, and freaks and circus people, with coat collars turned up against the chill, looking pale in the light of dawn. It wasn't only country boys who ran away to see the circus come to town! The son of a wealthy city family told me that the one great adventure of his guarded youth was when he slid down a drain-pipe from his third story bedroom before sunrise and made his way through the city's darkness to the railroad siding where the circus train was unloading. When he returned his father gave him something to remember it by, but that didn't mean a thing: he already had something he could never forget.

Naturally, a good many small boys thought the finest thing on earth would be to run away with the circus. James Otis knew there was another side to its life, and he thought if boys knew how hard things might be, they might not be so anxious to leave home. So he wrote this story about a lovable, fat little fellow named Toby Tyler, who thought Uncle Dan'l didn't treat him right and believed what one of the circus men told him about the fine time he would have with the show. It didn't take him long to find out how mistaken he had been: no one had been really unkind to him before, and he was quite unprepared for unkindness.

The boys and girls in our neighborhood followed Toby's experiences—and those of his friend and consoler, Mr. Stubbs the monkey, from one week to the next, while circus life, glittering and clattering, went on around us. And when the story ended, with every-thing coming out right, it took breath and started right over again with further adventures in *Mr. Stubbs's Brother*.

Toby Tyler has kept itself alive and loved by American children for more than fifty years. It isn't read all over the world like *Heidi*, *Pinocchio*, *Tom Sawyer*, or *Treasure Island*, but you can call it a chil-dren's classic, if you accept my definition of one. For when somebody once asked me the difference between a child's book and a children's classic, I was on a plat-form and had to think quickly. I said any child's book was read once, but a children's classic was a book that was re-read many times, by the same child or by suc-cessive generations of children. When *Toby Tyler* first came out we read it over and over—and since then three generations of children have read it.

Louis Glanzman, who illustrated this edition of *Toby Tyler*, grew up on an old farm in Virginia, which I suspect looks more than a little like Uncle Dan'l's farm in the drawings for this book. Mr. Glanzman was born in 1922, and began to draw long before he was old enough to go to school. His mother was an artist, too, and she encouraged him in his love for art. When the Second World War came along, he joined the Army Air Force, and for the next four years held down various jobs, from drawing to working as an aircraft mechanic.

Toby Tyler is the first book which Mr. Glanzman

has illustrated. I think you will agree with me when I say that his pictures of Toby and Mr. Stubbs make that pair look just as James Otis must have visualized them when he sat down to write his story of circus life.

Toby Tyler

1. *Toby's Introduction to the Circus*

"COULDN'T you give more'n six peanuts for a cent?" was a question asked by a very small boy, with big, staring eyes, of a candy vendor at a circus booth. And as he spoke, he looked wistfully at the quantity of nuts piled high up on the basket, and then at the six, each of which now looked so small as he held them in his hand.

"Couldn't do it," was the reply of the proprietor of the booth, as he put the boy's penny carefully away in the drawer.

The little fellow looked for another moment at his purchase, and then carefully cracked the largest one.

A shade—and a very deep shade it was—of disappointment passed over his face, and then, looking up anxiously, he asked, "Don't you swap 'em when they're bad?"

The man's face looked as if a smile had been a stranger to it for a long time; but one did pay it a visit just then, and he tossed the boy two nuts and asked him a question at the same time. "What is your name?"

The big, brown eyes looked up for an instant, as if to learn whether the question was asked in good faith, and then their owner said, as he carefully picked apart another nut, "Toby Tyler."

"Well, that's a queer name."

"Yes, I s'pose so, myself; but, you see, I don't expect that's the name that belongs to me. But the fellers call me so, an' so does Uncle Dan'l."

"Who is Uncle Daniel?" was the next question. In the absence of other customers the man seemed disposed to get as much amusement out of the boy as possible.

"He hain't my uncle at all; I only call him so because all the boys do, an' I live with him."

"Where's your father and mother?"

"I don't know," said Toby, rather carelessly. "I don't know much about 'em, an' Uncle Dan'l says they don't know much about me. Here's another bad nut; goin' to give me two more?"

The two nuts were given him, and he said, as he

put them in his pocket and turned over and over again those which he held in his hand, "I shouldn't wonder if all of these was bad. S'posen you give me two for each one of 'em before I crack 'em, an' then they won't be spoiled so you can't sell 'em again."

As this offer of barter was made, the man looked amused, and he asked, as he counted out the number which Toby desired, "If I give you these, I suppose you'll want me to give you two more for each one, and you'll keep that kind of trade going until you get my whole stock?"

"I won't open my head if every one of 'em's bad."

"All right; you can keep what you've got, and I'll give you these besides; but I don't want you to buy any more, for I don't want to do that kind of business."

Toby took the nuts offered, not in the least abashed, and seated himself on a convenient stone to eat them and at the same time to see all that was going on around him. The coming of a circus to the little town of Guilford was an event, and Toby had hardly thought of anything else since the highly colored posters had first been put up. It was yet quite early in the morning, and the tents were just being erected by the men. Toby had followed, with eager eyes, everything that looked as if it belonged to the circus, from the time the first wagon had entered the town until the street parade had been made and everything was being prepared for the afternoon's performance.

The man who had made the losing trade in peanuts seemed disposed to question the boy still further, probably owing to the fact that he had nothing better to do.

"Who is this Uncle Daniel you say you live with? Is he a farmer?"

"No; he's a deacon, an' he raps me over the head with the hymn book whenever I go to sleep in meetin', an' he says I eat four times as much as I earn. I blame him for hittin' so hard when I go to sleep, but I s'pose he's right about my eatin'. You see," and here his tone grew both confidential and mournful, "I am an awful eater, an' I can't seem to help it. Somehow I'm hungry all the time. I don't seem ever to get enough till carrot time comes, an' then I can get all I want without troublin' anybody."

"Didn't you ever have enough to eat?"

"I s'pose I did; but you see Uncle Dan'l he found me one mornin' on his hay, an' he says I was cryin' for something to eat then, an' I've kept it up ever since. I tried to get him to give me money enough to go into the circus with; but he said a cent was all he could spare these hard times, an' I'd better take that an' buy something to eat with it, for the show wasn't very good, anyway. I wish peanuts wasn't but a cent a bushel."

"Then you would make yourself sick eating them."

"Yes, I s'pose I should; Uncle Dan'l says I'd eat till I was sick, if I got the chance; but I'd like to try it once."

He was a very small boy, with a round head covered with short red hair, a face as speckled as any turkey's egg, but thoroughly good-natured looking. As he sat there on the rather sharp point of the rock, swaying his body to and fro as he hugged his knees with his hands and kept his eyes fastened on the tempting display of good things before him, it would have been a very hard-hearted man who would not have given him something. But Mr. Job Lord, the proprietor of the booth, was a hard-hearted man, and he did not make the slightest advance toward offering the little fellow anything.

Toby rocked himself silently for a moment, and then he said, hesitatingly, "I don't suppose you'd like to sell me some things, an' let me pay you when I get older, would you?"

Mr. Lord shook his head decidedly at this proposition.

"I didn't s'pose you would," said Toby, quickly, "but you didn't seem to be selling anything, an' I thought I'd just see what you'd say about it." And then he appeared suddenly to see something wonderfully interesting behind him, which served as an excuse to turn his reddening face away.

"I suppose your Uncle Daniel makes you work for your living, don't he?" asked Mr. Lord, after he had rearranged his stock of candy and had added a couple of slices of lemon peel to what was popularly supposed to be lemonade.

"That's what I think; but he says that all the work I do wouldn't pay for the meal that one chicken would eat, an' I s'pose it's so, for I don't like to work as well as a feller without any father and mother ought to. I don't know why it is, but I guess it's because I take up so much time eatin' that it kinder tires me out. I s'pose you go into the circus whenever you want to, don't you?"

"Oh, yes; I'm there at every performance, for I keep the stand under the big canvas as well as this one out here."

There was a great big sigh from out Toby's little round stomach, as he thought what bliss it must be to own all those good things and to see the circus wherever it went. "It must be nice," he said, as he faced the booth and its hard-visaged proprietor once more.

"How would you like it?" asked Mr. Lord, patronizingly, as he looked Toby over in a business way, very much as if he contemplated purchasing him.

"Like it!" echoed Toby, "why, I'd grow fat on it."

"I don't know as that would be any advantage," continued Mr. Lord, reflectively, "for it strikes me that you're about as fat now as a boy of your age ought to be. But I've a great mind to give you a chance."

"What!" cried Toby, in amazement, and his eyes opened to their widest extent, as this possible opportunity of leading a delightful life presented itself.

"Yes, I've a great mind to give you the chance. You see," and now it was Mr. Lord's turn to grow confidential, "I've had a boy with me this season, but he cleared out at the last town, and I'm running the business alone now."

Toby's face expressed all the contempt he felt for the boy who would run away from such a glorious life

as Mr. Lord's assistant must lead, but he said not a word, waiting in breathless expectation for the offer which he now felt certain would be made him.

"Now I ain't hard on a boy," continued Mr. Lord, still confidentially, "and yet that one seemed to think that he was treated worse and made to work harder than any boy in the world."

"He ought to live with Uncle Dan'l a week," said Toby, eagerly.

"Here I was just like a father to him," said Mr. Lord, paying no attention to the interruption, "and I gave him his board and lodging and a dollar a week besides."

"Could he do what he wanted to with the dollar?"

"Of course he could. I never checked him, no matter how extravagant he was, an' yet I've seen him spend his whole week's wages at this very stand in one afternoon. And even after his money had all gone that way, I've paid for peppermint and ginger out of my own pocket just to cure his stomachache."

Toby shook his head mournfully, as if deploring that depravity which could cause a boy to run away from such a tender-hearted employer and from such a desirable position. But even as he shook his head so sadly, he looked wistfully at the peanuts, and Mr. Lord observed the look.

It may have been that Mr. Job Lord was the tender-hearted man he prided himself upon being, or it may have been that he wished to purchase Toby's sympathy; but, at all events, he gave him a large handful of nuts, and Toby never bothered his little round head as to what motive prompted the gift. Now he could listen to the story of the boy's treachery and eat at the same time; therefore he was an attentive listener.

"All in the world that boy had to do," continued Mr. Lord, in the same injured tone he had previously used, "was to help me set things to rights when we struck a town in the morning, and then tend to the counter till we left the town at night, and all the rest of the time he had to himself. Yet that boy was ungrateful enough to run away."

Mr. Lord paused, as if expecting some expression of sympathy from his listener; but Toby was so busily engaged with his unexpected feast, and his mouth was so full that it did not seem even possible for him to shake his head.

"Now what should you say if I told you that you looked to me like a boy that was made especially to help run a candy counter at a circus, and if I offered the place to you?"

Toby made one frantic effort to swallow the very large mouthful, and in a choking voice he answered, quickly, "I should say I'd go with you, an' be mighty glad of the chance."

"Then it's a bargain, my boy, and you shall leave town with me tonight."

2. *Toby Runs Away from Home*

Toby could scarcely restrain himself at the prospect of this golden future that had so suddenly opened before him. He tried to express his gratitude, but could only do so by evincing his willingness to commence work at once.

"No, no, that won't do," said Mr. Lord, cautiously. "If your Uncle Daniel should see you working here, he might mistrust something, and then you couldn't get away."

"I don't believe he'd try to stop me," said Toby,

confidently, "for he's told me lots of times that it was a sorry day for him when he found me."

"We won't take any chances, my son," was the reply, in a very benevolent tone, as he patted Toby on the head and at the same time handed him a piece of pasteboard. "There's a ticket for the circus, and you come around to see me about ten o'clock tonight, I'll put you on one of the wagons, and by tomorrow morning your Uncle Daniel will have hard work to find you."

If Toby had followed his inclinations, the chances are that he would have fallen on his knees and kissed Mr. Lord's hands in the excess of his gratitude. But not knowing exactly how such a show of thankfulness might be received, he contented himself by repeatedly promising that he would be punctual to the time and place appointed.

He would have loitered in the vicinity of the candy stand in order that he might gain some insight into the business, but Mr. Lord advised that he remain away, lest his Uncle Daniel should see him and suspect where he had gone when he was missed in the morning.

As Toby walked around the circus grounds, whereon was so much to attract his attention, he could not prevent himself from assuming an air of proprietorship. His interest in all that was going on was redoubled, and in his anxiety that everything should be done correctly and in the proper order he actually, and perhaps for the first time in his life, forgot that he was hungry.

He was really to travel with a circus, to become a part, as it were, of the whole, and to be able to see its many wonderful and beautiful attractions every day.

Even the very tent ropes had acquired a new interest for him, and the faces of the men at work seemed suddenly to have become those of friends. How hard it was for him to walk around unconcernedly: and how especially hard to prevent his feet from straying toward that tempting display of dainties which he was to sell to those who came to see and enjoy, and who would look at him with wonder and curiosity! It was very hard not to be allowed to tell his playmates of his wonderfully good fortune; but silence meant success, and he locked his secret in his bosom, not even daring to talk with anyone he knew, lest he should betray himself by some incautious word.

He did not go home to dinner that day, and once or twice he felt impelled to walk past the candy stand, giving a mysterious shake of the head at the proprietor as he did so. The afternoon performance passed off as usual to all of the spectators save Toby. He imagined that each one of the performers knew that he was about to join them; and even as he passed the cage containing the monkeys, he fancied that one particularly old one knew all about his intention of running away.

Of course it was necessary for him to go home at the close of the afternoon's performance, in order to get one or two valuable articles of his own, such as a boat, a kite, and a pair of skates, and in order that his actions might not seem suspicious. Before he left the grounds, however, he stole slyly around to the candy stand and informed Mr. Job Lord in a very hoarse whisper that he would be on hand at the time appointed.

Mr. Lord patted him on the head, gave him two large sticks of candy, and, what was more kind and surprising, considering the fact that he wore glasses and was cross-eyed, he winked at Toby. A wink from Mr. Lord must have been intended to convey a great deal, because, owing to the defect in his eyes, it required no little exertion, and even then could not be considered as a really first-class wink.

That wink, distorted as it was, gladdened Toby's heart immensely and took away nearly all the sting of the scolding with which Uncle Daniel greeted him when he reached home.

That night, despite the fact that he was going to travel with the circus, despite the fact that his home was not a happy or cheerful one, Toby was not in a pleasant frame of mind. He began to feel for the first time that he was doing wrong. And as he gazed at Uncle Daniel's stern, forbidding-looking face, it seemed to have changed somewhat from its severity, and caused a great lump of something to come up in his throat as he thought that perhaps he should never see it again. Just then one or two kind words would have prevented him from running away, bright as the prospect of circus life appeared.

It was almost impossible for him to eat anything, and this very surprising state of affairs attracted the attention of Uncle Daniel.

"Bless my heart! What ails the boy?" asked the old man, as he peered over his glasses at Toby's well-filled plate, which was usually emptied so quickly. "Are ye sick, Toby, or what is the matter with ye?"

"No, I hain't sick," said Toby, with a sigh, "but I've been to the circus, an' I got a good deal to eat."

"Oho! You spent that cent I give ye, eh, an' got so much that it made ye sick?"

Toby thought of the six peanuts which he had bought with the penny Uncle Daniel had given him; and, amid all his homesickness, he could not help wondering if Uncle Daniel ever made himself sick with only six peanuts when he was a boy.

As no one paid any further attention to Toby, he pushed back his plate, arose from the table, and went with a heavy heart to attend to his regular evening chores. The cow, the hens, and even the pigs came in for a share of his unusually kind attention; and as he fed them all, the big tears rolled down his cheeks as he thought that perhaps never again would he see any of them. These dumb animals had all been Toby's confidants; he had poured out his griefs in their ears and fancied, when the world or Uncle Daniel had used him unusually hard, that they sympathized with him. Now he was leaving them forever, and as he locked the stable door, he could hear the sounds of music coming from the direction of the circus grounds, and he was angry at it, because it represented that which was taking him away from his home, even though it was not as pleasant as it might have been.

Still, he had no thought of breaking the engagement which he had made. He went to his room, made a bundle of his worldly possessions, and crept out of the back door, down the road to the circus.

Mr. Lord saw him as soon as he arrived on the grounds, and as he passed another ticket to Toby, he took his bundle from him, saying, as he did so, "I'll pack up your bundle with my things, and then you'll be sure not to lose it. Don't you want some candy?"

Toby shook his head; he had just discovered that there was possibly some connection between his heart and his stomach, for his grief at leaving home had taken from him all desire for good things. It is also more than possible that Mr. Lord had had experience enough with boys to know that they might be homesick on the eve of starting to travel with a circus; and in order to make sure that Toby would keep to his engagement, he was unusually kind.

That evening was the longest that Toby ever knew. He wandered from one cage of animals to another, then to see the performance in the ring, and back again to the animals, in the vain hope of passing the time pleasantly. But it was of no use; that lump in his throat would remain there, and the thoughts of what he was about to do would trouble him severely. The performance failed to interest him, and the animals did not attract until he had visited the monkey cage for the third or fourth time. Then he fancied that the same venerable monkey who had looked so knowing in the afternoon was gazing at him with a sadness which

Toby walked around the circus grounds. (Page 25)

could only have come from a thorough knowledge of all the grief and doubt that was in his heart.

There was no one around the cages, and Toby got just as near to the iron bars as possible. No sooner had he flattened his little pug nose against the iron than the aged monkey came down from the ring in which he had been swinging, and, seating himself directly in front of Toby's face, looked at him most compassionately.

It would not have surprised the boy just then if the animal had spoken; but as he did not, Toby did the next best thing and spoke to him.

"I s'pose you remember that you saw me this afternoon, an' somebody told you that I was goin' to join the circus, didn't they?"

The monkey made no reply, though Toby fancied that he winked an affirmative answer; and he looked so sympathetic that he continued, confidentially:

"Well, I'm the same feller, an' I don't mind telling you that I'm awfully sorry I promised that candy man I'd go with him. Do you know that I came near crying at the supper table tonight; an' Uncle Dan'l looked real good an' nice, though I never thought so before. I wish I wasn't goin', after all, 'cause it don't seem a bit like a good time now. But I s'pose I must, 'cause I promised to, an' 'cause the candy man has got all my things."

The big tears had begun to roll down Toby's cheeks, and as he ceased speaking, the monkey reached out one little paw, which Toby took as earnestly as if it had been done purposely to console him.

"You're real good, you are," continued Toby, "an' I hope I shall see you real often, for it seems to me now, when there hain't any folks around, as if you was the only friend I've got in this great, big world. It's awful when a feller feels the way I do, an' when he don't seem to want anything to eat. Now if you'll stick to me, I'll stick to you, an' then it won't be half so bad when we feel this way."

During this speech Toby had still clung to the little brown paw, which the monkey now withdrew and continued to gaze into the boy's face.

"The fellers all say I don't amount to anything," sobbed Toby, "an' Uncle Dan'l says I don't, an' I s'pose they know; but I tell you I feel just as bad, now that I'm goin' away from them all, as if I was as good as any of them."

At this moment Toby saw Mr. Lord enter the tent, and he knew that the summons to start was about to be given.

"Good-by," he said to the monkey, as he vainly tried to take him by the hand again, "remember what I've told you, an' don't forget that Toby Tyler is feelin' worse tonight than if he was twice as big an' twice as good."

Mr. Lord had come to summon him away, and he now told Toby that he would show him with which man he was to ride that night.

Toby looked another good-by at the venerable

monkey, who was watching him closely, and then
followed his employer out of the tent, among the ropes
and poles and general confusion attendant upon the
removal of a circus from one place to another.

3. *The Night Ride*

THE wagon on which Mr. Lord was to send his new-found employee was, by the most singular chance, the one containing the monkeys, and Toby accepted this as a good omen. He would be near his venerable friend all night, and there was some consolation in that. The driver instructed the boy to watch his movements, and when he saw him leading his horses around, "To look lively, and be on hand, for he never waited for anyone."

Toby not only promised to do as ordered, but he followed the driver around so closely that, had he desired, he could not have rid himself of his little companion.

The scene which presented itself to Toby's view was strange and weird in the extreme. Shortly after he had attached himself to the man with whom he was to ride, the performance was over, and the work of putting the show and its belongings into such a shape as could be conveyed from one town to another was soon in active operation. Toby forgot his grief, forgot that he was running away from the only home he had ever known, in fact, forgot everything concerning himself, so interested was he in that which was going on about him.

As soon as the audience had got out of the tent—and almost before—the work of taking down the canvas was begun.

Torches were stuck in the earth at regular intervals, the lights that had shone so brilliantly in and around the ring had been extinguished, the canvas sides had been taken off, and the boards that had formed the seats were being packed into one of the carts with a rattling sound that seemed as if a regular fusillade of musketry was being indulged in. Men were shouting, horses were being driven hither and thither, harnessed to the wagons, or drawing the huge carts away as soon as they were loaded. Everything seemed in the greatest state of confusion, while really the work was being done in the most systematic manner possible.

Toby had not long to wait before the driver informed him that the time for starting had arrived and assisted him to climb up to the narrow seat whereon he was to ride that night.

The scene was so exciting, and his efforts to stick to the narrow seat so great, that he really had no time to attend to the homesick feeling that had crept over him during the first part of the evening.

The long procession of carts and wagons drove slowly out of the town, and when the last familiar house had been passed, the driver spoke to Toby for the first time since they started.

"Pretty hard work to keep on—eh, sonny?"

"Yes," replied the boy, as the wagon jolted over a rock, bouncing him high in air, and he, by strenuous efforts, barely succeeded in alighting on the seat again, "it is pretty hard work; an' my name's Toby Tyler."

Toby heard a queer sound that seemed to come from the man's throat, and for a few moments he feared that his companion was choking. But he soon understood that this was simply an attempt to laugh, and he at once decided that it was a very poor style of laughing.

"So you object to being called sonny, do you?"

"Well, I'd rather be called Toby, for, you see, that's my name."

"All right, my boy, we'll call you Toby. I suppose you thought it was a mighty fine thing to run away an' jine a circus, didn't you?"

Toby started in affright, looked around cautiously, and then tried to peer down through the small, square aperture, guarded by iron rods, that opened into the cage just back of the seat they were sitting on. Then

he turned slowly around to the driver and asked in a voice sunk to a whisper, "How did you know that I was runnin' away? Did he tell you?" and Toby motioned with his thumb as if he were pointing out someone behind him.

It was the driver's turn now to look around in search of the "he" referred to by Toby.

"Who do you mean?" asked the man, impatiently.

"Why, the old feller; the one in the cart there. I think he knew I was runnin' away, though he didn't say anything about it; but he looked just as if he did."

The driver looked at Toby in perfect amazement for a moment, and then, as if suddenly understanding the boy, relapsed into one of those convulsive efforts that caused the blood to rush up into his face and gave him every appearance of having a fit.

"You must mean one of the monkeys," said the driver, after he had recovered his breath, which had been almost shaken out of his body by the silent laughter. "So you thought a monkey had told me what any fool could have seen if he had watched you for five minutes."

"Well," said Toby, slowly, as if he feared he might provoke one of those terrible laughing spells again, "I saw him tonight, an' he looked as if he knew what I was doin'; so I up an' told him, an' I didn't know but he'd told you, though he didn't look to me like a feller that would be mean."

There was another internal shaking on the part of the driver, which Toby did not fear so much, since he was getting accustomed to it, and then the man said, "Well, you are the queerest little cove I ever saw."

"I s'pose I am," was the reply, accompanied by a long-drawn sigh. "I don't seem to amount to so much as the other fellers do, an' I guess it's because I'm always hungry. You see, I eat awful, Uncle Dan'l says."

The only reply which the driver made to this plaintive confession was to put his hand down into the deepest recesses of one of his deep pockets and to draw therefrom a huge doughnut, which he handed to his companion.

Toby was so much at his ease by this time that the appetite which had failed him at supper had now returned in full force, and he devoured the doughnut in a most ravenous manner.

"You're too small to eat so fast," said the man, in a warning tone, as the last morsel of the greasy sweetness disappeared, and he fished up another for the boy. "Some time you'll get hold of one of the India-rubber doughnuts that they feed to circus people, an' choke yourself to death."

Toby shook his head and devoured this second cake as quickly as he had the first, craning his neck and uttering a funny little squeak as the last bit went down, just as a chicken does when he gets too large a mouthful of dough.

"I'll never choke," he said, confidently, "I'm used to it. And Uncle Dan'l says I could eat a pair of boots an' never wink at 'em; but I don't just believe that."

As the driver made no reply to this remark, Toby curled himself up on one corner of the seat and watched with no little interest all that was passing on around him. Each of the wagons had a lantern fastened to the hind axle, and these lights could be seen far ahead on the road, as if a party of fireflies had started in single file on an excursion. The trees by the side of the road stood out weird and ghostly looking in the darkness, and the rumble of the carts ahead and behind formed a musical accompaniment to the picture that sounded strangely doleful.

Mile after mile was passed over in perfect silence, save now and then when the driver would whistle a few bars of some very dismal tune that would fairly make Toby shiver with its mournfulness. Eighteen miles was the distance from Guilford to the town where the next performance of the circus was to be given, and as Toby thought of the ride before them, it seemed as if the time would be almost interminable. He curled himself up on one corner of the seat and tried very hard to go to sleep; but just as his eyes began to grow heavy, the wagon would jolt over some rock or sink deep in some rut, till Toby, the breath very nearly shaken out of his body and his neck almost dislocated, would sit bolt upright, clinging to the seat with both hands, as if he expected each moment to be pitched out into the mud.

The driver watched him closely and each time that he saw him shaken up and awakened so thoroughly, he would indulge in one of his silent laughing spells, until

Toby would wonder whether he would ever recover from it. Several times had Toby been awakened, and each time he had seen the amusement his sufferings caused, until he finally resolved to put an end to the sport by keeping awake.

"What is your name?" he asked of the driver, thinking a conversation would be the best way to rouse himself into wakefulness.

"Waal," said the driver, as he gathered the reins carefully in one hand and seemed to be debating in his mind how he should answer the question, "I don't know as I know myself, it's been so long since I've heard it."

Toby was wide enough awake now, as this rather singular problem was forced upon his mind. He revolved the matter silently for some moments, and at last he asked, "What do folks call you when they want to speak to you?"

"They always call me Old Ben, an' I've got so used to the name that I don't need any other."

Toby wanted very much to ask more questions, but he wisely concluded that it would not be agreeable to his companion.

"I'll ask the old man about it," said Toby to himself, referring to the aged monkey, whom he seemed to feel acquainted with. "He most likely knows, if he'll say anything." After this the conversation ceased, until Toby again ventured to suggest, "It's a pretty long drive, hain't it?"

"You want to wait till you've been in this business a

year or two," said Ben, sagely, "an then you won't think much of it. Why, I've known the show towns to be thirty miles apart, an' them was the times when we had lively work of it, riding all night and working all day kind of wears on a fellow."

"Yes, I s'pose so," said Toby, with a sigh, as he wondered whether he had got to work as hard as that, "but I s'pose you get all you want to eat, don't you?"

"Now you've struck it!" said Ben, with the air of one about to impart a world of wisdom, as he crossed one leg over the other, that his position might be as comfortable as possible while he was initiating his young companion into the mysteries of the life. "I've had all the boys ride with me since I've been with this show, an' I've tried to start them right; but they didn't seem to profit by it, an' always got sick of the show an' run away, just because they didn't look out for themselves as they ought to. Now listen to me, Toby, an' remember what I say. You see, they put us all in a hotel together, an' some of these places where we go don't have any too much stuff on the table. Whenever we strike a new town, you find out at the hotel what time they have the grub ready, an' you be on hand, so's to get in with the first. Eat all you can, an' fill your pockets."

"If that's all a feller has to do to travel with a circus," said Toby, "I'm just the one, 'cause I always used to do just that when I hadn't any idea of bein' a circus man."

"Then you'll get along all right," said Ben, as he

checked the speed of his horses and, looking carefully ahead, said, as he guided his team to one side of the road, "This is as far as we're going tonight."

Toby learned that they were within a couple of miles of the town and that the entire procession would remain by the roadside until time to make the grand entrée into the village, when every wagon, horse, and man would be decked out in the most gorgeous array, as they had been when they entered Guilford.

Under Ben's direction he wrapped himself in an old horse blanket and lay down on the top of the wagon. And he was so tired from the excitement of the day and night, that he had hardly stretched out at full length before he was fast asleep.

4. *The First Day with the Circus*

WHEN Toby awakened and looked around, he could hardly realize where he was or how he came there. As far ahead and behind on the road as he could see, the carts were drawn up on one side; men were hurrying to and fro, orders were being shouted, and everything showed that the entry into the town was about to be made. Directly opposite the wagon on which he had been sleeping were the four elephants and two camels, and close behind, contentedly munching their breakfasts, were a number of tiny ponies. Troops of horses were being groomed and attended to; the road was littered with saddles, flags, and general decorations, until it seemed to Toby that there must have been a smash-up, and that he now beheld ruins rather than systematic disorder.

How different everything looked now, compared to the time when the cavalcade marched into Guilford, dazzling everyone with the gorgeous display! Then the horses pranced gayly under their gaudy decorations, the wagons were bright with glass, gilt, and flags, the lumbering elephants and awkward camels were covered with fancifully embroidered velvets, and even the drivers of the wagons were resplendent in their uniforms of scarlet and gold. Now, in the gray light of the early morning, everything was changed. The horses were tired and muddy and wore old and dirty harness. The gilded chariots were covered with mud-bespattered canvas, which caused them to look like the most ordinary of market wagons. The elephants and camels looked dingy, dirty, almost repulsive. And the drivers were only a sleepy-looking set of men, who, in their shirt sleeves, were getting ready for the change which would dazzle the eyes of the inhabitants of the town.

Toby descended from his lofty bed, rubbed his eyes to awaken himself thoroughly, and under the guidance of Ben went to a little brook near by and washed his face. He had been with the circus not quite ten hours, but now he could not realize that it had ever seemed bright and beautiful. He missed his comfortable bed, the quiet and cleanliness, and the well-spread table. Although he had felt the lack of a parent's care, Uncle Daniel's home seemed the very abode of love and friendly feeling compared to this condition, where no one appeared to care even enough for him to scold at him. He was thoroughly homesick and heartily wished that he was back in his old native town.

While he was washing his face in the brook, he saw some of the boys who had come out from the town to catch the first glimpse of the circus, and he saw at once that he was the object of their admiring gaze. He heard one of the boys say when they first discovered him:

"There's one of them, an' he's only a little feller; so I'm going to talk to him."

The evident admiration which the boys had for Toby pleased him, and this pleasure was the only drop of comfort he had had since he started. He hoped that they would come and talk with him; and, that they might have the opportunity, he was purposely slow in making his toilet.

The boys approached him shyly, as if they had their doubts whether he was made of the same material as themselves, and when they got quite near to him and satisfied themselves that he was only washing his face in much the same way that any well-regulated boy would do, the one who had called attention to him said, half timidly, "Hello!"

"Hello!" responded Toby, in a tone that was meant to invite confidence.

"Do you belong to the circus?"

"Yes," said Toby, a little doubtfully.

Then the boys stared at him again as if he were one of the strange-looking animals, and the one who had been the spokesman drew a long breath of envy as he said, longingly, "My! What a nice time you must have!"

Toby remembered that only yesterday he himself had thought that boys must have a nice time with a circus, and he now felt what a mistake that thought was; but he concluded that he would not undeceive his new acquaintance.

"And do they give you frogs to eat, so's to make you limber?"

This was the first time that Toby had thought of breakfast, and the very mention of eating made him hungry. He was just at that moment so very hungry that he did not think he was replying to the question when he said, quickly, "Eat frogs! I could eat anything if I only had the chance."

The boys took this as an answer to their question, and felt perfectly convinced that the agility of circus riders and tumblers depended upon the quantity of frogs eaten, and they looked upon Toby with no little degree of awe.

Toby might have undeceived them as to the kind of food he ate, but just at that moment the harsh voice of Mr. Job Lord was heard calling him, and he hurried away to commence his first day's work.

Toby's employer was not the same pleasant, kindly-spoken man that he had been during the time they were in Guilford and before the boy was absolutely under his control. He looked cross, he acted cross, and it did not take the boy very long to find out that he was very cross.

He scolded Toby roundly and launched more oaths at his defenseless head than Toby had ever heard in his life. He was angry that the boy had not been on hand to help him and also that he had been obliged to hunt for him.

Toby tried to explain that he had no idea of what he was expected to do, and that he had been on the wagon to which he had been sent, only leaving it to wash his face; but the angry man grew still more furious.

"Went to wash your face, did yer? Want to set yourself up for a dandy, I suppose, and think that you must souse that speckled face of yours into every brook you come to? I'll soon break you of that; and the sooner you understand that I can't afford to have you wasting your time in washing, the better it will be for you."

Toby now grew angry, and not realizing how wholly he was in the man's power, he retorted, "If you think I'm going round with a dirty face, even if it is speckled, for a dollar a week, you're mistaken, that's all. How many folks would eat your candy if they knew you handled it over before you washed your hands?"

"Oho! I've picked up a preacher, have I? Now I want you to understand, my bantam, that I do all the preaching as well as the practicing myself, and this

is about as quick a way as I know of to make you understand it."

As the man spoke, he grasped the boy by the coat collar with one hand and with the other plied a thin rubber cane with no gentle force to every portion of Toby's body that he could reach.

Every blow caused the poor boy the most intense pain, but he determined that his tormentor should not have the satisfaction of forcing an outcry from him, and he closed his lips so tightly that not a single sound could escape from them.

This very silence enraged the man so much that he redoubled the force and rapidity of his blows, and it is impossible to say what might have been the consequences had not Ben come that way just then and changed the aspect of affairs.

"Up to your old tricks of whipping the boys, are you, Job?" he said, as he wrested the cane from the man's hand and held him off at arm's length, to prevent him from doing Toby more mischief.

Mr. Lord struggled to release himself and insisted that, since the boy was in his employ, he should do with him just as he saw fit.

"Now look here, Mr. Lord," said Ben, as gravely as if he was delivering some profound piece of wisdom, "I've never interfered with you before, but now I'm going to stop your game of thrashing your boy every morning before breakfast. You just tell this youngster what you want him to do, and if he don't do it, you can discharge him. If I hear of your flogging him, I shall attend to your case at once. You hear me?"

Ben shook the now terrified candy vendor much as if he had been a child, and then released him, saying to Toby as he did so, "Now, my boy, you attend to your business as you ought to, and I'll settle his account if he tries the flogging game again."

"You see, I don't know what there is for me to do," sobbed Toby, for the kindly interference of Ben had made him show more feeling than Mr. Lord's blows had done.

"Tell him what he must do," said Ben, sternly.

"I want him to go to work and wash the tumblers and fix up the things in that green box, so we can commence to sell as soon as we get into town," snarled Mr. Lord, as he motioned toward a large green chest that had been taken out of one of the carts, and which Toby saw was filled with dirty glasses, spoons, knives, and other utensils such as were necessary to carry on the business.

Toby got a pail of water from the brook, hunted around and found towels and soap, and devoted himself to his work with such industry that Mr. Lord could not repress a grunt of satisfaction as he passed him, however angry he felt because he could not administer the whipping which would have smoothed his ruffled temper.

By the time the procession was ready to start for the town, Toby had as much of his work done as he could find that it was necessary to do, and his master, in his surly way, half acknowledged that this last boy of his was better than any he had had before.

Although Toby had done his work so well, he was far from feeling happy. He was both angry and sad as he thought of the cruel blows that had been inflicted, and he had plenty of leisure to repent of the rash step he had taken, although he could not see very clearly how he was to get away from it. He thought that he could not go back to Guilford, for Uncle Daniel would not allow him to come to his house again, and the hot, scalding tears ran down his cheeks as he realized that he was homeless and friendless in this great, big world.

It was while he was in this frame of mind that the procession, all gaudy with flags, streamers, and banners, entered the town. Under different circumstances this would have been a most delightful day for him, for the entrance of a circus into Guilford had always been a source of one day's solid enjoyment; but now he was the most disconsolate and unhappy boy in all that crowd.

He did not ride throughout the entire route of the procession, for Mr. Lord was anxious to begin business, and the moment the tenting ground was reached, the wagon containing Mr. Lord's goods was driven into the enclosure, and Toby's day's work began.

He was obliged to bring water, to cut up the lemons, fetch and carry fruit from the booth in the big tent to the booth on the outside, until he was ready to drop with fatigue, and having had no time for breakfast, was nearly famished.

It was quite noon before he was permitted to go to the hotel for something to eat, and then Ben's advice to be one of the first to get to the tables was not needed.

In the eating line that day he astonished the servants, the members of the company, and even himself, and by the time he arose from the table, with both pockets and his stomach full to bursting, the tables had been set and cleared away twice while he was making one meal.

"Well, I guess you didn't hurry yourself much," said Mr. Lord, when Toby returned to the circus ground.

"Oh, yes, I did," was Toby's innocent reply, "I ate just as fast as I could," and a satisfied smile stole over the boy's face as he thought of the amount of solid food which he had consumed.

The answer was not one which was calculated to make Mr. Lord feel any more agreeably disposed toward his new clerk, and he showed his ill-temper very plainly as he said, "It must take a good deal to satisfy you."

"I s'pose it does," calmly replied Toby. "Sam Merrill used to say that I took after Aunt Olive and Uncle Dan'l. One ate a good while, an' the other ate awful fast."

Toby could not understand what it was that Mr. Lord said in reply, but he could understand that his employer was angry at somebody or something, and he tried unusually hard to please him. He talked to the boys who had gathered around, to induce them to buy, washed the glasses as fast as they were used, tried to keep off the flies, and in every way he could think of endeavored to please his master.

5. *The Counterfeit Ten-cent Piece*

WHEN the doors of the big tent were opened and the people began to crowd in, just as Toby had seen them do at Guilford, Mr. Lord announced to his young clerk that it was time for him to go into the tent to work. Then it was that Toby learned for the first time that he had two masters instead of one, and this knowledge caused him no little uneasiness. If the other one was anything like Mr. Lord, his lot would be just twice as bad, and he began to wonder whether he could even stand it one day longer.

As the boy passed through the tent on his way to

the candy stand, where he was really to enter upon the duties for which he had run away from home, he wanted to stop for a moment and speak with the old monkey who he thought had taken such an interest in him. But when he reached the cage in which his friend was confined, there was such a crowd around it that it was impossible for him to get near enough to speak without being overheard.

This was such a disappointment to the little fellow that the big tears came into his eyes, and in another instant would have gone rolling down his cheeks if his aged friend had not chanced to look toward him. Toby fancied that the monkey looked at him in the most friendly way, and then he was certain that he winked one eye. Toby felt that there was no mistake about that wink, and it seemed as if it was intended to convey comfort to him in his troubles. He winked back at the monkey in the most emphatic and grave manner possible and then went on his way, feeling wonderfully comforted.

The work inside the tent was far different and much harder than it was outside. He was obliged to carry around among the audience trays of candy, nuts, and lemonade for sale, and he was also expected to cry aloud the description of that which he offered. The partner of Mr. Lord, who had charge of the stand inside the tent, showed himself to be neither better nor worse than Mr. Lord himself. When Toby first presented himself for work, he handed him a tray filled with glasses of lemonade and told him to go among the audience, crying, "Here's your nice, cold lemonade, only five cents a glass!"

Toby started to do as he was bidden; but when he tried to repeat the words in anything like a loud tone of voice, they stuck in his throat, and he found it next to impossible to utter a sound above a whisper. It seemed to him that everyone in the audience was looking only at him, and the very sound of his own voice made him afraid.

He went entirely around the tent once without making a sale, and when he returned to the stand, he was at once convinced that one of his masters was quite as bad as the other. This one—and he knew that his name was Jacobs, for he heard someone call him so— very kindly told him that he would break every bone in his body if he didn't sell something, and Toby confidently believed that he would carry out his threat.

It was with a heavy heart that he started around again in obedience to Mr. Jacobs's angry command; but this time he did manage to cry out, in a very thin and very squeaky voice, the words which he had been told to repeat.

This time, perhaps owing to his pitiful and imploring look, certainly not because of the noise he made, he met with very good luck, and sold every glass of the mixture which Messrs. Lord and Jacobs called lemonade and went back to the stand for more.

He certainly thought he had earned a word of praise and fully expected it as he put the empty glasses and money on the stand in front of Mr. Jacobs. But, instead of the kind words, he was greeted with a volley of curses; and the reason for it was that he had taken in payment for two of the glasses a lead ten-cent piece. Mr. Jacobs, after scolding poor little Toby to his heart's content, vowed that the amount should be kept from his first week's wages, and then handed back the coin, with orders to give it to the first man who gave him money to change, under the penalty of a severe flogging if he failed to do so.

Poor Toby tried to explain matters by saying, "You see, I don't know anything about money; I never had more'n a cent at a time, an' you mustn't expect me to get posted all at once."

"I'll post you with a stick if you do it again; an' it won't be well for you if you bring that ten-cent piece back here!"

Now Toby was very well aware that to pass the coin, knowing it to be bad, would be a crime, and he resolved to take the consequences of which Mr. Jacobs had intimated, if he could not find the one who had given him the counterfeit and persuade him to give him good money in its stead. He remembered very plainly where he had sold each glass of lemonade, and he retraced his steps, glancing at each face carefully as he passed. At last he was confident that he saw the man who had gotten him into such trouble, and he climbed up the board seats, saying, as he stood in front of him and held out the coin, "Mister, this money that you gave me is bad. Won't you give me another one for it?"

The man was a rough-looking party who had taken

his girl to the circus, and who did not seem at all disposed to pay any heed to Toby's request. Therefore he repeated it, and this time more loudly.

"Get out of the way!" said the man, angrily. "How can you expect me to see the show if you stand right in front of me?"

"You'll like it better," said Toby, earnestly, "if you give me another ten-cent piece."

"Get out, an' don't bother me!" was the angry rejoinder, and the little fellow began to think that perhaps he would be obliged to "get out" without getting his money.

It was becoming a desperate case, for the man was growing angry very fast, and if Toby did not succeed in getting good money for the bad, he would have to take the consequences of which Mr. Jacobs had spoken.

"Please, mister," he said, imploringly, for his heart began to grow very heavy, and he was fearing that he should not succeed, "won't you please give me the money back? You know you gave it to me, an' I'll have to pay it if you don't."

The boy's lip was quivering, and those around began to be interested in the affair, while several in the immediate vicinity gave vent to their indignation that a man should try to cheat a boy out of ten cents by giving him counterfeit money.

The man whom Toby was speaking to was about to dismiss him with an angry reply, when he saw that those about him were not only interested in the matter but were evidently taking sides with the boy against him. And knowing well that he had given the counterfeit money, he took another coin from his pocket and, handing it to Toby, said, "I didn't give you the lead piece; but you're making such a fuss about it, that here's ten cents to make you keep quiet."

"I'm sure you did give me the money," said Toby, as he took the extended coin, "an' I'm much obliged to you for takin' it back. I didn't want to tell you before, 'cause you'd thought I was beggin'; but if you hadn't given me this, I 'xpect I'd have got an awful whippin', for Mr. Jacobs said he'd fix me if I didn't get the money for it."

The man looked sheepish enough as he put the bad money in his pocket, and Toby's innocently told story caused such a feeling in his behalf among those who sat near that he not only disposed of his entire stock then and there, but received from one gentleman twenty-five cents for himself. He was both proud and happy as he returned to Mr. Jacobs with empty glasses, and with the money to refund the amount of loss which would have been caused by the counterfeit.

But the worthy partner of Mr. Lord's candy business had no words of encouragement for the boy who was trying so hard to please.

"Let that make you keep your eyes open," he growled out sulkily, "an' if you get caught in that trap again, you won't be let off so easy."

Poor little Toby! His heart seemed ready to break, but his few hours' previous experience had taught him that there was but one thing to do and that was to work just as hard as possible, trusting to some good fortune to enable him to get out of the very disagreeable position in which he had voluntarily placed himself.

He took the basket of candy that Mr. Jacobs handed him and trudged around the circle of seats, selling far more because of the pitifulness of his face than because of the excellence of his goods; and even this worked to his disadvantage. Mr. Jacobs was keen enough to see why his little clerk sold so many goods, and each time that he returned to the stand he said something to him in an angry tone, which had the effect of deepening the shadow on the boy's face and at the same time increasing trade.

By the time the performance was over, Toby had in his pocket a dollar and twenty-five cents which had been given him for himself by some of the kind-hearted in the audience, and he kept his hand almost constantly upon it, for the money seemed to him like some kind friend who would help him out of his present difficulties.

After the audience had dispersed, Mr. Jacobs set Toby at work washing the glasses and clearing up generally, and then the boy started toward the other portion of the store—that watched over by Mr. Lord. Not a person save the watchmen was in the tent, and as Toby went toward the door, he saw his friend, the monkey, sitting in one corner of the cage and apparently watching his every movement.

It was as if he had suddenly seen one of the boys from home, and Toby, uttering an exclamation of delight, ran up to the cage and put his hand through the wires.

The monkey, in the gravest possible manner, took one of the fingers in his paw, and Toby shook hands with him very earnestly.

"I was sorry that I couldn't speak to you when I went in this noon," said Toby, as if making an apology, "but, you see, there were so many around here to see you that I couldn't get the chance. Did you see me wink at you?"

The monkey made no reply, but he twisted his face into such a funny little grimace that Toby was quite as well satisfied as if he had spoken.

"I wonder if you hain't some relation to Steve Stubbs?" Toby continued, earnestly, "for you look just like him, only he didn't have quite so many whiskers. What I want to say was, that I'm awful sorry I run away. I used to think that Uncle Dan'l was bad enough, but he was just a perfect good Samarathon to what Mr. Lord an' Mr. Jacobs are. An' when Mr. Lord looks at me with that crooked eye of his, I feel it 'way down in my boots. Do you know"—and here Toby put his mouth nearer to the monkey's head and whispered— "I'd run away from this circus if I could get the chance; wouldn't you?"

Just at this point, as if in answer to the question, the monkey stood up on his hind feet and reached out his paw to the boy, who seemed to think this was his way of being more emphatic in saying, "Yes."

Toby took the paw in his hand, shook it again

earnestly, and said as he released it, "I was pretty sure you felt just about the same way I did, Mr. Stubbs, when I passed you this noon. Look here"—and Toby took the money from his pocket which had been given him—"I got all that this afternoon, an' I'll try an' stick it out somehow till I get as much as ten dollars, an' then we'll run away some night, an' go 'way off as far as—as—as out West, an' we'll stay there too."

The monkey, probably tired with remaining in one position so long, started toward the top of the cage, chattering and screaming, joining the other monkeys, who had gathered in a little group in one of the swings.

"Now see here, Mr. Stubbs," said Toby, in alarm, you mustn't go to telling everybody about it, or Mr. Lord will know, an' then we'll be dished, sure."

The monkey sat quietly in the swing, as if he felt reproved by what the boy had said; and Toby, considerably relieved by his silence, said, as he started toward the door, "That's right—mum's the word; you keep quiet, an' so will I, an' pretty soon we'll get away from the whole crowd."

All the monkeys chattered, and Toby, believing that everything which he had said had been understood by the animals, went out of the door to meet his other taskmaster.

6. *A Tender-hearted Skeleton*

"Now, then, lazy bones," was Mr. Lord's warning cry as Toby came out of the tent, "if you've fooled away enough of your time, you can come here an' tend shop for me while I go to supper. You crammed yourself this noon, an' it'll teach you a good lesson to make you go without anything to eat tonight. It'll make you move round more lively in future."

Instead of becoming accustomed to such treatment as he was receiving from his employers, Toby's heart grew more tender with each brutal word, and this last punishment—that of losing his supper—caused the poor boy more sorrow than blows would. Mr. Lord started for the hotel as he concluded his cruel speech, and poor little Toby, going behind the counter, leaned his head upon the rough boards and cried as if his heart would break.

All the fancied brightness and pleasure of a circus life had vanished, and in its place was the bitterness of remorse that he had repaid Uncle Daniel's kindness by the ingratitude of running away. Toby thought that if he could only nestle his little red head on the pillows of his little bed in that rough room at Uncle Daniel's, he would be the happiest and best boy in the future, in all the great, wide world.

While he was still sobbing away at a most furious rate, he heard a voice close at his elbow and, looking up, saw the thinnest man he had ever seen in all his life. The man had flesh-colored tights on, and a spangled red velvet garment that was neither pants, because there were no legs to it, nor a coat, because it did not come above his waist, made up the remainder of his costume. Because he was so wonderfully thin, because of the costume which he wore, and because of a highly colored painting which was hanging in front of one of the small tents, Toby knew that the Living Skeleton was before him, and his big, brown eyes opened all the wider as he gazed at him.

"What is the matter, little fellow?" asked the man in a kindly tone. "What makes you cry so? Has Job been up to his old tricks again?"

"I don't know what his old tricks are," and Toby

sobbed, the tears coming again because of the sympathy which this man's voice expressed for him, "but
I know that he's a mean, ugly thing—that's what I
know. An' if I could only get back to Uncle Dan'l,
there hain't elephants enough in all the circuses in the
world to pull me away again."

"Oh, you run away from home, did you?"

"Yes, I did," sobbed Toby, "an' there hain't any boy
in any Sunday-school book that ever I read that was
half so sorry he'd been bad as I am. It's awful, an'
now I can't have any supper, 'cause I stopped to talk
with Mr. Stubbs."

"Is Mr. Stubbs one of your friends?" asked the
skeleton as he seated himself in Mr. Lord's own private chair.

"Yes, he is, an' he's the only one in this whole circus
who 'pears to be sorry for me. You'd better not let Mr.
Lord see you sittin' in that chair or he'll raise a row."

"Job won't raise any row with me," said the skeleton. "But who is this Mr. Stubbs? I don't seem to
know anybody by that name."

"I don't think that is his name. I only call him so,
'cause he looks so much like a feller I know who is
named Stubbs."

This satisfied the skeleton that this Mr. Stubbs must
be someone attached to the show, and he asked:

"Has Job been whipping you?"

"No; Ben, the driver on the wagon where I ride,
told him not to do that again; but he hain't going to
let me have any supper, 'cause I was so slow about my

work—though I wasn't slow. I only talked to Mr. Stubbs when there wasn't anybody round his cage."

"Sam! Sam! Sam-u-el!"

This name, which was shouted twice in a quick, loud voice and the third time in a slow manner, ending almost in a screech, did not come from either Toby or the skeleton, but from an enormously large woman, dressed in a gaudy red-and-black dress, cut very short and with low neck and an apology for sleeves, who had just come out from the tent whereon the picture of the Living Skeleton hung.

"Samuel," she screamed again, "come inside this minute, or you'll catch your death o' cold, an' I shall have you wheezin' around with the phthisic all night. Come in, Sam-u-el."

"That's her," said the skeleton to Toby, as he pointed his thumb in the direction of the fat woman, but paying no attention to the outcry she was making, "that's my wife, Lilly, an' she's the Fat Woman of the show. She's always yellin' after me that way the minute I get out for a little fresh air, an' she's always sayin' just the same thing. Bless you, I never have the phthisic, but she does awful. An' I s'pose 'cause she's so large she can't feel all over her, an' thinks it's me that has it."

"Is—is all that—is that your wife?" stammered Toby, in astonishment, as he looked at the enormously fat woman who stood in the tent door and then at the wonderfully thin man who sat beside him.

"Yes, that's her," said the skeleton. "She weighs

pretty nigh four hundred, though of course the show cards says it's over six hundred, an' she earns almost as much money as I do. Of course she can't get so much, for skeletons is much scarcer than fat folks; but we make a pretty good thing travelin' together."

"Sam-u-el!" again came the cry from the fat woman, "are you never coming in?"

"Not yet, my angel," said the skeleton, placidly, as he crossed one thin leg over the other and looked calmly at her. "Come here an' see Job's new boy."

"Your imprudence is wearin' me away so that I sha'n't be worth five dollars a week to any circus," she said, impatiently, at the same time coming toward the candy stand quite as rapidly as her very great size would admit.

"This is my wife Lilly—Mrs. Treat," said the skeleton, with a proud wave of his hand, as he rose from his seat and gazed admiringly at her. "This is my flower—my queen, Mr.—Mr.—"

"Tyler," said Toby, supplying the name which the skeleton—or Mr. Treat, as Toby now learned his name was—did not know, "Tyler is my name—Toby Tyler."

"Why, what a little chap you are!" said Mrs. Treat, paying no attention to the awkward little bend of the head which Toby intended for a bow. "How small he is, Samuel!"

"Yes," said the skeleton, reflectively, as he looked Toby over from head to foot, as if he were mentally trying to calculate exactly how many inches high he was, "he is small; but he's got all the world before him to grow in, an' if he only eats enough— There, that reminds me. Job isn't going to give him any supper, because he didn't work hard enough."

"He won't, won't he?" exclaimed the large lady, savagely. "Oh, he's a precious one, he is. An' some day I shall just give him a good shakin'-up, that's what I'll do. I get all out of patience with that man's ugliness."

"An' she'll do just what she says," said the skeleton to Toby, with an admiring shake of the head. "That woman hain't afraid of anybody, an' I wouldn't be a bit surprised if she did give Job a pretty rough time."

Toby thought, as he looked at her, that she was large enough to give 'most anyone a pretty rough time, but he did not venture to say so. While he was looking first at her and then at her very thin husband, the skeleton told his wife the little that he had learned regarding the boy's history; and when he had concluded, she waddled away toward her tent.

"Great woman that," said the skeleton, as he saw her disappear within the tent.

"Yes," said Toby, "she's the greatest I ever saw."

"I mean that she's got a great head. Now you'll see about how much she cares for what Job says."

"If I was as big as her," said Toby, with just a shade of envy in his voice, "I wouldn't be afraid of anybody."

"It hain't so much the size," said the skeleton, sagely, "it hain't so much the size, my boy; for I can scare that woman almost to death when I feel like it."

Toby looked for a moment at Mr. Treat's thin legs and arms and then he said, warningly, "I wouldn't feel like it very often if I was you, Mr. Treat, 'cause she might break some of your bones if you didn't happen to scare her enough."

"Don't fear for me, my boy—don't fear for me. You'll see how I manage her if you stay with the circus long enough. Now, I often——"

If Mr. Treat was about to confide a family secret to Toby, it was fated that he should not hear it then, for Mrs. Treat had just come out of her tent, carrying in her hands a large tin plate piled high with a miscellaneous assortment of pie, cake, bread, and meat.

She placed this in front of Toby, and as she did so, she handed him two pictures.

"There, little Toby Tyler," she said, "there's something for you to eat, if Mr. Job Lord and his precious partner Jacobs did say you shouldn't have any supper; an' I've brought you a picture of Samuel an' me. We sell 'em for ten cents apiece, but I'm going to give them to you, because I like the looks of you."

Toby was quite overcome with the presents and seemed at a loss how to thank her for them. He attempted to speak but could not get the words out at first. Then he said, as he put the two photographs in the same pocket with his money, "You're awful good to me, an' when I get to be a man, I'll give you lots of things. I wasn't so very hungry, if I am such a big eater, but I did want something."

In the gray light of the early morning,
everything was changed. (Page 45)

"Bless your dear little heart, and you *shall* have something to eat," said the Fat Woman, as she seized Toby, squeezed him close up to her, and kissed his freckled face as kindly as if it had been as fair and white as possible. "You shall eat all you want to; an' if you get the stomachache, as Samuel does sometimes when he's been eatin' too much, I'll give you some catnip tea out of the same dipper that I give him his. He's a great eater, Samuel is," she added, in a burst of confidence, "an' it's a wonder to me what he does with it all sometimes."

"Is he?" exclaimed Toby, quickly. "How funny that is, for I'm an awful eater. Why, Uncle Dan'l used to say that I ate twice as much as I ought to, an' it never made me any bigger. I wonder what's the reason?"

"I declare I don't know," said the Fat Woman, thoughtfully, "an' I've wondered at it time an' time again. Some folks is made that way, an' some folks is made different. Now, I don't eat enough to keep a chicken alive, an' yet I grow fatter an' fatter every day. Don't I, Samuel?"

"Indeed you do, my love," said the skeleton, with a world of pride in his voice, "but you mustn't feel bad about it, for every pound you gain, makes you worth just so much more to the show."

"Oh, I wasn't worryin', I was only wonderin'. But we must go, Samuel, for the poor child won't eat a bit while we are here. After you've eaten what there is there, bring the plate in to me," she said to Toby, as she took her lean husband by the arm and walked him off toward their own tent.

Toby gazed after them a moment, and then he commenced a vigorous attack upon the eatables which had been so kindly given him. Of the food which he had taken from the dinner table he had eaten some while he was in the tent, and after that he had entirely forgotten that he had any in his pocket; therefore, at the time that Mrs. Treat had brought him such a liberal supply he was really very hungry.

He succeeded in eating nearly all the food which had been brought to him, and the very small quantity which remained he readily found room for in his pockets. Then he washed the plate nicely, and seeing no one in sight, he thought he could leave the booth long enough to return the plate.

He ran with it quickly into the tent occupied by the thin man and fat woman and handed it to her, with a profusion of thanks for her kindness.

"Did you eat it all?" she asked.

"Well," hesitated Toby, "there was three doughnuts an' a piece of pie left over, an' I put them in my pocket. If you don't care, I'll eat them some time tonight."

"You shall eat it whenever you want to, an' any time that you get hungry again, you come right to me."

"Thank you, ma'am. I must go now, for I left the store all alone."

"Run, then; an' if Job Lord abuses you, just let me know it, an' I'll keep him from cuttin' up any monkey shines."

Toby hardly heard the end of her sentence, so great was his haste to get back to the booth. And just as he emerged from the tent on a quick run, he received a blow on the ear which sent him sprawling in the dust, and he heard Mr. Job Lord's angry voice as it said, "So, just the moment my back is turned, you leave the stand to take care of itself, do you, an' run around tryin' to plot some mischief against me, eh?" And the brute kicked the prostrate boy twice with his heavy boot.

"Please don't kick me again!" pleaded Toby. "I wasn't gone but a minute, an' I wasn't doing anything bad."

"You're lying now, an' you know it, you young cub!" exclaimed the angry man as he advanced to kick the boy again. "I'll let you know who you've got to deal with when you get hold of me!"

"And I'll let you know who you've got to deal with when you get hold of me!" said a woman's voice, and, just as Mr. Lord raised his foot to kick the boy again, the Fat Woman seized him by the collar, jerked him back over one of the tent ropes, and left him quite as prostrate as he had left Toby. "Now, Job Lord," said the angry woman, as she towered above the thoroughly enraged but thoroughly frightened man, "I want you to understand that you can't knock and beat this boy while I'm around. I've seen enough of your capers, an' I'm going to put a stop to them. That boy wasn't in this tent more than two minutes, an' he attends to his work better than anyone you have ever had, so see that you treat him decent. Get up," she said to Toby, who had not dared to rise from the ground, "and if he offers to strike you again, come to me."

Toby scrambled to his feet and ran to the booth in time to attend to one or two customers who had just come up. He could see from out the corner of his eye that Mr. Lord had arisen to his feet also and was engaged in an angry conversation with Mrs. Treat, the result of which he very much feared would be another and a worse whipping for him.

But in this he was mistaken, for Mr. Lord, after the conversation was ended, came toward the booth and began to attend to his business without speaking one word to Toby. When Mr. Jacobs returned from his supper, Mr. Lord took him by the arm and walked him out toward the rear of the tents; and Toby was very positive that he was to be the subject of their conversation, which made him not a little uneasy.

It was not until nearly time for the performance to begin that Mr. Lord returned and he had nothing to say to Toby, save to tell him to go into the tent and begin his work there. The boy was only too glad to escape so easily, and he went to his work with as much alacrity as if he were about entering upon some pleasure.

When he met Mr. Jacobs, that gentleman spoke to him very sharply about being late and seemed to think it no excuse at all that he had just been relieved from the outside work by Mr. Lord.

7. *An Accident and Its Consequences*

TOBY's experience in the evening was very similar to that of the afternoon, save that he was so fortunate as not to take any more bad money in payment for his goods. Mr. Jacobs scolded and swore alternately, and the boy really surprised him by his way of selling goods, though he was very careful not to say anything about it, but made Toby believe that he was doing only about half as much work as he ought to do. Toby's private hoard of money was increased that evening, by presents, ninety cents, and he began to look upon himself as almost a rich man.

When the performance was nearly over, Mr. Jacobs

called to him to help in packing up; and by the time
the last spectator had left the tent, the worldly possessions of Messrs. Lord and Jacobs were ready for removal, and Toby allowed to do as he had a mind to,
as long as he was careful to be on hand when Old Ben
was ready to start.

Toby thought that he would have time to pay a visit
to his friends, the skeleton and the Fat Woman, and to
that end started toward the place where their tent had
been standing. But to his sorrow he found that it was
already being taken down, and he had only time to
thank Mrs. Treat and to press the fleshless hand of her
shadowy husband as they entered their wagon to drive
away.

He was disappointed, for he had hoped to be able
to speak with his new-made friends a few moments
before the weary night's ride commenced; but, failing
in that, he went hastily back to the monkey's cage.
Old Ben was there, getting things ready for a start,
but the wooden sides of the cage had not been put up
and Toby had no difficulty in calling the aged monkey
up to the bars. He held one of the Fat Woman's doughnuts in his hand and said, as he passed it through to
the animal:

"I thought perhaps you might be hungry, Mr.
Stubbs, and this is some of what the skeleton's wife
give me. I hain't got very much time to talk with you
now, but the first chance I can get away tomorrow, an'
when there hain't anybody 'round, I want to tell you
something."

The monkey had taken the doughnut in his hand-like paws and was tearing it to pieces, eating small portions of it very rapidly.

"Don't hurry yourself," said Toby, warningly, "for Uncle Dan'l always told me the worst thing a feller could do was to eat fast. If you want any more before we start, just put your hand through the little hole up there near the seat, an' I'll give you all you want."

From the look on his face Toby confidently believed the monkey was about to make some reply, but just then Ben shut up the sides, separating Toby and Mr. Stubbs, and the order was given to start.

Toby clambered up on to the high seat, Ben followed him, and in another instant the team was moving along slowly down the dusty road, preceded and followed by the many wagons, with their tiny, swinging lights.

"Well," said Ben, when he had got his team well under way and felt that he could indulge in a little conversation, "how did you get along today?"

Toby related all of his movements and gave the driver a faithful account of all that had happened to him, concluding his story by saying, "That was one of Mrs. Treat's doughnuts that I just gave to Mr. Stubbs."

"To whom?" asked Ben, in surprise.

"To Mr. Stubbs—the old fellow here in the cart, you know, that's been so good to me."

Toby heard a sort of gurgling sound, saw the driver's body sway back and forth in a trembling way, and was just becoming thoroughly alarmed, when he thought of the previous night and understood that Ben was only laughing in his own peculiar way.

"How did you know his name was Stubbs?" asked Ben, after he had recovered his breath.

"Oh, I don't know that that is his real name," was the quick reply, "I only call him that because he looks so much like a feller with that name that I knew at home. He don't seem to mind because I call him Stubbs."

Ben looked at Toby earnestly for a moment, acting all the time as if he wanted to laugh again, but didn't dare to, for fear he might burst a blood vessel; and then he said, as he patted him on the shoulder, "Well, you are the queerest little fish that I ever saw in all my travels. You seem to think that that monkey knows all you say to him."

"I'm sure he does," said Toby, positively. "He don't say anything right out to me, but he knows everything I tell him. Do you suppose he could talk if he tried to?"

"Look here, Mr. Toby Tyler," and Ben turned half around in his seat and looked Toby full in the face, so as to give more emphasis to his words, "are you heathen enough to think that that monkey could talk if he wanted to?"

"I know I hain't a heathen," said Toby, thoughtfully, "for if I had been some of the missionaries would have found me out a good while ago; but I never saw anybody like this old Mr. Stubbs before, an' I thought he could talk if he wanted to, just as the Living Skeleton does, or his wife. Anyhow, Mr. Stubbs winks at me; an' how could he do that if he didn't know what I've been sayin' to him?"

"Look here, my son," said Ben, in a most fatherly fashion, "monkeys hain't anything but beasts, an' they don't know how to talk any more than they know what you say to 'em."

"Didn't you ever hear any of them speak a word?"

"Never. I've been in a circus, man an' boy, nigh on to forty years, an' I never seen nothin' in a monkey more'n any other beast, except their awful mischiefness."

"Well," said Toby, still unconvinced, "I believe Mr. Stubbs knows what I say to him, anyway."

"Now don't be foolish, Toby," pleaded Ben. "You can't show me one thing that a monkey ever did because you told him to."

Just at that moment, Toby felt someone pulling at the back of his coat and, looking round, he saw that it was a little brown hand reaching through the bars of the air hole of the cage, that was tugging away at his coat.

"There!" he said, triumphantly, to Ben. "Look there! I told Mr. Stubbs if he wanted anything more to eat, to tell me, an' I would give it to him. Now you can see for yourself that he's come for it." And Toby took a doughnut from his pocket and put it into the tiny hand, which was immediately withdrawn. "Now what do you think of Mr. Stubbs knowing what I say to him?"

"They often stick their paws up through there," said Ben, in a matter-of-fact tone. "I've had 'em pull my coat in the night till they made me as nervous as ever any old woman was. You see, Toby, my boy, monkeys is monkeys; an' you mustn't go to gettin' the idea that they're anything else, for it's a mistake. You think this old monkey in here knows what you say? Why, that's just the cuteness of the old fellow. He watches you to see if he can't do just as you do, an' that's all there is about it."

Toby was more than half convinced that Ben was putting the matter in its proper light, and he would have believed all that had been said if, just at that moment, he had not seen that brown hand reaching through the hole to clutch him again by the coat.

The action seemed so natural, so like a hungry boy who gropes in the dark pantry for something to eat, that it would have taken more arguments than Ben had at his disposal to persuade Toby that his Mr. Stubbs could not understand all that was said to him. Toby put another doughnut in the outstretched hand and then sat silently, as if in a brown study over some difficult problem.

For some time the ride was continued in silence. Ben was going through all the motions of whistling without uttering a sound—a favorite amusement of his—and Toby's thoughts were far away in the humble home he had scorned, with Uncle Daniel, whose virtues had increased in his esteem with every mile of distance which had been put between them, and whose faults had decreased in a corresponding ratio.

Toby's thoughtfulness had made him sleepy, and his eyes were almost closed in slumber, when he was startled by a crashing sound, was conscious of a feeling of being hurled from his seat by some great force, and then he lay senseless by the side of the road, while the wagon became a perfect wreck, from out of which a small army of monkeys was escaping. Ben's experienced ear had told him at the first crash that his wagon was breaking down, and, without having time to warn Toby of his peril, he had leaped clear of the wreck, keeping his horses under perfect control, and thus averting more trouble. It was the breaking of one of the axles which Toby had heard just before he was thrown from his seat and when the body of the wagon came down upon the hard road.

The monkeys, thus suddenly released from confinement, had scampered off in every direction, and by a singular chance, Toby's aged friend started for the woods in such a direction as to bring him directly before the boy's insensible form. The monkey, on coming up to Toby, stopped, urged by the well-known curiosity of its race, and began to examine the boy's person carefully, prying into pockets and trying to open the boy's half-closed eyelids. Fortunately for Toby, he had fallen upon a mud bank and was only stunned for the moment, having received no serious bruises. The attentions bestowed upon him by the monkey served the purpose of bringing him to his senses; and, after he had looked around him in the gray light of the coming morning, it would have taken far more of a philosopher than Old Ben was to persuade the boy that monkeys did not possess reasoning faculties.

The monkey was busy at Toby's ears, nose, and mouth, as monkeys will do when they get an opportunity, and the expression of its face was as grave as possible. Toby firmly believed that the monkey's face showed sorrow at his fall, and he imagined that the attentions which were bestowed upon him were for the purpose of learning whether he had been injured or not.

"Don't worry, Mr. Stubbs," said Toby, anxious to reassure his friend, as he sat upright and looked about him. "I didn't get hurt any; but I would like to know how I got 'way over here."

It really seemed as if the monkey was pleased to know that his little friend was not hurt, for he seated himself on his haunches, and his face expressed the liveliest pleasure that Toby was well again—or at least that was how the boy interpreted the look.

By this time the news of the accident had been shouted ahead from one team to the other, and all hands were hurrying to the scene for the purpose of rendering aid. As Toby saw them coming, he also saw a number of small forms, looking something like diminutive men, hurrying past him, and for the first time he understod how it was that the aged monkey was at liberty, and knew that those little dusky forms were the other occupants of the cage escaping to the woods.

"See there, Mr. Stubbs! See there!" he exclaimed, pointing toward the fugitives, "they're all going off into the woods! What shall we do?"

The sight of the runaways seemed to excite the old monkey quite as much as it did the boy. He sprang to his feet, chattering in the most excited way, screamed two or three times, as if he were calling them back, and then started off in vigorous pursuit.

"Now he's gone, too!" said Toby, disconsolately, believing that the old fellow had run away from him. "I didn't think Mr. Stubbs would treat me this way!"

8. *Capture of the Monkeys*

THE boy tried to rise to his feet, but his head whirled so and he felt so dizzy and sick from the effects of his fall, that he was obliged to sit down again until he should feel able to stand. Meanwhile the crowd around the wagon paid no attention to him, and he lay there quietly enough, until he heard the hateful voice of Mr. Lord, asking if his boy were hurt.

The sound of his voice affected Toby very much as the chills and fever affect a sufferer, and he shook so with fear and his heart beat so loudly, that he thought Mr. Lord must know where he was by the sound. Seeing, however, that his employer did not come directly toward him, the thought flashed upon his mind that now would be a good chance to run away, and he acted upon it at once. He rolled himself over in the mud until he reached a low growth of fir trees that skirted the road, and when beneath their friendly shade, he arose to his feet and walked swiftly toward the woods, following the direction the monkeys had taken.

He no longer felt dizzy and sick: the fear of Mr. Lord had dispelled all that, and he felt strong and active again.

He had walked rapidly for some distance and was nearly beyond the sound of the voices in the road, when he was startled by seeing quite a procession of figures emerge from the trees and come directly toward him.

He could not understand the meaning of this strange company, and it so frightened him that he attempted to hide behind a tree, in the hope that they might pass without seeing him. But no sooner had he secreted himself than a strange, shrill chattering came from the foremost of the group, and in an instant Toby emerged from his place of concealment.

He had recognized the peculiar sound as that of the old monkey who had left him a few moments before, and he knew now what he did not know then, owing to the darkness. The newcomers were the monkeys that had escaped from the cage and had been overtaken

Packing up. (Page 78)

and compelled to come back by the old monkey, who seemed to have the most perfect control over them.

The old fellow was leading the band, and all were linked "hand in hand" with each other, which gave the whole crowd a most comical appearance as they came up to Toby, half hopping, half walking upright, and all chattering and screaming like a crowd of children out for a holiday.

Toby stepped toward the noisy crowd, held out his hand gravely to the old monkey, and said, in tones of heartfelt sorrow:

"I felt awful bad because I thought you had gone off an' left me, when you only went off to find the other fellows. You're awful good, Mr. Stubbs, an' now, instead of runnin' away, as I was goin' to do, we'll all go back together."

The old monkey grasped Toby's extended hand with his disengaged paw and, clinging firmly to it, the whole crowd followed in unbroken line, chattering and scolding at the most furious rate, while every now and then Mr. Stubbs would look back and scream out something, which would cause the confusion to cease for an instant.

It was really a comical sight, but Toby seemed to think it the most natural thing in the world that they should follow him in this manner, and he chattered to the old monkey quite as fast as any of the others were doing. He told him very gravely all that he knew about the accident, explained why it was that he con-

ceived the idea of running away, and really believed that Mr. Stubbs understood every word he was saying.

Very shortly after Toby had started to run away, the proprietor of the circus drove up to the scene of disaster; and, after seeing that the wagon was being rapidly fixed up so that it could be hauled to the next town, he ordered that search should be made for the monkeys. It was very important that they should be captured at once, and he appeared to think more of the loss of the animals than of the damage done to the wagon.

While the men were forming a plan for a search for the truants, so that in case of a capture they could let each other know, the noise made by Toby and his party was heard, and the men stood still to learn what it meant.

The entire party burst into shouts of laughter as Toby and his companions walked into the circle of light formed by the glare of the lanterns, and the merriment was by no means abated at Toby's serious demeanor. The wagon was now standing upright, with the door open, and Toby therefore led his companions directly to it, gravely motioning them to enter.

The old monkey, instead of obeying, stepped back to Toby's side and screamed to the others in such a manner that they all entered the cage, leaving him on the outside with the boy.

Toby motioned him to get in, too, but he clung to his hand and scolded so furiously that it was apparent he had no idea of leaving his boy companion. One of

the men stepped up and was about to force him into
the wagon, when the proprietor ordered him to stop.

"What boy is that?" he asked.

"Job Lord's new boy," said someone in the crowd.

The man asked Toby how it was that he had succeeded in capturing all the runaways, and he answered,
gravely:

"Mr. Stubbs an' I are good friends, an' when he saw
the others runnin' away, he just stopped 'em an'
brought 'em back to me. I wish you'd let Mr. Stubbs
ride with me; we like each other a good deal."

"You can do just what you please with Mr. Stubbs,
as you call him. I expected to lose half the monkeys in
that cage, and you have brought back every one. That
monkey shall be yours, and you may put him in the
cage whenever you want to or take him with you, just
as you choose, for he belongs entirely to you."

Toby's joy knew no bounds; he put his arm around
the monkey's neck, and the monkey clung firmly to
him, until even Job Lord was touched at the evidence
of affection between the two.

While the wagon was being repaired, Toby and the
monkey stood hand in hand watching the work go on,
while those in the cage scolded and raved because they
had been induced to return to captivity. After a while
the old monkey seated himself on Toby's arm and
cuddled close up to him, uttering now and then a contented sort of little squeak as the boy talked to him.

That night Mr. Stubbs slept in Toby's arms, in
the band wagon, and both boy and monkey appeared

very well contented with their lot, which a short time previous had seemed so hard.

When Toby awakened to his second day's work with the circus, his monkey friend was seated by his side, gravely exploring his pockets, and all the boy's treasures were being spread out on the floor of the wagon by his side. Toby remonstrated with him on this breach of confidence, but Mr. Stubbs was more in the mood for sport than for grave conversation, and the more Toby talked, the more mischievous did he become, until at length the boy gathered up his little store of treasures, took the monkey by the paw, and walked him toward the cage from which he had escaped on the previous night.

"Now, Mr. Stubbs," said Toby, speaking in an injured tone, "you must go in here and stay till I have got more time to fool with you."

He opened the door of the cage, but the monkey struggled as well as he was able, and Toby was obliged to exert all his strength to put him in.

When once the door was fastened upon him, Toby tried to impress upon his monkey friend's mind the importance of being more sedate, and he was convinced that the words had sunk deep into Mr. Stubbs's heart, for, by the time he had concluded, the old monkey was seated in the corner of the cage, looking up from under his shaggy eyebrows in the most reproachful manner possible.

Toby felt sorry that he had spoken so harshly and was about to make amends for his severity, when Mr.

Lord's gruff voice recalled him to the fact that his time was not his own, and he therefore commenced his day's work, but with a lighter heart than he had had since he stole away from Uncle Daniel and Guilford.

This day was not very much different from the preceding one so far as the manner of Mr. Lord and his partner toward the boy was concerned. They seemed to have an idea that he was doing only about half as much work as he ought to, and both united in swearing at and abusing him as much as possible.

As far as his relations with other members of the company were concerned, Toby now stood in a much better position than before. Those who had witnessed the scene told the others how Toby had led in the monkeys on the night previous, and nearly every member of the company had a kind word for the little fellow whose head could hardly be seen above the counter of Messrs. Lord and Jacobs's booth.

9. *The Dinner Party*

AT NOON Toby was thoroughly tired out, for whenever anyone spoke kindly to him, Mr. Lord seemed to
take a malicious pleasure in giving him extra tasks to
do, until Toby began to hope that no one else would
pay any attention to him. On this day he was permitted to go to dinner first, and after he returned, he
was left in charge of the booth. Trade being dull, as it
usually was during the dinner hour, he had very little
work to do after he had cleaned the glasses and set
things to rights generally.

When, therefore, he saw the gaunt form of the

skeleton emerge from his tent and come toward him he was particularly pleased, for he had begun to think very kindly of the thin man and his fleshy wife.

"Well, Toby," said the skeleton, as he came up to the booth, carefully dusted Mr. Lord's private chair, and sat down very cautiously in it, as if he expected it would break down under his weight, "I hear you've been making quite a hero of yourself by capturing the monkeys last night."

Toby's freckled face reddened with pleasure as he heard these words and he stammered out with considerable difficulty, "I didn't do anything; it was Mr. Stubbs that brought 'em back."

"Mr. Stubbs!" And the skeleton laughed so heartily that Toby was afraid he would dislocate some of his thinly covered joints. "When you was tellin' about Mr. Stubbs yesterday, I thought you meant someone belonging to the company. You ought to have seen my wife, Lilly, shake with laughing when I told her who Mr. Stubbs was!"

"Yes," said Toby, at a loss to know just what to say, "I should think she *would* shake when she laughs."

"She does," replied the skeleton. "If you could see her when something funny strikes her, you'd think she was one of those big plates of jelly that they have in the bakeshop windows." And Mr. Treat looked proudly at the gaudy picture which represented his wife in all her monstrosity of flesh. "She's a great woman, Toby, an' she's got a great head."

Toby nodded his head in assent. He would have

The two reveled in their freedom! (Page 100)

liked to have said something nice regarding Mrs. Treat, but he really did not know what to say, so he simply contented himself and the fond husband by nodding.

"She thinks a good deal of you, Toby," continued the skeleton, as he moved his chair to a position more favorable for him to elevate his feet on the edge of the counter, and placed his handkerchief under him as a cushion, "she's talking of you all the time, and if you wasn't such a little fellow I should begin to be jealous of you—I should, upon my word."

"You're—both—very—good," stammered Toby, so weighted down by a sense of the honor heaped upon him as to be at a loss for words.

"An' she wants to see more of you. She made me come out here now, when she knew Mr. Lord would be away, to tell you that we're goin' to have a little kind of a friendly dinner in our tent tomorrow—she's cooked it all herself, or she's going to—and we want you to come in an' have some with us."

Toby's eyes glistened at the thought of the unexpected pleasure, and then his face grew sad as he replied, "I'd like to come first-rate, Mr. Treat, but I don't s'pose Mr. Lord would let me stay away from the shop long enough."

"Why, you won't have any work to do tomorrow, Toby—it's Sunday."

"So it is!" said the boy, with a pleased smile, as he thought of the day of rest which was so near. And then he added, quickly, "An' this is Saturday afternoon.

What fun the boys at home are havin'! You see there hain't any school Saturday afternoons, an' all the fellers go out in the woods."

"And you wish you were there to go with them, don't you?" asked the skeleton, sympathetically.

"Indeed I do!" exclaimed Toby, quickly. "It's twice as good as any circus that ever was."

"But you didn't think so before you came with us, did you?"

"I didn't know so much about circuses then as I do now," replied the boy, sadly.

Mr. Treat saw that he was touching on a sore subject and one which was arousing sad thoughts in his little companion's mind, and he hastened to change it at once.

"Then I can tell Lilly that you'll come, can I?"

"Oh, yes, I'll be sure to be there; an' I want you to know just how good I think you both are to me."

"That's all right, Toby," said Mr. Treat, with a pleased expression on his face, "an' you may bring Mr. Stubbs with you, if you want to."

"Thank you," said Toby, "I'm sure Mr. Stubbs will be just as glad to come as I shall. But where will we be tomorrow?"

"Right here. We always stay over Sunday at the place where we show Saturday. But I must be going, or Lilly will worry her life out of her for fear I'm somewhere getting cold. She's awful careful of me, that woman is. You'll be on hand tomorrow at one o'clock, won't you?"

"Indeed I will," said Toby, emphatically, "an' I'll bring Mr. Stubbs with me, too."

With a friendly nod of the head, the skeleton hurried away to reassure his wife that he was safe and well. And before he had hardly disappeared within the tent, Toby had another caller, who was none other than his friend Old Ben, the driver.

"Well, my boy," shouted Ben, in his cheery, hearty tones, "I haven't seen you since you left the wagon so sudden last night. Did you get shook up much?"

"Oh, no," replied Toby, "you see I hain't very big, an' then I struck in the mud; so I got off pretty easy."

"That's a fact; an' you can thank your lucky stars for it, too, for I've seen grown-up men get pitched off a wagon in that way an' break their necks doin' it. But has Job told you where you was going to sleep tonight? You know we stay over here till tomorrow."

"I didn't think anything about that; but I s'pose I'll sleep in the wagon, won't I?"

"You can sleep at the hotel, if you want to; but the beds will likely be dirty. An' if you take my advice, you'll crawl into some of the wagons in the tent."

Ben then explained to him that, after his work was done that night, he would not be expected to report for duty until the time for starting on Sunday night, and concluded his remarks by saying:

"Now you know what your rights are, an' don't you let Job impose on you in any way. I'll be round here after you get through work, an' we'll bunk in somewhere together."

The arrival of Messrs. Lord and Jacobs put a stop
to the conversation and was the signal for Toby's time
of trial. It seemed to him, and with good reason, that
the chief delight these men had in life was to torment
him, for neither ever spoke a pleasant word to him.
And when one was not giving him some difficult work
to do or finding fault in some way, the other would
be sure to do so; and Toby had very little comfort from
the time he began work in the morning until he
stopped at night.

It was not until after the evening performance was
over that Toby had a chance to speak with Mr. Stubbs,
and then he was so tired that he simply took the old
monkey from the cage, nestled him under his jacket,
and lay down with him to sleep in the place which Old
Ben had selected.

When the morning came, Mr. Stubbs aroused his
young master at a much earlier hour than he would
have awakened had he been left to himself, and the
two went out for a short walk before breakfast. They
went instinctively toward the woods; and when the
shade of the trees was once reached, how the two reveled in their freedom! Mr. Stubbs climbed into the
trees, swung himself from one to the other by means
of his tail, gathered half-ripe nuts, which he threw at
his master, tried to catch the birds, and had a good
time generally.

Toby, stretched at full length on the mossy bank,
watched the antics of his pet, laughing boisterously at
times as Mr. Stubbs would do some one thing more

comical than usual, and forgot there was in this world such a thing as a circus or such a man as Job Lord. It was to Toby a morning without a flaw, and he took no heed of the time, until the sound of the church bells warned him of the lateness of the hour, reminding him at the same time of where he should be—where he would be, if he were at home with Uncle Daniel.

In the meantime the old monkey had been trying to attract his young master's attention, and, failing in his efforts, he came down from the tree, crept softly up to Toby, and nestled his head under the boy's arm.

This little act of devotion seemed to cause Toby's grief to burst forth afresh, and clasping the monkey around the neck, hugging him close to his bosom, he sobbed:

"O Mr. Stubbs, Mr. Stubbs, how lonesome we are! If we was only at Uncle Dan'l's, we'd be the two happiest people in all this world. We could play on the hay or go up to the pasture or go down to the village; an' I'd work my fingers off if I could only be there just once more. It was wicked for me to run away, an' now I'm gettin' paid for it."

He hugged the monkey closely, swaying his body to and fro, and presenting a perfect picture of grief. The monkey, not knowing what to make of this changed mood, cowered whimperingly in his arms, looking up into his face and licking the boy's hands whenever he had the opportunity.

It was some time before Toby's grief exhausted itself; and then, still clasping the monkey, he hurried out of the woods toward the town and the now thoroughly hated circus tents.

The clocks were just striking one as Toby entered the enclosure used by the show as a place of performance, and, remembering his engagement with the skeleton and his wife, he went directly to their tent. From the odors which assailed him as he entered, it was very evident that a feast of no mean proportions was in course of preparation and Toby's keen appetite returned in full vigor. Even the monkey seemed affected by the odor, for he danced about on his master's shoulder and chattered so that Toby was obliged to choke him a little in order to make him present a respectable appearance.

When Toby reached the interior of the tent, he was astonished at the extent of the preparations that were being made, and gazed around him in surprise. The platform on which the lean man and fat woman were in the habit of exhibiting themselves now bore a long table loaded with eatables; and, from the fact that eight or ten chairs were ranged around it, Toby understood that he was not the only guest invited to the feast. Some little attempt had also been made at decoration by festooning the end of the tent where the platform was placed with two or three flags and some streamers, and the tent poles also were fringed with tissue paper of the brightest colors.

Toby had only time enough to notice this when the skeleton advanced toward him, and, with the liveliest appearance of pleasure, said, as he took him by the hands with a grip that made him wince:

"It gives me great joy, Mr. Tyler, to welcome you at one of our little home reunions, if one can call a tent, that is moved every day in the week, home."

Toby hardly knew whom Mr. Treat referred to when he said, "Mr. Tyler," but by the time his hands were released from the bony grasp, he understood that it was himself who was spoken to.

The skeleton then formally introduced him to the other guests present, who were sitting at one end of the tent and evidently anxiously awaiting the coming feast.

"These," said Mr. Treat, as he waved his hand toward two white-haired, pink-eyed young ladies, who sat with their arms twined around each other's waist, and had been eying the monkey with some appearance of fear, "are the Miss Cushings, known to the world as the Albino Children. They command a large salary and form a very attractive feature of our exhibition."

The young ladies arose at the same time, as if they had been the Siamese Twins and could not act independently of each other, and bowed.

Toby made the best bow he was capable of, and the monkey made frantic efforts to escape, as if he would enjoy twisting his paws in their perpendicular hair.

"And this," continued Mr. Treat, pointing to a sickly, sour-looking individual, who was sitting apart from the others, with his arms folded, and looking as if he was counting the very seconds before the dinner should begin, "is the wonderful Signor Castro, whose sword-swallowing feats you have doubtless heard of."

Toby stepped back just one step, as if overwhelmed by awe at beholding the signor in the guise of a humble individual; and the gentleman who gained his livelihood by swallowing swords unbent his dignity so far as to unfold his arms and present a very, dirty-looking hand for Toby to shake. The boy took hold of the outstretched hand, wondering why the signor never used soap and water, and Mr. Stubbs, apparently afraid of the sour-looking man, retreated to Toby's shoulder, where he sat chattering and scolding about the introduction.

Again the skeleton waved his hand, and this time he introduced "Mademoiselle Spelletti, the wonderful snake charmer, whose exploits in this country and before the crowned heads of Europe had caused the whole world to stand aghast at her daring."

Mademoiselle Spelletti was a very ordinary-looking young lady of about twenty-five years of age, who looked very much as if her name might originally have been Murphy, and she too extended a hand for Toby to grasp—only her hand was clean, and she appeared to be a very much more pleasant acquaintance than the gentleman who swallowed swords.

This ended the introductions, and Toby was just looking around for a seat, when Mrs. Treat, the fat lady, and the giver of the feast which was about to

come and which already smelled so invitingly, entered from behind a curtain of canvas, where the cooking stove was supposed to be located.

She had every appearance of being the cook for the occasion. Her sleeves were rolled up, her hair tumbled and frowzy, and there were several unmistakable marks of grease on the front of her calico dress.

She waited for no ceremony, but rushed up to Toby and, taking him in her arms, gave him such a squeeze that there seemed to be every possibility that she would break all the bones in his body. And she kept him so long in this bearlike embrace that Mr. Stubbs reached his little brown paws over and got such a hold of her hair that all present, save Signor Castro, rushed forward to release her from the monkey's grasp.

"You dear little thing!" said Mrs. Treat, paying but slight attention to the hair pulling she had just undergone and holding Toby at arm's length, so that she could look into his face, "you were so late that I was afraid you wasn't coming, and my dinner wouldn't have tasted half so good if you hadn't been here to eat some."

Toby hardly knew what to say for this hearty welcome, but he managed to tell the large and kind-hearted lady that he had had no idea of missing the dinner and that he was very glad she wanted him to come.

"Want you to come, you dear little thing!" she exclaimed, as she gave him another hug, but careful not to give Mr. Stubbs a chance of grasping her hair again. "Of course I wanted you to come, for this dinner has been got up so that you could meet these people here, and so that they could see you."

Toby was entirely at a loss to know what to say to this overwhelming compliment, and for that reason did not say anything, only submitting impatiently to the third hug, which was all Mrs. Treat had time to give him, for she was obliged to run behind the canvas screen again, as there were unmistakable sounds of something boiling over on the stove.

"You'll excuse me," said the skeleton, with an air of dignity, waving his hand once more toward the assembled company, "but, while introducing you to Mr. Tyler, I had almost forgotten to introduce him to you. This, ladies and gentlemen"——and here he touched Toby on the shoulder, as if he were some living curiosity whose habits and mode of capture he was about to explain to a party of spectators——"is Mr. Toby Tyler, of whom you heard on the night when the monkey cage was smashed, and who now carries with him the identical monkey which was presented to him by the manager of this great show as a token of esteem for his skill and bravery in capturing the entire lot of monkeys without a single blow."

By the time that Mr. Treat got through with this long speech Toby felt very much as if he were some wonderful creature whom the skeleton was exhibiting; but he managed to rise to his feet and duck his little red head in his best imitation of a bow. Then he sat down and hugged Mr. Stubbs to cover his confusion.

One of the Albino Children now came forward and, while stroking Mr. Stubbs's hair, looked so intently at Toby that for the life of him he couldn't say which she regarded as the curiosity, himself or the monkey. Therefore he hastened to say, modestly:

"I didn't do much toward catchin' the monkeys; Mr. Stubbs here did almost all of it, an' I only led 'em in."

"There, there, my boy," said the skeleton, in a fatherly tone, "I've heard the whole story from Old Ben, an' I sha'n't let you get out of it like that. We all know what you did, an' it's no use for you to deny any part of it."

10. *Mr. Stubbs at a Party*

Toby was about to say that he did not intend to represent the matter other than it really was, when a voice from behind the canvas screen arrested further conversation.

"Sam-u-el, come an' help me carry these things in."

Something very like a smile of satisfaction passed over Signor Castro's face as he heard this, which told him that the time for the feast was near at hand; and the snake charmer, as well as the Albino Children, seemed quite as much pleased as did the sword swallower.

CLEVELAND HEIGHTS
PUBLIC LIBRARY

"You will excuse me, ladies and gentlemen," said the skeleton, in an important tone, "I must help Lilly, and then I shall have the pleasure of helping you to some of her cooking, which, if I do say it, that oughtn't, is as good as can be found in this entire country."

Then he, too, disappeared behind the canvas screen.

Left alone, Toby looked at the ladies, and the ladies looked at him, in perfect silence, while the sword swallower grimly regarded them all, until Mr. Treat reappeared, bearing on a platter an immense turkey, as nicely browned as any Thanksgiving turkey Toby ever saw. Behind him came his fat wife, carrying several dishes, each of which emitted a most fragrant odor. And as these were placed upon the table the spirits of the sword swallower seemed to revive, and he smiled pleasantly; while even the ladies appeared animated by the sight and odor of the good things which they were to be called upon so soon to pass judgment.

Several times did Mr. and Mrs. Treat bustle in and out from behind the screen, and each time they made some addition to that which was upon the table, until Toby feared they would never finish, and the sword swallower seemed unable to restrain his impatience.

At last the finishing touch had been put to the table, the last dish placed in position, and then, with a certain kind of grace, which no one but a man as thin as Mr. Treat could assume, he advanced to the edge of the platform and said:

"Ladies and gentlemen, nothing gives me greater pleasure than to invite you all, including Mr. Tyler's friend Stubbs, to the bountiful repast which my Lilly has prepared for——"

At this point, Mr. Treat's speech——for it certainly seemed as if he had commenced to make one——was broken off in a most summary manner. His wife had come up behind him, and, with as much ease as if he had been a child, lifted him from off the floor and placed him gently in the chair at the head of the table.

"Come right up and get dinner," she said to her guests. "If you had waited until Samuel had finished his speech, everything on the table would have been stone cold."

The guests proceeded to obey her kindly command; and it is to be regretted that the sword swallower had no better manners than to jump on to the platform with one bound and seat himself at the table with the most unseemly haste. The others, and more especially Toby, proceeded in a leisurely and more dignified manner.

A seat had been placed by the side of the one intended for Toby for the accommodation of Mr. Stubbs, who suffered a napkin to be tied under his chin and behaved generally in a manner that gladdened the heart of his young master.

Mr. Treat cut generous slices from the turkey for each guest, and Mrs. Treat piled their plates high with all sorts of vegetables, complaining, after the manner of housewives generally, that the food was not cooked as she would like to have had it, and declaring that she had had poor luck with everything that morning, when she firmly believed in her heart that her table had never looked better.

After the company had had the edge taken off their appetites—which effect was produced on the sword swallower only after he had been helped three different times, the conversation began by the Fat Woman asking Toby how he got along with Mr. Lord.

Toby could not give a very good account of his employer, but he had the good sense not to cast a damper on a party of pleasure by reciting his own troubles; so he said, evasively:

"I guess I shall get along pretty well, now that I have got so many friends."

Just as he had commenced to speak, the skeleton had put into his mouth a very large piece of turkey—very much larger in proportion than himself—and when Toby had finished speaking, he started to say something evidently not very complimentary to Mr. Lord. But what it was the company never knew; for just as he opened his mouth to speak, the food went down the wrong way, his face became a bright purple, and it was quite evident that he was choking.

Toby was alarmed and sprung from his chair to assist his friend, upsetting Mr. Stubbs from his seat, causing him to scamper up the tent pole, with the napkin still tied around his neck, and to scold in his most vehement manner. Before Toby could reach the skeleton, however, the Fat Woman had darted toward

her lean husband, caught him by the arm, and was pounding his back, by the time Toby got there, so vigorously, that the boy was afraid her enormous hand would go through his tissue-paper-like frame.

"I wouldn't," said Toby, in alarm, "you may break him."

"Don't you get frightened," said Mrs. Treat, turning her husband completely over and still continuing the drumming process. "He's often taken this way; he's such a glutton that he'd try to swallow the turkey whole if he could get it in his mouth, an' he's so thin that 'most anything sticks in his throat."

"I should think you'd break him all up," said Toby, apologetically, as he resumed his seat at the table. "He don't look as if he could stand very much of that sort of thing."

But apparently Mr. Treat could stand very much more than Toby gave him credit for, because at this juncture he stopped coughing, and his face fast assumed its natural hue.

His attentive wife, seeing that he had ceased struggling, lifted him in her arms, and sat him down in his chair with a force that threatened to snap his very head off.

"There!" she said, as he wheezed a little from the effects of the shock, "now see if you can behave yourself, an' chew your meat as you ought to! One of these days when you're alone you'll try that game, and that'll be the last of you."

"If he'd try to do one of my tricks long enough, he'd

get so that there wouldn't hardly anything choke him," the sword swallower ventured to suggest, mildly, as he wiped a small stream of cranberry sauce from his chin and laid a well-polished turkey bone by the side of his plate.

"I'd like to see him try it!" said the fat lady, with just a shade of anger in her voice. Then turning toward her husband, she said, emphatically, "Samuel, don't you ever let me catch *you* swallowing a sword!"

"I won't, my love, I won't; and I will try to chew my meat more," replied the very thin glutton, in a feeble tone.

Toby thought that perhaps the skeleton might keep the first part of that promise, but he was not quite sure about the last.

It required no little coaxing on the part of both Toby and Mrs. Treat to induce Mr. Stubbs to come down from his lofty perch. But the task was accomplished at last, and by the gift of a very large doughnut he was induced to resume his seat at the table.

The time had now come when the duties of a host, in his own peculiar way of viewing them, devolved upon Mr. Treat, and he said, as he pushed his chair back a short distance from the table and tried to polish the front of his vest with his napkin:

"I don't want this fact lost sight of, because it is an important one: everyone must remember that we have gathered here to meet and become better acquainted with the latest and best addition to this circus, Mr. Toby Tyler."

Poor Toby! As the company all looked directly at him, and Mrs. Treat nodded her enormous head energetically, as if to say that she agreed exactly with her husband, the poor boy's face grew very red and the squash pie lost its flavor.

"Although Mr. Tyler may not be exactly one of us, owing to the fact that he does not belong to the profession, but is only one of the adjuncts to it, so to speak," continued the skeleton, in a voice which was fast being raised to its highest pitch, "we feel proud, after his exploits at the time of the accident, to have him with us, and gladly welcome him now, through the medium of this little feast prepared by my Lilly."

Here the Albino Children nodded their heads in approval, and the sword swallower gave a grunt of assent. Thus encouraged, the skeleton proceeded:

"I feel, when I say that we like and admire Mr. Tyler, all present will agree with me, and all would like to hear him say a word for himself."

The skeleton seemed to have expressed the views of those present remarkably well, judging from their expressions of pleasure and assent, and all waited for the honored guest to speak.

Toby knew that he must say something, but he couldn't think of a single thing. He tried over and over again to call to his mind something which he had read as to how people acted and what they said when they were expected to speak at a dinner table, but his thoughts refused to go back for him, and the silence was actually becoming painful. Finally, and with the greatest effort, he managed to say, with a very perceptible stammer, and while his face was growing very red:

"I know I ought to say something to pay for this big dinner that you said was gotten up for me, but I don't know what to say, unless to thank you for it. You see I hain't big enough to say much, an', as Uncle Dan'l says, I don't amount to very much 'cept for eatin', an' I guess he's right. You're all real good to me, an' when I get to be a man, I'll try to do as much for you."

Toby had risen to his feet when he began to make his speech, and while he was speaking, Mr. Stubbs had crawled over into his chair. When he finished, he sat down again without looking behind him and of course sat plump on the monkey. There was a loud outcry from Mr. Stubbs, a little frightened noise from Toby, an instant's scrambling, and then boy, monkey, and chair tumbled off the platform, landing on the ground in an indescribable mass, from which the monkey extricated himself more quickly than Toby could, and again took refuge on the top of the tent pole.

Of course all the guests ran to Toby's assistance, and while the Fat Woman poked him all over to see that none of his bones were broken, the skeleton brushed the dirt from his clothes.

All this time the monkey screamed, yelled, and danced around on the tent pole and ropes as if his feelings had received a shock from which he could never recover.

"I didn't mean to end it up that way, but it was Mr. Stubbs's fault," said Toby, as soon as quiet had been restored, and the guests, with the exception of the monkey, were seated at the table once more.

"Of course you didn't," said Mrs. Treat, in a kindly tone. "But don't you feel bad about it one bit, for you ought to thank your lucky stars that you didn't break any of your bones."

"I s'pose I did," said Toby, soberly, as he looked back at the scene of his disaster and then up at the chattering monkey that had caused all the trouble.

Shortly after this, Mr. Stubbs having again been coaxed down from his lofty position, Toby took his departure, promising to call as often during the week as he could get away from his exacting employers.

Just outside the tent he met Old Ben, who said, as he showed signs of indulging in another of his internal laughing spells:

"Hello! Has the skeleton an' his lily of a wife been givin' a blowout to you, too?"

"They invited me in there to dinner," said Toby, modestly.

"Of course they did—of course they did," replied Ben, with a chuckle. "They carries a cookin' stove along with 'em, so's they can give these little spreads whenever we stay over a day in a place. Oh, I've been there!"

"And did they ask you to make a speech?"

"Of course. Did they try it on you?"

"Yes," said Toby, mournfully, "an' I tumbled off the platform when I got through."

"I didn't do exactly that," replied Ben, thoughtfully, "but I s'pose you got too much steam on, seein' 's how it was likely your first speech. Now, you'd better go into the tent an' try to get a little sleep, 'cause we've got a long ride tonight over a rough road, an' you won't get more'n a cat nap all night."

"But where are you going?" asked Toby, as he shifted Mr. Stubbs over to his other shoulder, preparatory to following his friend's advice.

"I'm goin' to church," said Ben, and then Toby noticed for the first time that the old driver had made some attempt at dressing up. "I've been with the circus, man an' boy, for nigh to forty years, an' I allus go to meetin' once on Sunday. It's somethin' I promised my old mother I would do, an' I hain't broke my promise yet."

"Why don't you take me with you?" asked Toby, wistfully, as he thought of the little church on the hill at home, and wished—oh, so earnestly!—that he was there then, even at the risk of being thumped on the head with Uncle Daniel's book.

"If I'd seen you this mornin', I would," said Ben, "but now you must try to bottle up some sleep agin tonight, an' next Sunday I'll take you."

With these words Old Ben started off, and Toby

proceeded to carry out his wishes, although he rather doubted the possibility of "bottling up" any sleep that afternoon.

He lay down on the top of the wagon, after having put Mr. Stubbs inside with the others of his tribe, and in a very few moments the boy was sound asleep, dreaming of a dinner party at which Mr. Stubbs made a speech and he himself scampered up and down the tent pole.

11. *A Stormy Night*

WHEN Toby awoke, it was nearly dark, and the bustle around him told very plainly that the time for departure was near at hand. He rubbed his eyes just enough to make sure that he was thoroughly awake and then jumped down from his rather lofty bed and ran around to the door of the cage to assure himself that Mr. Stubbs was safe. This done, his preparations for the journey were made.

Now Toby noticed that each one of the drivers was clad in rubber clothing, and, after listening for a moment, he learned the cause of their waterproof garments. It was raining very hard, and Toby thought with dismay of the long ride that he would have to take on the top of the monkey's cage, with no protection whatever save that afforded by his ordinary clothing.

While he was standing by the side of the wagon, wondering how he should get along, Old Ben came in. The water was pouring from his clothes in little rivulets, and he offered most unmistakable evidence of the damp state of the weather.

"It's a nasty night, my boy," said the old driver, in much the same cheery tone that he would have used had he been informing Toby that it was a beautiful moonlight evening.

"I guess I'll get wet," said Toby, ruefully, as he looked up at the lofty seat which he was to occupy.

"Bless me!" said Ben, as if the thought had just come to him, "it won't do for you to ride outside on a night like this. Wait here, an' I'll see what I can do for you."

The old man hurried off to the other end of the tent, and almost before Toby thought he had time to go as far as the ring he returned.

"It's all right," he said, and this time in a gruff voice, as if he were announcing some misfortune, "you're to ride in the women's wagon. Come with me."

Toby followed without a question, though he was wholly at a loss to understand what the "women's wagon" was, for he had never seen anything which looked like one.

He soon learned, however, when Old Ben stopped in front—or, rather, at the end—of a long, covered wagon that looked like an omnibus, except that it was considerably longer, and the seats inside were divided by arms, padded, to make them comfortable to lean against.

"Here's the boy," said Ben, as he lifted Toby up on the step, gave him a gentle push to intimate that he was to get inside, and then left him.

As Toby stepped inside, he saw that the wagon was nearly full of women and children. And fearing lest he should take a seat that belonged to someone else, he stood in the middle of the wagon, not knowing what to do.

"Why don't you sit down, little boy?" asked one of the ladies, after Toby had remained standing nearly five minutes and the wagon was about to start.

"Well," said Toby, with some hesitation, as he looked around at the two or three empty seats that remained, "I didn't want to get in anybody else's place, an' I didn't know where to sit."

"Come right here," said the lady, as she pointed to a seat by the side of a little girl who did not look any older than Toby, "the lady who usually occupies that seat will not be here tonight, and you can have it."

"Thank you, ma'am," said Toby, as he sat timidly down on the edge of the seat, hardly daring to sit back comfortably and feeling very awkward meanwhile, but congratulating himself on being thus protected from the pouring rain.

The wagon started, and as each one talked with her neighbor, Toby felt a most dismal sense of loneliness and almost wished that he was riding on the monkey cart with Ben, where he could have someone to talk with. He gradually pushed himself back into a more comfortable position and had then an opportunity of seeing more plainly the young girl who rode by his side.

She was quite as young as Toby and small of her age; but there was an old look about her face that made the boy think of her as being an old woman cut down to fit children's clothes. Toby had looked at her so earnestly that she observed him, and asked, "What is your name?"

"Toby Tyler."

"What do you do in the circus?"

"Sell candy for Mr. Lord."

"Oh! I thought you was a new member of the company."

Toby knew by the tone of her voice that he had fallen considerably in her estimation by not being one of the performers, and it was some little time before he ventured to speak. And then he asked, timidly, "What do you do?"

"I ride one of the horses with mother."

"Are you the little girl that comes out with the lady an' four horses?" asked Toby, in awe that he should be conversing with so famous a person.

"Yes, I am. Don't I do it nicely?"

"Why, you're a perfect little—little—fairy!" exclaimed Toby, after hesitating a moment to find some word which would exactly express his idea.

This praise seemed to please the young lady, and in a short time the two became very good friends, even if Toby did not occupy a more exalted position than that of candy seller. She had learned from him all about the accident to the monkey cage and about Mr. Stubbs, and in return had told him that her name was Ella Mason, though on the bills she was called, "Mademoiselle Jeannette."

For a long time the two children sat talking together, and then Mademoiselle Jeannette curled herself up on the seat, with her head in her mother's lap, and went to sleep.

Toby had resolved to keep awake and watch her, for he was struck with admiration at her face; but sleep got the better of him in less than five minutes after he had made the resolution, and he sat bolt upright, with his little round head nodding and bobbing until it seemed almost certain that he would shake it off.

When Toby awoke, the wagon was drawn up by the side of the road, the sun was shining brightly, preparations were being made for the entrée into town, and the harsh voice of Mr. Job Lord was shouting his name in a tone that boded no good for poor Toby when he should make his appearance.

Toby would have hesitated before meeting his angry employer but that he knew it would only make matters worse for him when he did show himself, and he mentally braced himself for the trouble which he

knew was coming. The little girl whose acquaintance
he had made the night previous was still sleeping.
And wishing to say good-by to her in some way without awakening her, he stooped down and gently kissed
the skirt of her dress. Then he went out to meet his
master.

Mr. Lord was thoroughly enraged when Toby left
the wagon and saw the boy just as he stepped to the
ground. The angry man gave a quick glance around,
to make sure that none of Toby's friends were in sight,
and then caught him by the coat collar and commenced to whip him severely with the small rubber
cane that he usually carried.

Mr. Job Lord lifted the poor boy entirely clear of
the ground, and each blow that he struck could be
heard almost the entire length of the circus train.

"You've been makin' so many acquaintances here
that you hain't willin' to do any work," he said, savagely, as he redoubled the force of his blows.

"Oh, please stop! please stop!" shrieked the poor
boy in his agony. "I'll do everything you tell me to,
if you won't strike me again!"

This piteous appeal seemed to have no effect upon
the cruel man, and he continued to whip the boy, despite his cries and entreaties until his arm fairly ached
from the exertion, and Toby's body was crossed and
recrossed with the livid marks of the cane.

"Now, let's see whether you'll 'tend to your work
or not!" said the man as he flung Toby from him with
such force that the boy staggered, reeled, and nearly

fell into the little brook that flowed by the roadside. "I'll make you understand that all the friends you've whined around in this show can't save you from a lickin' when I get ready to give you one! Now go an' do your work that ought to have been done an hour ago!"

Mr. Lord walked away with the proud consciousness of a man who has achieved a great victory, and Toby was limping painfully along toward the cart that was used in conveying Mr. Lord's stock in trade, when he felt a tiny hand slip into his, and heard a childish voice say:

"Don't cry, Toby. Some time, when I get big enough, I'll make Mr. Lord sorry that he whipped you as he did. And I'm big enough now to tell him just what kind of man I think he is."

Looking around, Toby saw his little acquaintance of the evening previous, and he tried to force back the big tears that were rolling down his cheeks as he said in a voice choked with grief, "You're awful good, an' I don't mind the lickin' when you say you're sorry for me. I s'pose I deserve it for runnin' away from Uncle Dan'l."

"Did it hurt you much?" she asked, feelingly.

"It did when he was doin' it," replied Toby, manfully, "but it don't a bit now that you've come."

"Then I'll go and talk to that Mr. Lord, and I'll come and see you again after we get into town," said the little miss, as she hurried away to tell the candy vendor what she thought of him.

He sat timidly on the edge of the seat. (Page 123)

That day, as on all others since he had been with the circus, Toby went to his work with a heavy heart, and time and time again did he count the money which had been given him by kind-hearted strangers, to see whether he had enough to warrant his attempting to run away. Three dollars and twenty-five cents was the total amount of his treasure, and, large as that sum appeared to him, he could not satisfy himself that he had sufficient to enable him to get back to the home which he had so wickedly left. Whenever he thought of his home, of the Uncle Daniel who had in charity cared for him—a motherless, fatherless boy—and of returning to it, with not even as much right as the Prodigal Son, of whom he had heard Uncle Daniel tell, his heart sank within him. And he doubted whether he would be allowed to remain, even if he should be so fortunate as ever to reach Guilford again.

This day passed, so far as Toby was concerned, very much as had the others: he could not satisfy either of his employers, try as hard as he might; but, as usual, he met with two or three kindly disposed people, who added to the fund that he was accumulating for his second venture of running away by the little gifts of money, each one of which gladdened his heart and made his trouble a trifle less hard to bear.

During the entire week he was thus equally fortunate. Each day added something to his fund, and each night it seemed to Toby that he was one day nearer the freedom for which he so ardently longed.

The skeleton, the fat lady, Old Ben, the Albino

Children, little Ella, and even the sword swallower all gave him a kindly word as they passed him while he was at his work or saw him as the preparations for the grand entrée were being made.

The time had passed slowly to Toby, and yet Sunday came again—as Sundays always come; and on this day Old Ben hunted him up, made him wash his face and hands until they fairly shone from very cleanliness, and then took him to church. Toby was surprised to find that it was really a pleasant thing to be able to go to church after being deprived of it, and was more light-hearted than he had yet been since he left Guilford when he returned to the tent at noon.

The skeleton had invited him to another dinner party; but Toby had declined the invitation, agreeing to present himself in time for supper instead. He hardly cared to go through the ordeal of another state dinner; and besides, he wanted to go off to the woods with the old monkey, where he could enjoy the silence of the forest, which seemed like a friend to him, because it reminded him of home.

Taking the monkey with him as usual, he inquired the nearest way to a grove, and, without waiting for dinner, started off for an afternoon's quiet enjoyment.

12. *Toby's Great Misfortune*

THE town in which the circus remained over Sunday was a small one, and a brisk walk of ten minutes sufficed to take Toby into a secluded portion of a very thickly grown wood, where he could lie upon the mossy ground and fairly revel in freedom.

As he lay upon his back, his hands under his head and his eyes directed to the branches of the trees above, where the birds twittered and sung, and the squirrels played in fearless sport, the monkey enjoyed himself, in his way, by playing all the monkey antics he knew of. He scrambled from tree to tree, swung himself from one branch to the other by the aid of his tail, and amused both himself and his master, until, tired by his exertions, he crept down by Toby's side and lay there in quiet, restful content.

One of Toby's reasons for wishing to be by himself that afternoon was that he wanted to think over some plan of escape, for he believed that he had nearly money enough to enable him to make a bold stroke for freedom and Uncle Daniel's. Therefore, when the monkey nestled down by his side, he was all ready to confide in him that which had been occupying his busy little brain for the past three days.

"Mr. Stubbs," he announced to the monkey, in a very solemn tone, "we're goin' to run away in a day or two."

Mr. Stubbs did not seem to be moved in the least at this very startling piece of intelligence, but winked his bright eyes in unconcern. And Toby, seeming to think that everything which he said had been understood by the monkey, continued: "I've got a good deal of money now, an' I guess there's enough for us to start out on. We'll get away some night an' stay in the woods till they get through hunting for us, an' then we'll go back to Guilford an' tell Uncle Dan'l if he'll only take us back we'll never go to sleep in meetin' any more, an' we'll be just as good as we know how. Now let's see how much money we've got.

Toby drew from a pocket, which he had been at a great deal of trouble to make in his shirt, a small bag of silver and spread it upon the ground, where he could count it at his leisure.

The glittering coin instantly attracted the monkey's attention, and he tried by every means to thrust his little black paw ino the pile; but Toby would allow nothing of that sort, and pushed him away quite roughly. Then he grew excited and danced and scolded around Toby's treasure, until the boy had hard work to count it.

He did succeed, however, and as he carefully replaced it in the bag, he said to the monkey, "There's seven dollars an' thirty cents in that bag, an' every cent of it is mine. That ought to take care of us for a good while, Mr. Stubbs; an' by the time we get home we shall be rich men."

The monkey showed his pleasure at this intelligence by putting his hand inside Toby's clothes to find the bag of treasure that he had seen secreted there, and two or three times, to the great delight of both himself and the boy, he drew forth the bag, which was immediately taken away from him.

The shadows were beginning to lengthen in the woods, and, heeding this warning of the coming night, Toby took the monkey on his arm and started for home, or for the tent, which was the only place he could call home.

As he walked along, he tried to talk to his pet in a serious manner, but the monkey, remembering where he had seen the bright coins secreted, tried so hard to get at them that finally Toby lost all patience and gave him quite a hard cuff on the ear, which had the effect of keeping him quiet for a time.

That night Toby took supper with the skeleton and his wife, and he enjoyed the meal, even though it was made from what had been left of the turkey that served as the noonday feast, more than he did the state dinner, where he was obliged to pay for what he ate by the torture of making a speech.

There were no guests but Toby present; and Mr. and Mrs. Treat were not only very kind, but so attentive that he was actually afraid he should eat so much as to stand in need of some of the catnip tea which Mrs. Treat had said she gave to her husband when he had been equally foolish. The skeleton would pile his plate high with turkey bones from one side, and the fat lady would heap it up, whenever she could find a chance, with all sorts of food from the other, until Toby pushed back his chair, his appetite completely satisfied, as if it never had been so before.

Toby had discussed the temper of his employer with his host and hostess, and, after some considerable conversation, confided in them his determination to run away.

"I'd hate awfully to have you go," said Mrs. Treat, reflectively, "but it's a good deal better for you to get away from that Job Lord if you can. It wouldn't do to let him know that you had any idea of goin', for he'd watch you as a cat watches a mouse, an' never let you go so long as he saw a chance to keep you. I heard him tellin' one of the drivers the other day that you sold more goods than any other boy he ever had an' he was going to keep you with him all summer."

"Be careful in what you do, my boy," said the skeleton, sagely, as he arranged a large cushion in an armchair and proceeded to make ready for his after-dinner nap, "be sure that you're all ready before you start, an', when you do go, get a good ways ahead of him; for if he should ever catch you, the trouncin' you'd get would be awful."

Toby assured his friends that he would use every endeavor to make his escape successful when he did start, and Mrs. Treat, with an eye to the boy's comfort, said, "Let me know the night you're goin', an' I'll fix you up something to eat, so's you won't be hungry before you come to a place where you can buy something."

As these kind-hearted people talked with him and were ready thus to aid him in every way that lay in their power, Toby thought that he had been very fortunate in thus having made so many kind friends in a place where he was having so much trouble.

It was not until he heard the sounds of preparation for departure that he left the skeleton's tent, and then, with Mr. Stubbs clasped tightly to his breast, he hurried over to the wagon where Old Ben was nearly ready to start.

"All right, Toby," said the old driver, as the boy came in sight, "I was afraid you was going to keep me waitin' for the first time. Jump right up on the box, for there hain't no time to lose, an' I guess you'll have to carry the monkey in your arms, for I don't want to stop to open the cage now."

"I'd just as soon carry him, an' a little rather," said Toby, as he clambered up on the high seat and arranged a comfortable place in his lap for his pet to sit.

In another moment the heavy team had started, and nearly the entire circus was on the move. "Now tell me what you've been doin' since I left you," said Old Ben, after they were well clear of the town, and he could trust his horses to follow the team ahead. "I s'pose you've been to see the skeleton an' his mountain of a wife?"

Toby gave a clear account of where he had been and what he had done, and when he concluded, he told Old Ben of his determination to run away and asked his advice on the matter.

"My advice," said Ben, after he had waited some time, to give due weight to his words, "is that you clear out from this show just as soon as you can. This hain't no fit place for a boy of your age to be in, an' the sooner you get back where you started from, an' get to school, the better. But Job Lord will do all he can to keep you from goin', if he thinks you have any idea of leavin' him."

Toby assured Ben, as he had assured the skeleton and his wife, that he would be very careful in all he did, and lay his plans with the utmost secrecy; and then he asked whether Ben thought the amount of money which he had would be sufficient to carry him home.

"Waal, that depends," said the driver, slowly. "If you go to spreadin' yourself all over creation, as boys are very apt to do, your money won't go very far; but if you look at your money two or three times afore you spend it, you ought to get back and have a dollar or two left."

The two talked, and Old Ben offered advice, until Toby could hardly keep his eyes open, and almost before the driver concluded his sage remarks, the boy had stretched himself on the top of the wagon, where he had learned to sleep without being shaken off, and was soon in dreamland.

The monkey, nestled down snug in Toby's bosom, did not appear to be as sleepy as was his master, but popped his head in and out from under the coat, as if watching whether the boy was asleep or not.

Toby was awakened by a scratching on his face, as if the monkey was dancing a hornpipe on that portion of his body, and by a shrill, quick chattering, which caused him to assume an upright position instantly.

He was frightened, although he knew not at what, and looked around quickly to discover the cause of the monkey's excitement.

Old Ben was asleep on his box, while the horses jogged along behind the other teams, and Toby failed to see anything whatever which should have caused his pet to become so excited.

"Lie down an' behave yourself," said Toby, as sternly as possible, and as he spoke, he took his pet by the collar, to oblige him to obey his command.

The moment that he did this he saw the monkey throw something out into the road, and the next instant he also saw that he held something tightly clutched in his other paw.

It required some little exertion and active movement on Toby's part to enable him to get hold of that paw, in order to discover what it was which Mr. Stubbs had captured; but the instant he did succeed there went up from his heart such a cry of sorrow as caused Old Ben to start up in alarm, and the monkey to cower and whimper like a whipped dog.

"What is it, Toby? What's the matter?" asked the old driver, as he peered out into the darkness ahead, as if he feared some danger threatened them from that quarter. "I don't see anything. What is it?"

"Mr. Stubbs has thrown all my money away," cried Toby, holding up the almost empty bag, which a short time previous had been so well filled with silver.

"Stubbs—thrown—the—money—away?" repeated Ben, with a pause between each word, as if he could not understand that which he himself was saying.

"Yes," sobbed Toby, as he shook out the remaining contents of the bag, "there's only half a dollar, an' all the rest is gone."

"The rest gone!" again repeated Ben. "But how come the monkey to have the money?"

"He tried to get at it out in the woods, an' I s'pose the moment I got asleep, he felt for it in my pockets. This is all there is left, an' he threw away some just as I woke up."

Again Toby held the bag up where Ben could see it, and again his grief broke out anew.

Ben could say nothing. He realized the whole situation: that the monkey had got at the money bag while Toby was sleeping, that in his play he had thrown it away piece by piece, and he knew that that small amount of silver represented liberty in the boy's eyes. He felt that there was nothing he could say which would assuage Toby's grief and he remained silent.

"Don't you s'pose we could go back an' get it?" asked the boy, after the intensity of his grief had somewhat subsided.

"No, Toby, it's gone," replied Ben, sorrowfully. "You couldn't find it if it was daylight, an' you don't stand a ghost of a chance now in the dark. Don't take on so, my boy. I'll see if we can't make it up to you in some way."

Toby gave no heed to this last remark of Ben's. He hugged the monkey convulsively to his breast, as if he would seek consolation from the very one who had wrought the ruin, and, rocking himself to and fro, he said, in a voice full of tears and sorrow:

"O Mr. Stubbs, why did you do it? Why did you do it? That money would have got us away from this hateful place, an' we'd gone back to Uncle Dan'l's, where we'd have been *so* happy, you an' me. An' now it's all gone—all gone. What made you, Mr. Stubbs— what made you do such a bad, cruel thing? Oh! what made you?"

"Don't, Toby. Don't take on so," said Ben, soothingly. "There wasn't so very much money there, after all, an' you'll soon get as much more."

"But it won't be for a good while, an' we could have been in the good old home long before I can get so much again."

"That's true, my boy, but you must kinder brace up an' not give way so about it. Perhaps I can fix it so the fellers will make it up to you. Give Stubbs a good poundin', an' perhaps that'll make you feel better."

"That won't bring back my money, an' I don't want to whip him," cried Toby, hugging his pet the closer because of this suggestion. "I know what it is to get a whippin', an' I wouldn't whip a dog, much less Mr. Stubbs, who didn't know any better."

"Then you must try to take it like a man," said Ben, who could think of no other plan by which the boy might soothe his feelings. "It hain't half so bad as it might be, an' you must try to keep a stiff upper lip, even if it does seem hard at first."

This keeping a stiff upper lip in the face of all the trouble he was having was all very well to talk about, but Toby could not reduce it to practice, or, at least, not so soon after he knew of his loss, and he continued to rock the monkey back and forth, to whisper in his ear now and then, and to cry as if his heart was breaking, for nearly an hour.

Ben tried, in his rough, honest way, to comfort him, but without success, and it was not until the boy's grief had spent itself that he would listen to any reasoning.

All this time the monkey had remained perfectly quiet, submitting to Toby's squeezing without making any effort to get away and behaving as if he knew he had done wrong and was trying to atone for it. He looked up into the boy's face every now and then with such a penitent expression that Toby finally assured him of forgiveness and begged him not to feel so badly.

13. *Toby Attempts to Resign His Situation*

AT LAST it was possible for Toby to speak of his loss with some degree of calmness, and then he immediately began to reckon up what he could have done with the money if he had not lost it.

"Now see here, Toby," said Ben, earnestly, "don't go to doin' anything of that kind. The money's lost, an' you can't get it back by talkin'. So the very best thing for you is to stop thinkin' what you could do if you had it, an' just to look at it as a goner."

"But—" persisted Toby.

"I tell you there's no buts about it," said Ben, rather sharply. "Stop talkin' about what's gone, an' just go to thinkin' how you'll get more. Do what you've a mind to the monkey, but don't keep broodin' over what you can't help."

Toby knew that the advice was good, and he struggled manfully to carry it into execution, but it was very hard work. At all events, there was no sleep for his eyes that night, and when, just about daylight, the train halted to wait a more reasonable hour in which to enter the town, the thought of what he might have done with his lost money was still in Toby's mind.

Only once did he speak crossly to the monkey, and that was when he put him into the cage preparatory to commencing his morning's work. Then he said:

"You wouldn't had to go into this place many times more if you hadn't been so wicked, for by tomorrow night we'd been away from this circus an' on the way to home an' Uncle Dan'l. Now you've spoiled my chance an' your own for a good while to come, an' I hope before the day is over, you'll feel as bad about it as I do."

It seemed to Toby as if the monkey understood just what he said to him, for he sneaked over into one corner, away from the other monkeys, and sat there looking very penitent and very dejected.

Then, with a heavy heart, Toby began his day's work.

Hard as had been Toby's lot previous to losing his

money and difficult as it had been to bear the cruelty of Mr. Job Lord and his precious partner, Mr. Jacobs, it was doubly hard now while this sorrow was fresh upon him.

Previous to this, when he had been kicked or cursed by one or the other of the partners, Toby thought exultantly that the time was not very far distant when he should be beyond the reach of his brutal taskmasters, and that thought had given him strength to bear all that had been put upon him.

Now the time of his deliverance from this bondage seemed very far off, and each cruel word or blow caused him the greater sorrow, because of the thought that but for the monkey's wickedness he would have been nearly free from that which made his life so very miserable.

If he had looked sad and mournful before, he looked doubly so now, as he went his dreary round of the tent, crying, "Here's your cold lemonade," or "Fresh-baked peanuts, ten cents a quart," and each day there were some in the audience who pitied the boy because of the misery which showed so plainly in his face, and they gave him a few cents more than his price for what he was selling or gave him money without buying anything at all, thereby aiding him to lay up something again toward making his escape.

Those few belonging to the circus who knew of Toby's intention to escape tried their best to console him for the loss of his money, and that kind-hearted couple, the skeleton and his fat wife, tried to force him to take a portion of their scanty earnings in the place of that which the monkey had thrown away. But this Toby positively refused to do, and to the arguments which they advanced as reasons why they should help him along, he only replied that until he could get the money by his own exertions, he would remain with Messrs. Lord and Jacobs and get along as best he could.

Every hour in the day the thought of what might have been if he had not lost his money so haunted his mind that finally he resolved to make one bold stroke and tell Mr. Job Lord that he did not want to travel with the circus any longer.

As yet he had not received the two dollars which had been promised him for his two weeks' work, and another one was nearly due. If he could get this money, it might, with what he had saved again, suffice to pay his railroad fare to Guilford, and if it would not, he resolved to accept from the skeleton sufficient to make up the amount needed.

He naturally shrunk from the task; but the hope that he might possibly succeed gave him the necessary amount of courage, and when he had gotten his work done on the third morning after he had lost his money and Mr. Lord appeared to be in an unusually good temper, he resolved to try the plan.

It was just before the dinner hour. Trade had been exceptionally good, and Mr. Lord had even spoken in a pleasant tone to Toby when he told him to fill up the lemonade pail with water, so that the stock might not be disposed of too quickly and with too little profit.

Toby poured in quite as much water as he thought the already weak mixture could receive and retain any flavor of lemon; and then, as his employer motioned him to add more, he mixed another quart in, secretly wondering what it would taste like.

"When you're mixin' lemonade for circus trade," said Mr. Lord, in such a benign, fatherly tone that one would have found it difficult to believe that he ever spoke harshly, "don't be afraid of water, for there's where the profit comes in. Always have a piece of lemon peel floatin' on the top of every glass, an' it tastes just as good to people as if it cost twice as much."

Toby could not agree exactly with that opinion, neither did he think it wise to disagree, more especially since he was going to ask the very great favor of being discharged. Therefore he nodded his head gravely and began to stir up what it pleased Mr. Lord to call lemonade, so that the last addition might be more thoroughly mixed with the others.

Two or three times he attempted to ask the favor which seemed such a great one, and each time the words stuck in his throat, until it seemed to him that he should never succeed in getting them out.

Finally, in his despair, he stammered out:

"Don't you think you could find another boy in this town, Mr. Lord?"

Mr. Lord moved round sideways, in order to bring his crooked eye to bear squarely on Toby, and then there was a long interval of silence, during which time the boy's color rapidly came and went and his heart beat very fast with suspense and fear.

"Well, what if I could?" he said at length. "Do you think that trade is so good I could afford to keep two boys, when there isn't half work enough for one?"

Toby stirred the lemonade with renewed activity, as if by this process he was making both it and his courage stronger, and said, in a low voice, which Mr. Lord could scarcely hear:

"I didn't think that; but you see I ought to go home, for Uncle Dan'l will worry about me, an', besides, I don't like a circus very well."

Again there was silence on Mr. Lord's part, and again the crooked eye glowered down on Toby.

"So," he said, and Toby could see that his anger was rising very fast, "you don't like a circus very well an' you begin to think that your Uncle Daniel will worry about you, eh? Well, I want you to understand that it don't make any difference to me whether you like a circus or not, and I don't care how much your Uncle Daniel worries. You mean that you want to get away from me, after I've been to all the trouble and expense of teaching you the business?"

Toby bent his head over the pail, and stirred away as if for dear life.

"If you think you're going to get away from here until you've paid me for all you've eat, an' all the time I've spent on you, you're mistaken, that's all. You've had an easy time with me, too easy, in fact, and that's what ails you. Now, you just let me hear two words

more out of your head about going away, only two
more, an' I'll show you what a whipping is. I've only
been playing with you before when you thought you
was getting a whipping, but you'll find out what it
means if I so much as see a thought in your eyes about
goin' away. An' don't you dare to try to give me the
slip in the night an' run away, for if you do, I'll follow
you an' have you arrested. Now you mind your eye
in the future."

It is impossible to say how much longer Mr. Lord
might have continued this tirade, had not a member
of the company, one of the principal riders, called him
to one side to speak with him.

Poor Toby was so much confused by the angry words
which had followed his very natural and certainly very
reasonable suggestion that he paid no attention to anything around him, until he heard his own name mentioned. Then, fearing lest some new misfortune was
about to befall him, he listened intently.

"I'm afraid you couldn't do much of anything with
him," he heard Mr. Lord say. "He's had enough of
this kind of life already, so he says, an' I expect the
next thing he does will be to try to run away."

"I'll risk his getting away from you, Job," he heard
the other say, "but of course I've got to take my
chances. I'll take him in hand from eleven to twelve
each day, just your slack time of trade, and I'll not only
give you half of what he can earn in the next two years,
but I'll pay you for his time if he gives us the slip
before the season is out."

Toby knew that they were speaking of him, but what it all meant he could not imagine.

"What are you going to do with him first?" Job asked.

"Just put him right into the ring and teach him what riding is. I tell you, Job, the boy's smart enough, and before the season's over I'll have him so that he can do some of the bareback acts, and perhaps we'll get some money out of him before we go into winter quarters."

Toby understood the meaning of their conversation only too well, and he knew that his lot, which before seemed harder than he could bear, was about to be intensified through this Mr. Castle, of whom he had frequently heard, and who was said to be a rival of Mr. Lord's, so far as brutality went. The two men now walked toward the large tent, and Toby was left alone with his thoughts and the two or three little boy customers, who looked at him wonderingly and envied him because he belonged to the circus.

During the ride that night he told Old Ben what he had heard, confidently expecting that that friend at least would console him, but Ben was not the champion which he had expected. The old man who had been with a circus, "man and boy, nigh to forty years," did not seem to think it any calamity that he was to be taught to ride.

"That Mr. Castle is a little rough on boys," Old Ben said, thoughtfully, "but it'll be a good thing for you, Toby. Just so long as you stay with Job Lord you won't be nothin' more'n a candy boy; but after you know how to ride, it'll be another thing, an' you can earn a good deal of money, an' be your own boss."

"But I don't want to stay with the circus," whined Toby, "I don't want to learn to ride an' I do want to get back to Uncle Dan'l."

"That may all be true, an' I don't dispute it," said Ben, "but you see you didn't stay with your Uncle Daniel when you had the chance, an' you did come with the circus. You've told Job you wanted to leave, an' he'll be watchin' you all the time to see that you don't give him the slip. Now, what's the consequence? Why, you can't get away for a while, anyhow, an' you'd better try to amount to something while you are here. Perhaps after you've got so you can ride, you may want to stay; an' I'll see to it that you get all of your wages, except enough to pay Castle for learnin' of you."

"I sha'n't want to stay," said Toby. "I wouldn't stay if I could ride all the horses at once, an' was gettin' a hundred dollars a day."

"But you can't ride one horse, an' you hain't gettin' but a dollar a week, an' still I don't see any chance of your gettin' away yet awhile," said Ben, in a matter-of-fact tone, as he devoted his attention again to his horses, leaving Toby to his own sad reflections and the positive conviction that boys who run away from home do not have a good time, except in stories.

The next forenoon, while Toby was deep in the excitement of selling to a boy no larger than himself and with just as red hair, three cents' worth of peanuts and two sticks of candy, and while the boy was trying to induce him to "throw in" a piece of gum, because of the quantity purchased, Job Lord called him aside, and Toby knew that his troubles had begun.

"I want you to go in an' see Mr. Castle; he's goin' to show you how to ride," said Mr. Lord, in as kindly a tone as if he were conferring some favor on the boy.

If Toby had dared to, he would have rebelled then and there and refused to go, but, as he hadn't the courage for such proceeding, he walked meekly into the tent and toward the ring.

14. *Mr. Castle Teaches Toby to Ride*

WHEN Toby got within sight of the ring, he was astonished at what he saw. A horse with a broad wooden saddle was being led slowly around the ring. Mr. Castle was standing on one side with a long whip in his hand, and on the tent pole, which stood in the center of the ring, was a long arm, from which dangled a leathern belt attached to a long rope that was carried through the end of the arm and run down to the base of the pole.

Toby knew well enough why the horse, the whip, and the man were there, but the wooden projection from the tent pole, which looked so much like a gallows, he could not understand at all.

"Come, now," said Mr. Castle, cracking his whip ominously as Toby came in sight, "why weren't you here before?"

"Mr. Lord just sent me in," said Toby, not expecting that his excuse would be received, for they never had been since he had arrived at the height of his ambition by joining the circus.

"Then I'll make Mr. Job understand that I am to have my full hour of your time, and if I don't get it, there'll be trouble between us."

It would have pleased Toby very well to have had Mr. Castle go out with his long whip just then and make trouble for Mr. Lord, but Mr. Castle had not the time to spare, because of the trouble which he was about to make for Toby, and that he commenced on at once.

"Well, get in here and don't waste any more time," he said, sharply.

Toby looked around curiously for a moment, and not understanding exactly what he was expected to get in and do, asked, "What shall I do?"

"Pull off your boots, coat, and vest."

Since there was no other course than to learn to ride, Toby wisely concluded that the best thing he could do would be to obey his new master without question, so he began to take off his clothes with as much alacrity as if learning to ride was the one thing upon which he had long set his heart.

Mr. Castle was evidently accustomed to prompt obedience, for he not only took it as a matter of course but endeavored to hurry Toby in the work of undressing.

With his desire to please and urged by Mr. Castle's words and the ominous shaking of his whip, Toby's preparations were soon made and he stood before his instructor clad only in his shirt, trousers, and stockings.

The horse was led around to where he stood, and when Mr. Castle held out his hand to help him to mount, Toby jumped up quickly without aid, thereby making a good impression at the start as a willing lad.

"Now," said the instructor, as he pulled down the leathern belt which hung from the rope and fastened it around Toby's waist, "stand up in the saddle and try to keep there. You can't fall, because the rope will hold you up, even if the horse goes out from under you; but it isn't hard work to keep on, if you mind what you are about, and if you don't, this whip will help you. Now stand up."

Toby did as he was bid, and as the horse was led at a walk and as he had the long bridle to aid him in keeping his footing, he had no difficulty in standing during the time that the horse went once around the ring; but that was all.

Mr. Castle seemed to think that this was preparation enough for the boy to be able to understand how to

ride and he started the horse into a canter. As might have been expected, Toby lost his balance, the horse went on ahead, and he was left dangling at the end of the rope, very much like a crab that has just been caught by the means of a pole and line.

Toby kicked, waved his hands, and floundered about generally, but all to no purpose, until the horse came around again, and then he made frantic efforts to regain his footing, which efforts were aided, or perhaps it would be more proper to say retarded, by the long lash of Mr. Castle's whip that played around his legs with merciless severity.

"Stand up! Stand up!" cried his instructor, as Toby reeled first to one side and then to the other, now standing erect in the saddle and now dangling at the end of the rope, with the horse almost out from under him.

This command seemed needless, as it was exactly what Toby was trying to do; but as it was given, he struggled all the harder, until it seemed to him that the more he tried the less did he succeed.

And this first lesson progressed in about the same way until the hour was over, save that now and then Mr. Castle would give him some good advice, but oftener he would twist the long lash of the whip around the boy's legs with such force that Toby believed the skin had been taken entirely off.

It may have been a relief to Mr. Castle when this first lesson was concluded and it certainly was to Toby, for he had had all the teaching in horsemanship that he wanted, and he thought, with deepest sorrow, that this would be of daily occurrence during all the time he remained with the circus.

As he went out of the tent, he stopped to speak with his friend, the old monkey, and his troubles seemed to have increased when he stood in front of the cage calling, "Mr. Stubbs! Mr. Stubbs!" and the old fellow would not even come down from off the lofty perch where he was engaged in monkey gymnastics with several younger companions. It seemed to him, as he afterward told Ben, "as if Mr. Stubbs had gone back on him because he knew that he was in trouble."

When he went toward the booth, Mr. Lord looked at him around the corner of the canvas, for it seemed to Toby that his employer could look around a square corner with much greater ease than he could straight ahead, with a disagreeable leer in his eye, as if he enjoyed the misery which he knew his little clerk had just undergone.

"Can you ride yet?" he asked, mockingly, as Toby stepped behind the counter to attend to his regular line of business.

Toby made no reply, for he knew that the question was only asked sarcastically and not through any desire for information. In a few moments Mr. Lord left him to attend to the booth alone and went into the tent, where Toby rightly conjectured he had gone to question Mr. Castle upon the result of the lesson just given.

That night Old Ben asked him how had got on while under the teaching of Mr. Castle; and Toby, knowing that the question was asked because of the real interest which Ben had in his welfare, replied:

"If I was tryin' to learn how to swing around the ring, strapped to a rope, I should say that I got along first-rate. But I don't know much about the horse, for I was only on his back a little while at a time."

"You'll get over that soon," said Old Ben, patronizingly, as he patted him on the back. "You remember my words, now. I say that you've got it in you, an' if you've a mind to take hold an' try to learn, you'll come out on the top of the heap yet an' be one of the smartest riders they've got in this show."

"I don't want to be a rider," said Toby, sadly, "I only want to get back home once more, an' then you'll see how much it'll take to get me away again."

"Well," said Ben, quietly, "be that as it may, while you're here the best thing you can do is to take hold an' get ahead just as fast as you can. It'll make it a mighty sight easier for you while you're with the show an' it won't spoil any of your chances for runnin' away whenever the time comes."

Toby fully appreciated the truth of this remark, and he assured Ben that he should do all in his power to profit by the instruction given and to please this new master who had been placed over him.

And with this promise he lay back on the seat and went to sleep, not to awaken until the preparations were being made for the entrée into the next town and Mr. Lord's harsh voice had cried out his name, with no gentle tone, several times.

The time of his deliverance from this bondage seemed very far off. (Page 145)

Toby's first lesson with Mr. Castle was the most pleasant one he had, for after the boy had once been into the ring, his master seemed to expect that he could do everything which he was told to do. And when he failed in any little particular, the long lash of the whip would go curling around his legs or arms, until the little fellow's body and limbs were nearly covered with the blue and black stripes.

For three lessons only was the wooden upright used to keep him from falling. After that he was forced to ride standing erect on the broad wooden saddle, or pad, as it is properly called, and whenever he lost his balance and fell, there was no question asked as to whether or not he had hurt himself, but he was mercilessly cut with the whip.

Messrs. Lord and Jacobs gained very much by comparison with Mr. Castle in Toby's mind. He had thought that his lot could not be harder than it was with them, but when he had experienced the pains of two or three of Mr. Castle's lessons in horsemanship, he thought that he would stay with the candy vendors all the season cheerfully rather than take six more lessons of Mr. Castle.

Night after night he fell asleep from the sheer exhaustion of crying, as he had been pouring out his woes in the old monkey's ears and laying his plans to run away. Now, more than ever, was he anxious to get away, and yet each day was taking him farther from home and consequently necessitating a larger amount of money with which to start. As Old Ben did not give him as much sympathy as Toby thought he ought to give—for the old man, while he would not allow Mr. Job Lord to strike the boy if he was near, thought it a necessary portion of the education for Mr. Castle to lash him all he had a mind to—he poured out all his troubles in the old monkey's ears and kept him with him from the time he ceased work at night until he was obliged to commence again in the morning.

The skeleton and his wife thought Toby's lot a hard one and tried by every means in their power to cheer the poor boy. Neither one of them could say to Mr. Castle what they had said to Mr. Lord, for the rider was a far different sort of person and one whom they would not be allowed to interfere with in any way. Therefore poor Toby was obliged to bear his troubles and his whippings as best he might, with only the thought to cheer him of the time when he could leave them all by running away.

But, despite all his troubles, Toby learned to ride faster than his teacher had expected he would, and in three weeks he found little or no difficulty in standing erect while his horse went around the ring at his fastest gait. After that had been accomplished, his progress was more rapid and he gave promise of becoming a very good rider—a fact which pleased both Mr. Castle and Mr. Lord very much, as they fancied that in another year Toby would be the source of a very good income to them.

The proprietor of the circus took considerable interest in Toby's instruction and promised Mr. Castle that Mademoiselle Jeannette and Toby should do an act together in the performance just as soon as the latter was sufficiently advanced. The boy's costume had been changed after he could ride without falling off, and now while he was in the ring, he wore the same as that used by the regular performers.

The little girl had, after it was announced that she and Toby were to perform together, been an attentive observer during the hour that Toby was under Mr. Castle's direction, and she gave him many suggestions that were far more valuable and quicker to be acted upon than those given by the teacher himself.

"Tomorrow you two will go through the exercise together," said Mr. Castle to Toby and Ella, at the close of one of Toby's lessons, after he had become so skilful that he could stand with ease on the pad and even advanced so far that he could jump through a hoop without falling more than twice out of three times.

The little girl appeared highly delighted by this information and expressed her joy.

"It will be real nice," she said to Toby after Mr. Castle had left them alone. "I can help you lots, and it won't be very long before we can do an act all by ourselves in the performance and then won't the people clap their hands when we come in!"

"It'll be better for you tomorrow than it will for me," said Toby, rubbing his legs sorrowfully, still feeling the sting of the whip. "You see, Mr. Castle won't dare to whip you, an' he'll make it all count on me, 'cause he knows Mr. Lord likes to have him whip me."

"But I sha'n't make any mistake," said Ella, confidently, "and so you won't have to be whipped on my account. And while I am on the horse, you can't be whipped, for he couldn't do it without whipping me, so you see you won't get only half as much."

Toby brightened up a little under the influence of this argument, but his countenance fell again as he thought that his chances of getting away from the circus were growing less each day.

"You see, I want to get back to Uncle Dan'l an' Guilford," he said, confidentially, "I don't want to stay here a single minute."

Ella opened her eyes in wide astonishment as she cried, "Don't want to stay here? Why don't you go home, then?"

" 'Cause Job Lord won't let me," said Toby, wondering if it was possible that his little companion did not know exactly what sort of man his master was.

Then he told her, after making her give him all kinds of promises, including the ceremony of crossing her throat, that she would never tell a single soul, that he had had many thoughts and had formed all kinds of plans for running away. He told her about losing his money, about his friendship for the skeleton and the fat lady, and at last he confided in her that he was intending to take the old monkey with him when he should make the attempt.

She listened with the closest attention, and when he

told her that his little hoard had now reached the sum of seven dollars and ten cents—almost as much as he had before—she said, eagerly, "I've got three little gold dollars in my trunk, an' you shall have them all. They're my very own, for Mamma gave them to me to do just what I wanted to with them. But I don't see how you can take Mr. Stubbs with you, for that would be stealing."

"No, it wouldn't, neither," said Toby, stoutly. "Wasn't he give to me to do just as I wanted to with? An' didn't the boss say he was all mine?"

"Oh, I'd forgotten that," said Ella, thoughtfully. "I suppose you can take him; but he'll be awfully in the way, won't he?"

"No," said Toby, anxious to say a good word for his pet. "He always does just as I want him to, an' when I tell him what I'm tryin' to do, he'll be as good as anything. But I can't take your dollars."

"Why not?"

" 'Cause that wouldn't be right for a boy to let a girl littler than himself help him. I'll wait till I get money enough of my own, an' then I'll go."

"But I want you to take my money, too; I want you to have it."

"No, I can't take it," said Toby, shaking his head resolutely as he put the golden temptation from him. And then, as a happy thought occurred to him, he said, quickly, "I tell you what to do with your dollars: you keep them till you grow up to be a woman, an' when I'm a man, I'll come, an' then we'll buy a circus of our own. I think, perhaps, I'd like to be with a circus if I owned one myself. We'll have lots of money then, an' we can do just what we want to."

This idea seemed to please the little girl, and the two began to lay all sorts of plans for that time when they should be man and woman, have lots of money, and be able to do just as they wanted to.

They had been sitting on the edge of the newly made ring while they were talking, and before they had half finished making plans for the future, one of the attendants came in to put things to order, and they were obliged to leave their seats, she going to the hotel to get ready for the afernoon's performance and Toby to try to do such work as Mr. Job Lord had laid out for him.

Just ten weeks from the time Toby had first joined the circus, Mr. Castle informed him and Ella that they were to appear in public on the following day. They had been practicing daily, and Toby had become so skilful that both Mr. Castle and Mr. Lord saw that the time had come when he could be made to earn some money for them.

15. *Toby's Friends Present Him with a Costume*

DURING this time Toby's funds had accumulated rather slower than on the first few days he was in the business, but he had saved eleven dollars, and Mr. Lord had paid him five dollars of his salary, so that he had the to him enormous sum of sixteen dollars. And he had about made up his mind to make one effort for liberty, when the news came that he was to ride in public.

He had, in fact, been ready to run away any time within the past week, but, as if they had divined his intentions, both Mr. Castle and Mr. Lord had kept a very strict watch over him, one or the other keeping him in sight from the time he got through with his labors at night until they saw him on the cart with Old Ben.

"I was just gettin' ready to run away," said Toby to Ella, on the day Mr. Castle gave his decision as to their taking part in the performance, and while they were walking out of the tent, "an' I shouldn't wonder now if I got away tonight."

"O Toby!" exclaimed the girl, as she looked reproachfully at him, "after all the work we've had to get ready, you won't go off and leave me before we've had a chance to see what the folks will say when they see us together?"

It was impossible for Toby to feel any delight at the idea of riding in public, and he would have been willing to have taken one of Mr. Lord's most severe whippings if he could have escaped. But he and Ella had become such firm friends and he had conceived such a boyish admiration for her, that he felt as if he were willing to bear almost anything for the sake of giving her pleasure. Therefore he said, after a few moments' reflection, "Well, I won't go tonight, anyway, even if I have the best chance that ever was. I'll stay one day more, anyhow, an' perhaps I'll have to stay a good many."

"That's a nice boy," said Ella, positively, as Toby thus gave his decision, "and I'll kiss you for it."

Before Toby fully realized what she was about,

almost before he had understood what she said, she had put her arms around his neck and given him a good, sound kiss right on his freckled face.

Toby was surprised, astonished, and just a little bit ashamed. He had never been kissed by a girl before— very seldom by anyone, save the fat lady—and he hardly knew what to do or say. He blushed until his face was almost as red as his hair, and this color had the effect of making his freckles stand out with startling distinctness. Then he looked carefully around to see if anyone had seen them.

"I never had a girl kiss me before," said Toby, hesitatingly, "an' you see it made me feel kinder queer to have you do it out here, where everybody could see."

"Well, I kissed you because I like you very much, and because you are going to stay and ride with me tomorrow," she said, positively, and then she added, slyly, "I may kiss you again, if you don't get a chance to run away very soon."

"I wish it wasn't for Uncle Dan'l an' the rest of the folks at home, an' there wasn't any such men as Mr. Lord an' Mr. Castle, an' then I don't know but I might want to stay with the circus, 'cause I like you awful much."

And as he spoke, Toby's heart grew very tender toward the only girl friend he had ever known.

By this time they had reached the door of the tent, and as they stepped outside, one of the drivers told them that Mr. Treat and his wife were very anxious to see both of them in their tent.

"I don't believe I can go," said Toby, doubtfully, as he glanced toward the booth where Mr. Lord was busy in attending to customers and evidently waiting for Toby to relieve him so that he could go to his dinner, "I don't believe Mr. Lord will let me."

"Go and ask him," said Ella, eagerly. "We won't be gone but a minute."

Toby approached his employer with fear and trembling. He had never before asked leave to be away from his work, even for a moment, and he had no doubt but that his request would be refused with blows.

"Mr. Treat wants me to come in his tent for a minute. Can I go?" he asked in a timid voice and in such a low tone as to render it almost inaudible.

Mr. Lord looked at him for an instant, and Toby was sure that he was making up his mind whether to kick him or catch him by the collar and use the rubber cane on him. But he had no such intention, evidently, for he said in a voice unusually mild, "Yes, an' you needn't come to work again until it's time to go into the tent."

Toby was almost alarmed at this unusual kindness, and it puzzled him so much that he would have forgotten he had permission to go away if Ella had not pulled him gently by the coat.

If he had heard a conversation between Mr. Lord and Mr. Castle that very morning, he would have understood why it was that Mr. Lord had so suddenly become kind. Mr. Castle had told Job that the boy had really shown himself to be a good rider and that in order to make him more contented with his lot and to keep him from running away, he must be used more kindly and perhaps be taken from the candy business altogether, which latter advice Mr. Lord did not look upon with favor, because of the large sales which the boy made.

When they reached the skeleton's tent, they found to their surprise that no exhibition was being given at that hour, and Ella said, with some concern, "How queer it is that the doors are not open! I do hope that they are not sick."

Toby felt a strange sinking at his heart at the possibility suggested itself that one or both of his kind friends might be ill, for they had both been so kind and attentive to him that he had learned to love them very dearly.

But the fears of both the children were dispelled when they tried to get in at the door and were met by the smiling skeleton himself who said, as he threw the canvas aside as far as if he were admitting his own enormous Lilly:

"Come in, my friends, come in. I have had the exhibition closed for one hour, in order that I might show my appreciation of my friend, Mr. Tyler."

Toby looked around in some alarm, fearing that Mr. Treat's friendship was about to be displayed in one of his state dinners, which he had learned to fear rather than enjoy. But, as he saw no preparations for dinner, he breathed more freely and wondered what all this ceremony could possibly mean.

Neither he nor Ella was long left in doubt, for as soon as they had entered, Mrs. Treat waddled from behind the screen which served them as a dressing room, with a bundle in her arms, which she handed to her husband.

He took it and, quickly mounting the platform, leaving Ella and Toby below, he commenced to speak with very many flourishes of his thin arms.

"My friends," he began, as he looked down upon his audience of three, who were listening in the following attitudes: Ella and Toby were standing upon the ground at the foot of the platform, looking up with wide-open, staring eyes. His fleshy wife was seated on a bench which had evidently been placed in such a position below the speaker's stand that she could hear and see all that was going on without the fatigue of standing up, which, for one of her size, was really very hard work. "My friends," repeated the skeleton, as he held his bundle in front of him with one hand and gesticulated with the other, "we all of us know that tomorrow our esteemed and worthy friend, Mr. Toby Tyler, makes his first appearance in any ring, and we all of us believe that he will soon become a bright and shining light in the profession which he is so soon to enter."

The speaker was here interrupted by loud applause from his wife, and he profited by the opportunity to wipe a stray drop of perspiration from his fleshless face. Then, as the fat lady ceased the exertion of clapping her hands, he continued:

"Knowing that our friend, Mr. Tyler, was being instructed, preparatory to dazzling the public with his talents, my wife and I began to prepare for him some slight testimonial of our esteem. And, being informed by Mr. Castle some days ago of the day on which he was to make his first appearance before the public, we were enabled to complete our little gift in time for the great and important event."

Here the skeleton paused to take a breath, and Toby began to grow most uncomfortably red in the face. Such praise made him feel very awkward.

"I hold in this bundle," continued Mr. Treat as he waved the package on high, "a costume for our bold and worthy equestrian and a sash to match for his beautiful and accomplished companion. In presenting these little tokens my wife, who has embroidered every inch of the velvet herself, and I feel proud to know that, when the great and auspicious occasion occurs tomorrow, the worthy Mr. Tyler will step into the ring in a costume which we have prepared expressly for him. Thus, when he does himself honor by his performance and earns the applause of the multitude, he will be doing honor and earning applause for the work of our hands—my wife, Lilly, and myself. Take them, my boy, and when you array yourself in them tomorrow, you will remember that the only Living Skeleton and the wonder of the nineteenth century in the shape of the Mammoth Lady, are present in their works if not in their persons."

As he finished speaking, Mr. Treat handed the bundle to Toby and then joined in the applause which was being given by Mrs. Treat and Ella.

Toby unrolled the package and found that it contained a circus rider's costume of pink tights and blue velvet trunks, collar and cuffs, embroidered in white and plentifully spangled with silver. In addition was a wide blue sash for Ella, embroidered to correspond with Toby's costume.

The little fellow was both delighted with the gift and at a loss to know what to say in response. He looked at the costume over and over again, and the tears of gratitude that these friends should have been so good to him came into his eyes. He saw, however, that they were expecting him to say something in reply and, laying the gift on the platform, he said to the skeleton and his wife:

"You've been so good to me ever since I've been with the circus that I wish I was big enough to say somethin' more than that I'm much obliged, but I can't. One of these days, when I'm a man, I'll show you how much I like you, an' then you won't be sorry that you was good to such a poor little runaway boy as I am."

Here the skeleton broke in with such loud applause and so many cries of "Hear! hear!" that Toby grew still more confused and forgot entirely what he was intending to say next.

"I want you to know how much obliged I am," he said, after some hesitation, "an' when I wear 'em, I'll ride just the best I know how, even if I don't want to, an' you shan't be sorry that you gave them to me."

As Toby concluded, he made a funny little awkward bow and then seemed to be trying to hide himself behind a chair from the applause which was given so generously.

"Bless your dear little heart!" said the fat lady, after the confusion had somewhat subsided. "I know you will do your best, anyway, and I'm glad to know that you're going to make your first appearance in something that Samuel and I made for you."

Ella was quite as well pleased with her sash as Toby was with his costume and thanked Mr. and Mrs. Treat in a pretty little way that made Toby wish he could say anything half so nicely.

The hour which the skeleton had devoted for the purpose of the presentation and accompanying speeches having elapsed, it was necessary that Ella and Toby should go, and that the doors of the exhibition be opened at once, in order to give any of the public an opportunity of seeing what the placards announced as two of the greatest curiosities on the face of the globe.

That day, while Toby performed his arduous labors, his heart was very light, for the evidences which the skeleton and his wife had given of their regard for him were very gratifying. He determined that he would do his very best to please as long as he was with the circus, and then, when he got a chance to run away, he would do so, but not until he had said good-by to Mr. and Mrs. Treat and thanked them again for their interest in him.

When he had finished his work in the tent that night, Mr. Lord said to him as he patted him on the back in the most fatherly fashion and as if he had never spoken a harsh word to him, "You can't come in here to sell candy now that you are one of the performers, my boy; an' if I can find another boy tomorrow, you won't have to work in the booth any longer. An' your salary of a dollar a week will go on just the same, even if you don't have anything to do but to ride."

This was a bit of news that was as welcome to Toby as it was unexpected, and he felt more happy then than he had for the ten weeks that he had been traveling under Mr. Lord's cruel mastership.

But there was one thing that night that rather damped his joy and that was that he noticed that Mr. Lord was unusually careful to watch him, not even allowing him to go outside the tent without following. He saw at once that, if he was to have a more easy time, his chances for running away were greatly diminished, and no number of beautiful costumes would have made him content to stay with the circus one moment longer than was absolutely necessary.

That night he told Old Ben of the events of the day

and expressed the hope that he might acquit himself creditably when he made his first appearance on the following day.

Ben sat thoughtfully for some time and then, making all the preparations which Toby knew so well signified a long bit of advice, he said, "Toby, my boy, I've been with a circus, man an' boy, nigh to forty years, an' I've seen lots of youngsters start in just as you're goin' to start in tomorrow; but the most of them petered out because they got to knowin' more'n them that learned 'em did. Now, you remember what I say, an' you'll find it good advice. Whatever business you get into, don't think you know all about it before you've begun. Remember that you can always learn somethin', no matter how old you are, an' keep your eyes an' ears open an' your tongue between your teeth, an' you'll amount to somethin', or my name hain't Ben."

16. *Toby's First Appearance in the Ring*

WHEN the circus entered the town which had been selected as the place where Toby was to make his début as a circus rider the boy noticed a new poster among the many glaring and gaudy bills which set forth the varied and numerous attractions that were to be found under one canvas for a trifling admission fee, and he noticed it with some degree of interest, not thinking for a moment that it had any reference to him.

"Look there!" said Toby to Ben, as he pointed out

the poster, which was printed in very large letters, with gorgeous coloring and surmounted by a picture of two very small people performing all kinds of impossible feats on horseback. "They've got someone else to ride with Ella today. I wonder who it can be?"

MADEMOISELLE JEANNETTE
A N D
MONSIEUR AJAX

two of the youngest equestrians in the world, will perform their graceful, dashing, and daring act entitled

THE TRIUMPH OF
THE INNOCENTS!

This is the first appearance of these daring young riders together since their separation in Europe last season, and their performance in this town will have a new and novel interest. See

MADEMOISELLE JEANNETTE
A N D
MONSIEUR AJAX

Ben looked at Toby for a moment, as if to assure himself that the boy was in earnest in asking the question, and then he relapsed into the worst fit of silent laughing that Toby had ever seen. After he had quite recovered, he asked, "Don't you know who Monsieur Ajax is? Hain't you never seen him?"

"No," replied Toby, at a loss to understand what there was so very funny in this very natural question. "I thought that I was goin' to ride with Ella."

"Why, that's you!" almost screamed Ben, in delight. "Monsieur Ajax means you, didn't you know it? You don't suppose they would go to put 'Toby Tyler' on the bills, do you? How it would look! 'Mademoiselle Jeannette an' Monsieur Toby Tyler!'"

Ben was off in one of his laughing spells again, and Toby sat there, stiff and straight, hardly knowing whether to join in the mirth or to get angry at the sport which had been made of his name.

"I don't care," he said at length. "I'm sure I think Toby Tyler sounds just as well as Monsieur Ajax, an' I'm sure it fits me a good deal better."

"That may be," said Ben, soothingly, "but you see it wouldn't go down so well with the public. They want furrin riders, an' they must have 'em, even if it does spoil your name."

Despite the fact that he did not like the new name that had been given him, Toby could not but feel pleased at the glowing terms in which his performance was set off, but he did not at all relish the lie that was told about his having been with Ella in Europe, and he would have been very much better pleased if that portion of it had been left off.

During the forenoon he did not go near Mr. Lord nor his candy stand, for Mr. Castle kept him and Ella busily engaged in practicing the feat which they were to perform in the afternoon, and it was almost time for the performance to begin before they were allowed even to go to their dinner.

Ella, who had performed several years, was very much more excited over the coming début than Toby was, and the reason why he did not show more interest was probably because of his great desire to leave the circus as soon as possible. And during that forenoon he thought very much more of how he should get back to Guilford and Uncle Daniel than he did of how he should get along when he stood before the audience.

Mr. Castle assisted his pupil to dress, and when that was done to his entire satisfaction, he said, in a stern voice, "Now, you can do this act all right, and if you slip up on it and don't do it as you ought to, I'll give you such a whipping when you come out of the ring that you'll think Job was only fooling with you when he tried to whip you."

Toby had been feeling reasonably cheerful before this, but these words dispelled all his cheerful thoughts and he was looking most disconsolate when Old Ben came into the dressing tent.

"All ready are you, my boy?" said the old man in his cheeriest voice. "Well, that's good, an' you look as nice as possible. Now remember what I told you last night, Toby, an' go in there to do your level best an' make a name for yourself. Come out here with me an' wait for the young lady."

These cheering words of Ben's did Toby as much

good as Mr. Castle's had the reverse, and as he stepped out of the dressing room to the place where the horses were being saddled, Toby resolved that he would do his very best that afternoon, if for no other reason than to please his old friend.

Toby was not naturally what might be called a pretty boy, for his short red hair and his freckled face prevented any great display of beauty, but he was a good, honest-looking boy, and in his tasteful costume looked very nice indeed—so nice that, could Mrs. Treat have seen him just then, she would have been very proud of her handiwork and hugged him harder than ever.

He had been waiting but a few moments when Ella came from her dressing room, and Toby was very much pleased when he saw by the expression of her face that she was perfectly satisfied with his appearance.

"We'll both do just as well as we can," she whispered to him, "and I know the people will like us and make us come back after we get through. And if they do, Mamma says she'll give each one of us a gold dollar."

She had taken hold of Toby's hand as she spoke, and her manner was so earnest and anxious that Toby was more excited than he ever had been about his début; and, had he gone into the ring just at that moment, the chances are that he would have surprised even his teacher by his riding.

"I'll do just as well as I can," said Toby, in reply

to his little companion, "an' if we earn the dollars, I'll have a hole bored in mine, an' you shall wear it around your neck to remember me by."

"I'll remember you without that," she whispered, "and I'll give you mine, so that you shall have so much the more when you go to your home."

There was no time for further conversation, for Mr. Castle entered just then to tell them that they must go in in another moment. The horses were all ready—a black one for Toby and a white one for Ella —and they stood champing their bits and pawing the earth in their impatience until the silver bells with which they were decorated rung out quick, nervous little chimes that accorded very well with Toby's feelings.

Ella squeezed Toby's hand as they stood waiting for the curtain to be raised that they might enter, and he had just time to return it when the signal was given, and almost before he was aware of it, they were standing in the ring, kissing their hands to the crowds that packed the enormous tent to its utmost capacity.

Thanks to the false announcement about the separation of the children in Europe and their reunion in this particular town, the applause was long and loud, and before it had died away, Toby had time to recover a little from the queer feeling which this sea of heads gave him.

He had never seen such a crowd before, except as he had seen them as he walked around at the foot of the seats, and then they had simply looked like so many human beings. But as he saw them now from the ring, they appeared like strange rows of heads without bodies, and he had hard work to keep from running back behind the curtain whence he had come.

Mr. Castle acted as the ringmaster this time, and after he had introduced them, very much after the fashion of the posters, and the clown had repeated some funny joke, the horses were led in, and they were assisted to mount.

"Don't mind the people at all," said Mr. Castle, in a low voice, "but ride just as if you were alone here with me."

The music struck up, the horses cantered around the ring, and Toby had really started as a circus rider.

"Remember," said Ella to him in a low tone, just as the horses started, "you told me that you would ride just as well as you could, and we must earn the dollars Mamma promised."

It seemed to Toby at first as if he could not stand up; but by the time they had ridden around the ring once and Ella had again cautioned him against making any mistake, for the sake of the money which they were going to earn, he was calm and collected enough to carry out his part of the "act" as well as if he had been simply taking a lesson.

The act consisted in their riding side by side, jumping over banners and through hoops covered with paper, and then the most difficult portion began.

The saddles were taken off the horses, and they were to ride first on one horse and then on the other, until

they concluded their performance by riding twice around the ring side by side, standing on their horses, each one with a hand on the other's shoulder.

All this was successfully accomplished without a single error, and when they rode out of the ring, the applause was so great as to leave no doubt but that they would be recalled and thus earn the promised money.

In fact, they had hardly got inside the curtain when one of the attendants called to them, and before they had time even to speak to each other, they were in the ring again, repeating the last portion of their act.

When they came out of the ring for the second time, they found Old Ben, the skeleton, the fat lady, and Mr. Job Lord waiting to welcome them. But before anyone could say a word, Ella had stood on tiptoe again and given Toby just such another kiss as she did when he told her that he would surely stay long enough to appear in the ring with her once.

"That's because you rode so well and helped me so much," she said, as she saw Toby's cheeks growing a fiery red, and then she turned to those who were waiting to greet her.

Mrs. Treat took her in her enormous arms and having kissed her, put her down quickly and clasped Toby as if he had been a very small walnut and her arms a very large pair of nut crackers.

"Bless the boy!" she exclaimed, as she kissed him again and again with an energy and force that made her kisses sound like the crack of the whip, and caused the horses to stamp in affright. "I knew he'd amount to something one of these days, an' Samuel an' I had to come out, when business was dull, just to see how he got along."

It was some time before she would unloose him from her motherly embrace, and when she did, the skeleton grasped him by the hand and said, in the most pompous and affected manner:

"Mr. Tyler, we're proud of you, and when we saw that costume of yours that my Lilly embroidered with her own hands, we was both proud of it and what it contained. You're a great rider, my boy, a great rider, and you'll stand at the head of the profession some day, if you only stick to it."

"Thank you, sir," was all Toby had time to say before Old Ben had him by the hand, and the skeleton was pouring out his congratulations in little Miss Ella's ear.

"Toby, my boy, you did well, an' now you'll amount to something, if you only remember what I told you last night," said Ben, as he looked upon the boy whom he had come to think of as his protégé, with pride. "I never seen anybody of your age do any better. An' now, instead of bein' only a candy peddler, you're one of the stars of the show."

"Thank you, Ben," was all that Toby could say, for he knew that his old friend meant every word that he said, and it pleased him so much that he could say no more than, "Thank you" in reply.

"I feel as if your triumph was mine," said Mr.

Lord, looking benignly at Toby from out his crooked eye and assuming the most fatherly tone at his command, "I have learned to look upon you almost as my own son, and your success is very gratifying to me."

Toby was not at all flattered by this last praise. If he had never seen Mr. Lord before, he might, and probably would, have been deceived by his words, but he had seen him too often and under too many painful circumstances to be at all swindled by his words.

Toby was very much pleased with his success and by the praise he received from all, and when the proprietor of the circus came along, patted him on the head and told him that he rode very nicely, he was quite happy, until he chanced to see the greedy twinkle in Mr. Lord's eye. Then he knew that all this success and all this praise were only binding him faster to the show which he was so anxious to escape from; his pleasure vanished very quickly, and in its stead came a bitter, homesick feeling which no amount of praise could banish.

It was Old Ben who helped him to undress after the skeleton and the fat lady had gone back to their tent, and Ella had gone to dress for her appearance with her mother, for now she was obliged to ride twice at each performance. When Toby was in his ordinary clothes again, Ben said:

"Now that you're one of the performers, Toby, you won't have to sell candy any more, an' you'll have the most of your time to yourself, so let's you an' I go out an' see the town."

"Don't you s'pose Mr. Lord expects me to go to work for him again today?"

"An' s'posin' he does?" said Ben, with a chuckle. "You don't s'pose the boss would let anyone that rides in the ring stand behind Job Lord's counter, do you? You can do just as you have a mind to, my boy, an' I say to you, let's go out an' see the town. What do you say to it?"

"I'd like to go first-rate, if I dared to," replied Toby, thinking of the many whippings he had received for far less than that which Ben now proposed he should do.

"Oh, I'll take care that Job don't bother you, so come along," and Ben started out of the tent and Toby followed, feeling considerably frightened at this first act of disobedience against his old master.

17. *Off for Home*

DURING this walk Toby learned many things that were of importance to him, so far as his plan for running away was concerned. In the first place, he gleaned from the railroad posters that were stuck up in the hotel to which they went that he could buy a ticket for Guilford for seven dollars, and also that, by going back to the town from which they had just come, he could go to Guilford by steamer for five dollars.

By returning to this last town, and Toby calculated that the fare on the stage back there could not be more than a dollar, he would have ten dollars left, and that

surely ought to be sufficient to buy food enough for
two days for the most hungry boy that ever lived.

When they returned to the circus grounds, the performance was over, and Mr. Lord in the midst of the
brisk trade which he usually had after the afternoon
performance, and yet, so far from scolding Toby for
going away, he actually smiled and bowed at him as he
saw him go by with Ben.

"See there, Toby," said the old driver to the boy, as
he gave him a vigorous poke in the ribs and then went
off into one of his dreadful laughing spells, "see what
it is to be a performer an' not workin' for such an old
fossil as Job is! He'll be so sweet to you now that sugar
won't melt in his mouth, an' there's no chance of his
ever attemptin' to whip you again."

Toby made no reply, for he was too busily engaged
thinking of something which had just come into his
mind to know that his friend had spoken.

But as Old Ben hardly knew whether the boy had
answered him or not, owing to his being obliged to
struggle with his breath lest he should lose it in the
second laughing spell that attacked him, the boy's
thoughtfulness was not particularly noticed.

Toby walked around the show grounds for a little
while with his old friend, and then the two went to
supper, where Toby performed quite as great wonders
in the way of eating as he had in the afternoon by
riding.

As soon as the supper was over, he quietly slipped
away from Old Ben, and at once paid a visit to Mr. and

Toby ran toward home. (Page 238)

Mrs. Treat, whom he found cosily engaged with their supper behind the screen.

They welcomed Toby most cordially, and, despite his assertions that he had just finished a very hearty meal, the fat lady made him sit down to the box which served as table, and insisted on his trying some of her doughnuts.

Under all these pressing attentions it was some time before Toby found a chance to say that which he had come to say, and when he did, he was almost at a loss how to proceed. But at last he commenced by starting abruptly on his subject with the words, "I've made up my mind to leave tonight."

"Leave tonight?" repeated the skeleton, inquiringly, not for a moment believing that Toby could think of running away after the brilliant success he had just made. "What do you mean, Toby?"

"Why, you know that I've been wantin' to get away from the circus," said Toby, a little impatient that his friend should be so wonderfully stupid, "an' I think that I'll have as good a chance now as ever I shall, so I'm goin' to try it."

"Bless us!" exclaimed the fat lady, in a gasping way. "You don't mean to say that you're goin' off just when you've started in the business so well? I thought you'd want to stay after you'd been so well received this afternoon."

"No," said Toby, and one quick little sob popped right up from his heart and out before he was aware of it, "I learned to ride because I had to, but I never give up runnin' away. I must see Uncle Dan'l an' tell him how sorry I am for what I did; an' if he won't have anything to say to me, then I'll come back, but if he'll let me, I'll stay there, an' I'll be *so* good that by-'n'-by he'll forget that I run off and left him without sayin' a word."

There was such a touch of sorrow in his tones, so much pathos in his way of speaking, that good Mrs. Treat's heart was touched at once, and putting her arms around the little fellow as if to shield him from some harm, she said, tenderly, "And so you shall go, Toby, my boy. But if you ever want a home or anybody to love you, come right here to us, and you'll never be sorry. So long as Sam keeps thin and I fat enough to draw the public, you never need say that you're homeless, for nothing would please us better than to have you come to live with us."

For reply Toby raised his head and kissed her on the cheek, a proceeding which caused her to squeeze him harder than ever.

During this conversation the skeleton had remained very thoughtful. After a moment or two he got up from his seat, went outside the tent, and presently returned with a quantity of silver ten-cent pieces in his hand.

"Here, Toby," he said, and it was to be seen that he was really too much affected even to attempt one of his speeches, "it's right that you should go, for I've known what it is to feel just as you do. What Lilly said about your having a home with us I say, an' here's five dollars that I want you to take to help you along."

At first Toby stoutly refused to take the money, but they both insisted to such a degree that he was actually forced to, and then he stood up to go.

"I'm goin to try to slip off after Job packs up the outside booth if I can," he said, "an' it was to say good-by that I come around here."

Again Mrs. Treat took the boy in her arms, as if it were one of her own children who was leaving her, and as she stroked his hair back from his forehead, she said, "Don't forget us, Toby, even if you never do see us again. Try an' remember how much we cared for you an' how much comfort you're taking away from us when you go; for it was a comfort to see you around, even if you wasn't with us very much. Don't forget us, Toby, an' if you ever get the chance, come an' see us. Good-by, Toby, good-by." And the kind-hearted woman kissed him again and again and then turned her back resolutely upon him, lest it should be bad luck to him if she again saw him after saying good-by.

The skeleton's parting was not quite so demonstrative. He clasped Toby's hand with one set of his flesh-less fingers, while with the other he wiped one or two suspicious-looking drops of moisture from his eyes, as he said, "I hope you'll get along all right, my boy, and I believe you will. You will get home to Uncle Daniel and be happier than ever, for now you know what it is to be entirely without a home. Be a good boy, mind your uncle, go to school, and one of these days you'll make a good man. Good-by, my boy."

The tears were now streaming down Toby's face very rapidly. He had not known, in his anxiety to get home, how very much he cared for this strangely assorted couple, and now it made him feel very miserable and wretched that he was going to leave them. He tried to say something more, but the tears choked his utterance and he left the tent quickly to prevent himself from breaking down entirely.

In order that his grief might not be noticed and the cause of it suspected, Toby went out behind the tent and, sitting there on a stone, he gave way to the tears which he could no longer control.

While he was thus engaged, heeding nothing which passed around him, he was startled by a cheery voice which cried, "Halloo! Down in the dumps again? What is the matter now, my bold equestrian?"

Looking up, he saw Ben standing before him, and he wiped his eyes hastily, for here was another from whom he must part and to whom a good-by must be spoken.

Looking around to make sure that no one was within hearing, he went up very close to the old driver, and said, in almost a whisper, "I was feelin' bad 'cause I just come from Mr. and Mrs. Treat, an' I've been sayin' good-by to them. I'm goin' to run away tonight."

Ben looked at him for a moment, as if he doubted whether the boy knew exactly what he was talking about, and then said, "So you still want to go home, do you?"

"Oh, yes, Ben, *so* much," was the reply, in a tone which expressed how dear to him was the thought of being in his old home once more.

"All right, my boy. I won't say one word agin it, though it do seem too bad, after you've turned out to be such a good rider," said the old man, thoughtfully. "It's better for you, I know, for a circus hain't no place for a boy, even if he wants to stay, an' I can't say but I'm glad you're still determined to go."

Toby felt relieved at the tone of this leave-taking. He had feared that Old Ben, who thought a circus rider was almost on the topmost round of Fortune's ladder, would have urged him to stay, since he had made his début in the ring, and he was almost afraid that he might take some steps to prevent his going.

"I wanted to say good-by now," said Toby, in a choking voice, " 'cause perhaps I shan't see you again."

"Good-by, my boy," said Ben as he took the boy's hand in his. "Don't forget this experience you've had in runnin' away. An' if ever the time comes that you feel as if you wanted to know that you had a friend, think of Old Ben, an' remember that his heart beats just as warm for you as if he was your father. Good-by, my boy, good-by, an' may the good God bless you!"

"Good-by, Ben," said Toby, and then, as the old driver turned and walked away, wiping something from his eye with the cuff of his sleeve, Toby gave full vent to his tears and wondered why it was that he was such a miserable little wretch.

There was one more good-by to be said and that

Toby dreaded more than all the others. It was to Ella. He knew that she would feel badly to have him go, because she liked to ride the act with him that gave them such applause, and he felt certain that she would urge him to stay.

Just then the thought of another of his friends, one who had not yet been warned of what very important matter was to occur, came into his mind, and he hastened toward the old monkey's cage. His pet was busily engaged in playing with some of the younger members of his family and for some moments could not be induced to come to the bars of the cage.

At last, however, Toby did succeed in coaxing him forward and then, taking him by the paw and drawing him as near as possible, Toby whispered, "We're goin' to run away tonight, Mr. Stubbs, an' I want you to be all ready to go the minute I come for you."

The old monkey winked both eyes violently and then showed his teeth to such an extent that Toby thought he was laughing at the prospect, and he said, a little severely, "If you had as many friends as I have got in this circus you wouldn't laugh when you was goin' to leave them. Of course I've got to go, an' I want to go; but it makes me feel bad to leave the skeleton an' the fat woman an' Old Ben an' little Ella. But I mustn't stand here. You be ready when I come for you, an' by mornin' we'll be so far off that Mr. Lord nor Mr. Castle can't catch us."

The old monkey went toward his companions, as if he were in high glee at the trip before him, and Toby went into the dressing tent to prepare for the evening's performance, which was about to commence.

It appeared to the boy as if everyone was unusually kind to him that night, and, feeling sad at leaving those in the circus who had befriended him, Toby was unusually attentive to everyone around him. He ran on some trifling errand for one, helped another in his dressing, and in a dozen kind ways seemed as if trying to atone for leaving them secretly.

When the time came for him to go into the ring and he met Ella, bright and happy at the thought of riding with him and repeating her triumphs of the afternoon, nothing save the thought of how wicked he had been to run away from good old Uncle Daniel and a desire to right that wrong in some way, prevented him from giving up his plan of going back.

The little girl observed his sadness, and she whispered, "Has anyone been whipping you, Toby?"

Toby shook his head. He had thought that he would tell her what he was about to do just before they went into the ring, but her kind words seemed to make that impossible. And he had said nothing, when the blare of the trumpets, the noisy demonstrations of the audience, and the announcement of the clown that the wonderful children riders were now about to appear, ushered them into the ring.

If Toby had performed well in the afternoon, he accomplished wonders on this evening, and they were called back into the ring, not once, but twice, and when finally they were allowed to retire, everyone behind the curtain overwhelmed them with praise.

Ella was so profuse with her kind words, her admiration for what Toby had done, and so delighted at the idea that they were to ride together, that even then the boy could not tell her what he was going to do, but went into his dressing room, resolving that he would tell her all when they both had finished dressing.

Toby made as small a parcel as possible of the costume which Mr. and Mrs. Treat had given him, for he determined that he would take it with him, and, putting it under his coat, went out to wait for Ella. As she did not come out as soon as he expected, he asked someone to tell her that he wanted to see her, and he thought to himself that when she did come she would be in a hurry and could not stop long enough to make any very lengthy objections to his leaving.

But she did not come at all—her mother sent out word that Toby could not see her until after the performance was over, owing to the fact that it was now nearly time for her to go into the ring and she was not dressed yet.

Toby was terribly disappointed. He knew that it would not be safe for him to wait until the close of the performance if he were intending to run away that night, and he felt that he could not go until he had said a few last words to her.

He was in a great perplexity, until the thought came to him that he could write a good-by to her, and by this means any unpleasant discussion would be avoided.

After some little difficulty he procured a small piece
of not very clean paper and a very short bit of lead
pencil, and using the top of one of the wagons as he sat
on the seat for a desk, he indited the following epistle:

> deaR ella I Am goin to Run away two night,
> & i want two say good by to yu & your mother. i am
> Small & unkle Danil says i dont mount two much,
> but i am old enuf two know that you have bin good
> two me, & when i Am a man i will buy you a whole
> cirkus, and we Will ride together. dont forgit me
> & I wont yu in haste
>
> TOBY TYLER

Toby had no envelope in which to seal this precious
letter, but he felt that it would not be seen by prying
eyes and would safely reach its destination, if he in-
trusted it to Old Ben.

It did not take him many moments to find the old
driver, and he said, as he handed him the letter, "I
didn't see Ella to tell her I was goin', so I wrote this
letter, an' I want to know if you will give it to her?"

"Of course I will. But see here, Toby," and Ben
caught him by the sleeve and led him aside where he
would not be overheard, "have you got money enough
to take you home? For if you haven't, I can let you
have some." And Ben plunged his hand into his capa-
cious pocket, as if he was about to withdraw from there
the entire United States Treasury.

Toby assured him that he had sufficient for all his
wants; but the old man would not be satisfied until
he had seen for himself and then, taking Toby's hand

again, he said, "Now, my boy, it won't do for you to
stay around here any longer. Buy something to eat
before you start an' go into the woods for a day or two
before you take the train or steamboat. You're too big
a prize for Job or Castle to let you go without a word,
an' they'll try their level best to find you. Be careful,
now, for if they should catch you, good-by any more
chances to get away. There," and here Ben suddenly
lifted him high from the ground and kissed him, "now
get away as fast as you can."

Toby pressed the old man's hand affectionately, and
then, without trusting himself to speak, walked swiftly
out toward the entrance.

He resolved to take Ben's advice and go into the
woods for a short time, and therefore he must buy
some provisions before he started.

As he passed the monkeys' cage, he saw his pet sitting near the bars and he stopped long enough to whisper, "I'll be back in ten minutes, Mr. Stubbs, an' you
be all ready then."

Then he went on, and just as he got near the
entrance one of the men told him that Mrs. Treat
wished to see him.

Toby could hardly afford to spare the time just
then, but he would probably have obeyed the summons
if he had known that by so doing he would be caught,
and he ran as fast as his little legs would carry him
toward the skeleton's tent.

The exhibition was open, and both the skeleton and
his wife were on the platform when Toby entered;

but he crept around at the back and up behind Mrs. Treat's chair, telling her as he did so that he had just received her message and that he must hurry right back, for every moment was important then to him.

"I put up a nice lunch for you," she said as she kissed him, "and you'll find it on top of the biggest trunk. Now go, and if my wishes are of any good to you, you will get to your Uncle Daniel's house without any trouble. Good-by again, little one."

Toby did not dare to trust himself any longer where everyone was so kind to him. He slipped down from the platform as quickly as possible, found the bundle— and a good-sized one it was too—without any difficulty, and went back to the monkeys' cage.

As orders had been given by the proprietor of the circus that the boy should do as he had a mind to with the monkey, he called Mr. Stubbs, and as he was in the custom of taking him with him at night, no one thought that it was anything strange that he should take him from the cage now.

Mr. Lord or Mr. Castle might possibly have thought it queer had either of them seen the two bundles which Toby carried, but, fortunately for the boy's scheme, they both believed that he was in the dressing tent and consequently thought that he was perfectly safe.

Toby's hand shook so that he could hardly undo the fastening of the cage, and when he attempted to call the monkey to him, his voice sounded so strange and husky that it startled him.

The old monkey seemed to prefer sleeping with Toby rather than with those of his kind in the cage; and as the boy took him with him almost every night, he came on this particular occasion as soon as Toby called, regardless of the strange sound of his master's voice.

With his bundles under his arm and the monkey on his shoulder, with both paws tightly clasped around his neck, Toby made his way out of the tent with beating heart and bated breath.

Neither Mr. Lord, Castle, nor Jacobs was in sight, and everything semed favorable for his flight. During the afternoon he had carefully noted the direction of the woods, and he started swiftly toward them now, stopping only long enough, as he was well clear of the tents, to say, in a whisper:

"Good-by, Mr. Treat, an' Mrs. Treat, an' Ella, an' Ben. Sometime, when I'm a man, I'll come back an' bring you lots of nice things an' I'll never forget you —never. When I have a chance to be good to some little boy that felt as bad as I did, I'll do it, an' tell him that it was you did it. Good-by."

Then, turning around, he ran toward the woods as swiftly as if his escape had been discovered and the entire company were in pursuit.

18. *A Day of Freedom*

TOBY ran at the top of his speed over the rough road, and the monkey, jolted from one side to the other, clutched his paws more tightly around the boy's neck, looking around into his face as if to ask what was the meaning of this very singular proceeding.

When he was so very nearly breathless as to be able to run no more but was forced to walk, Toby looked behind him and there he could see the bright lights of the circus and hear the strains of the music as he had heard them on the night when he was getting ready to run away from Uncle Daniel. Those very sounds, which reminded him forcibly of how ungrateful he had been to the old man who had cared for him when there was no one else in the world who would do so, made it more easy for him to leave those behind who had been so kind to him when he stood so much in need of kindness.

"We are goin' home, Mr. Stubbs!" he said, exultantly, to the monkey, "home to Uncle Dan'l an' the boys. An' won't you have a good time when we get there! You can run all over the barn an' up in the trees an' do just what you want to, an' there'll be plenty of fellows to play with you. You don't know half how good a place Guilford is, Mr. Stubbs."

The monkey chattered away as if he were anticipating lots of fun on his arrival at Toby's home, and the boy chattered back, his spirits rising at every step which took him farther away from the collection of tents where he had spent so many wretched hours.

A brisk walk of half an hour sufficed to take Toby to the woods, and after some little search he found a thick clump of bushes in which he concluded he could sleep without the risk of being seen by anyone who might pass that way before he should be awake in the morning.

He had not much choice in the way of a bed, for it was so dark in the woods that it was impossible to collect moss or leaves to make a soft resting place, and the few leaves and pine boughs which he did gather made his place for sleeping but very little softer.

But during the ten weeks that Toby had been with

the circus his bed had seldom been anything softer than the seat of the wagon, and it troubled him very little that he was to sleep with nothing but a few leaves between himself and the earth.

Using the bundle in which was his riding costume for a pillow and placing the lunch Mrs. Treat had given him near by, where the monkey could not get at it conveniently, he cuddled Mr. Stubbs up in his bosom and lay down to sleep.

"Mr. Lord won't wake us up in the mornin' an' swear at us for not washin' the tumblers," said Toby, in a tone of satisfaction, to the monkey, "an' we won't have to go into the tent tomorrow an' sell sick lemonade an' poor peanuts. But," and here his tone changed to one of sorrow, "there'll be some there that'll be sorry not to see us in the mornin', Mr. Stubbs, though they'll be glad to know that we got away all right. But won't Mr. Lord swear, an' won't Mr. Castle crack his whip, when they come to look round for us in the mornin' and find that we hain't there!"

The only reply which the monkey made to this was to nestle his head closer under Toby's coat and to show, in the most decided manner, that he was ready to go to sleep.

And Toby was quite as ready to go to sleep as he was. He had worked hard that day, but the excitement of escaping had prevented him from realizing his fatigue until after he had lain down. And almost before he had got through congratulating himself upon the ease with which he had gotten free, both he and the

monkey were as sound asleep as if they had been tucked up in the softest bed that was ever made.

Toby's very weariness was a friend to him that night, for it prevented him from waking, which, if he had done so, might have been unpleasant when he fully realized that he was all alone in the forest, and the sounds that are always heard in the woods might have frightened him just the least bit.

The sun was shining directly in his face when Toby awoke on the following morning, and the old monkey was still snugly nestled under his coat. He sat up rather dazed at first and then, as he fully realized that he was actually free from all that had made his life such a sad and hard one for so many weeks, he shouted aloud, reveling in his freedom.

The monkey, awakened by Toby's cries, started from his sleep in affright and jumped into the nearest tree, only to chatter, jump, and swing from the boughs when he saw that there was nothing very unusual going on, save that he and Toby were out in the woods again, where they could have no end of a good time and do just as they liked.

After a few moments spent in a short jubilee at their escape, Toby took the monkey on his shoulder and the bundles under his arm again and went cautiously out to the edge of the thicket, where he could form some idea as to whether or no they were pursued.

He had entered the woods at the brow of a small hill when he had fled so hastily on the previous evening and looking down, he could see the spot whereon the tents of the circus had been pitched, but not a sign of them was now visible. He could see a number of people walking around, and he fancied that they looked up every now and then to where he stood concealed by the foliage.

This gave him no little uneasiness, for he feared that Mr. Lord or Mr. Castle might be among the number and he believed that they would begin a search for him at once, and that the spot where their attention would first be drawn was exactly where he was then standing.

"This won't do, Mr. Stubbs," he said, as he pushed the monkey higher up on his shoulder and started into the thickest part of the woods, "we must get out of this place, an' go farther down, where we can hide till tomorrow mornin'. Besides, we must find some water where we can wash our faces."

The old monkey would hardly have been troubled if they had not had their faces washed for the next month to come, but he grinned and talked as Toby trudged along, attempting to catch hold of the leaves as they were passed and in various other ways impeding his master's progress, until Toby was obliged to give him a most severe scolding in order to make him behave himself in anything like a decent manner.

At last, after fully half an hour's rapid walking, Toby found just the place he wanted in which to pass the time he concluded it would be necessary to spend before he dare venture out to start for home.

It was a little valley entirely filled by trees, which

grew so thickly, save in one little spot, as to make it almost impossible to walk through. The one clear spot was not more than ten feet square, but it was just at the edge of a swiftly running brook, and a more beautiful or convenient place for a boy and a monkey to stop who had no tent, nor means to build one, could not well be imagined.

Toby's first act was to wash his face, and he tried to make the monkey do the same, but Mr. Stubbs had no idea of doing any such foolish thing. He would come down close to the edge of the water and look in, but the moment that Toby tried to make him go in, he would rush back among the trees, climb out on some slender bough, and then swing himself down by the tail and chatter away as if making sport of his young master for thinking that he would be so foolish as to soil his face with water.

After Toby had made his toilet, he unfastened the bundle which the fat lady had given him, for the purpose of having breakfast. As much of an eater as Toby was, he could not but be surprised at the quantity of food which Mrs. Treat called a lunch. There were two whole pies and half of another, as many as two dozen doughnuts, several large pieces of cheese, six sandwiches, with a plentiful amount of meat, half a dozen biscuits, nicely buttered, and a large piece of cake.

The monkey had come down from the tree as soon as he saw Toby untying the bundle, and there was quite as much pleasure depicted on his face when he saw the good things that were spread out before him, as there was on Toby's. And he showed his thankfulness at Mrs. Treat's foresight by suddenly snatching one of the doughnuts and running with it up the tree where he knew Toby could not follow.

"Now look here, Mr. Stubbs!" said Toby, sternly, "you can have all you want to eat, but you must take it in a decent way, an' not go to cuttin' up any such shines as that."

And after giving this command—which, by the way, was obeyed just about as well as it was understood—Toby devoted his time to his breakfast and he reduced the amount of eatables very considerably before he had finished.

Toby cleared off his table by gathering the food together and putting it back into the paper as well as possible, and then he sat down to think over the situation, and to decide what he had better do.

He felt rather nervous about venturing out when it was possible for Mr. Lord or Mr. Castle to get hold of him again, and as the weather was yet warm during the night, his camping place everything that could be desired, and the stock of food likely to hold out, he concluded that he had better remain there for two days at least. Then he would be reasonably sure that if either of the men whom he so dreaded to see had remained behind for the purpose of catching him, he would have got tired out and gone on.

This point decided upon, the next was to try to fix up something soft for a bed. He had his pocket knife with him, and in his little valley were pine and hem-

lock trees in abundance. From the tips of their branches
he knew that he could make a bed as soft and fragrant
as any that could be thought of, and he set to work
at once, while Mr. Stubbs continued his antics above
his head.

After about two hours' steady work he had cut
enough of the tender branches to make himself a bed
into which he and the monkey could burrow and sleep
as comfortably as if they were in the softest bed in
Uncle Daniel's house.

When Toby first began to cut the boughs, he had
an idea that he might possibly make some sort of hut,
but the two hours' work had blistered his hands, and
he was perfectly ready to sit down and rest, without the
slightest desire for any other kind of hut than that
formed by the trees themselves.

Toby imagined that in that beautiful place he could,
with the monkey, stay contented for any number of
days, but after he had rested a time, played with his
pet a little, and eaten just a trifle more of the lunch,
the time passed so slowly that he soon made up his
mind to run the risk of meeting Mr. Lord or Mr.
Castle again by going out of the woods the first thing
the next morning.

Very many times before the sun set that day, was
Toby tempted to run the risk that night, for the sake
of the change, if no more, but as he thought the matter
over, he saw how dangerous such a course would be and
he forced himself to wait.

That night he did not sleep as soundly as on the

previous one, for the very good reason that he was not as tired. He awoke several times, and the noise of the night birds alarmed him to such an extent that he was obliged to awaken the old monkey for company.

But the night passed despite his fears, as all nights will, whether a boy is out in the woods alone or tucked up in his own little bed at home. In the morning Toby made all possible haste to get away, for each moment that he stayed now made him more impatient to be moving toward home.

He washed himself as quickly as possible, ate his breakfast with the most unseemly haste, and, taking up his bundles and the monkey, once more started, as he supposed, in the direction from which he had entered the woods.

Toby walked briskly along, in the best possible spirits, for his running away was now an accomplished fact and he was going toward Uncle Daniel and home just as fast as possible. He sang "Old Hundred" through five or six times by way of showing his happiness. It is quite likely that he would have sung something a little more lively had he known anything else, but "Old Hundred" was the extent of his musical education, and he kept repeating that, which was quite as satisfactory as if he had been able to go through with every opera that was ever written.

The monkey would jump from his shoulder into the branches above, run along on the trees for a short distance, and then wait until Toby came along, when he would drop down on his shoulder suddenly, and in every other way of displaying monkey delight he showed that he was just as happy as was possible.

Toby trudged on in this contented way for nearly an hour, and every moment expected to step out to the edge of the woods, where he could see houses and men once more. But instead of doing so the forest seemed to grow more dense, and nothing betokened his approach to the village. There was a great fear came into Toby's heart just then, and for a moment he halted in helpless perplexity. His lips began to quiver, his face grew white, and his hand trembled so that the old monkey took hold of one of his fingers and looked at it wonderingly.

19. *Mr. Stubbs's Mischief and His Sad Fate*

Toby had begun to realize that he was lost in the woods, and the thought was sufficient to cause alarm in the mind of one much older than the boy. He said to himself that he would keep on in the direction he was then traveling for fifteen minutes; and as he had no means of computing time, he sat down on a log, took out the bit of pencil with which he had written the letter to Ella, and multiplied sixty by fifteen. He knew that there were sixty seconds to the minute and that he could ordinarily count one to each second; therefore, when he learned there were nine hundred seconds in fifteen minutes, he resolved to walk as straight ahead as possible until he should have counted that number.

He walked on, counting as regularly as he could, and thought to himself that he never before realized how long fifteen minutes were. It really seemed to him that an hour had passed before he finished counting, and then when he stopped, there were no more signs that he was near a clearing than there had been before.

"Ah, Mr. Stubbs, we're lost! We're lost!" he cried, as he laid his cheek on the monkey's head and gave way to the lonesome grief that came over him. "What shall we do? Perhaps we won't ever find our way out, but will die here, an' then Uncle Dan'l won't ever know how sorry I was that I run away."

Then Toby lay right down on the ground and cried so hard that the monkey acted as if it were frightened and tried to turn the boy's face over, and finally leaned down and licked Toby's ear.

This little act, which seemed so much like a kiss, caused Toby to feel no small amount of comfort, and he sat up again, took the monkey in his arms, and began seriously to discuss some definite plan of action.

"It won't do to keep on the way we've been goin', Mr. Stubbs," said Toby, as he looked full in his pet's face—and the old monkey sat as still and looked as grave as it was possible for him to look and sit— "for we must be goin' into the woods deeper. Let's start off this way," and Toby pointed at right angles with the course they had been pursuing, "an' keep right on that way till we come to something or till we drop right down an' die."

It is fair to presume that the old monkey agreed to Toby's plan, for although he said nothing in favor of it he certainly made no objections to it, which to Toby was the same as if his companion had assented to it in the plainest English.

Both the bundles and the monkey were rather a heavy load for a small boy like Toby to carry. But he clung manfully to them, walked resolutely on, without looking to the right or to the left, glad when the old monkey would take a run among the trees, for then he would be relieved of his weight; and glad when he returned, for then he had his company, and that repaid him for any labor which he might have to perform.

Toby was in a hard plight as it was, but without the old monkey for a companion he would have thought his condition was a hundred times worse and would hardly have had the courage to go on as he was going.

On and on he walked, until it seemed to him that he could really go no farther, and yet he could see no signs which indicated the end of the woods. At last he sunk upon the ground, too tired to walk another step, saying to the monkey, who was looking as if he would like to know the reason of this pause, "It's no use, Mr. Stubbs, I've got to sit down here an' rest awhile, anyhow. Besides, I'm awfully hungry."

Then Toby commenced to eat his dinner and to give the monkey his, until the thought came to him that he neither had any water nor did he know where to find it, and then, of course, he immediately became so thirsty that it was impossible for him to eat any more.

"We can't stand this," moaned Toby to the monkey. "We've got to have something to drink or else we can't eat all these sweet things, an' I'm so tired that I can't go any farther. Don't let's eat dinner now, but let's stay here an' rest an' then we can keep on an' look for water."

Toby's resting spell was a long one, for as soon as he stretched himself out on the ground, he was asleep from actual exhaustion and he did not awaken until the sun was just setting. Then he saw that, hard as his troubles had been before, they were about to become, or in fact had become, worse.

He had paid no attention to his bundles when he lay down, and when he awoke, he was puzzled to make out what it was that was strewn around the ground so thickly.

He had looked at it but a very short time when he saw that it was what had been the lunch he had carried so far. After having had the sad experience of losing his money, he understood very readily that the old monkey had taken the lunch while he slept and had amused himself by picking it apart into the smallest particles possible, and then strewn them around on the ground where he now saw them.

Toby looked at them in almost speechless surprise and then he turned to where the old monkey lay, apparently asleep, but as the boy watched him intently, he could see that the cunning animal was really watching him out of one half-closed eye.

"Now you have killed us, Mr. Stubbs," wailed Toby. "We never can find our way out of here. An' now we hain't got anything to eat and by tomorrow we shall be starved to death. Oh, dear! Wasn't you bad enough when you threw all the money away, so you had to go an' do this just when we was in awful trouble?"

Mr. Stubbs now looked up as if he had just been awakened by Toby's grief, looked around him leisurely as if to see what could be the matter, and then, apparently seeing for the first time the crumbs that were lying around on the ground, took up some and examined them intently.

"Now don't go to makin' believe that you don't know how they come there," said Toby, showing anger toward his pet for the first time. "You know it was you who did it, for there wasn't anyone else here, an' you can't fool me by lookin' so surprised."

It seemed as if the monkey had come to the conclusion that his little plan of ignorance wasn't the most perfect success, for he walked meekly toward his young master, climbed up on his shoulder, and sat there kissing his ear, or looking down into his eyes, until the boy could resist the mute appeal no longer, but took him into his arms and hugged him closely as he said:

"It can't be helped now, I s'pose, an' we shall have

to get along the best way we can, but it was awful wicked of you, Mr. Stubbs, an' I don't know what we're going to do for something to eat."

While the destructive fit was on him, the old monkey had not spared the smallest bit of food but had picked everything into such minute shreds that none of it could be gathered up, and everything was surely wasted.

While Toby sat bemoaning his fate and trying to make out what was to be done for food, the darkness, which had just begun to gather when he first awoke, now commenced to settle around, and he was obliged to seek for some convenient place in which to spend the night before it became so dark as to make the search impossible.

Owing to the fact that he had slept nearly the entire afternoon and also rendered wakeful by the loss he had just sustained, Toby lay awake on the hard ground, with the monkey on his arm, hour after hour, until all kinds of fancies came to him. And in every sound he feared he heard someone from the circus coming to capture him or some wild beast intent on picking his bones.

The cold sweat of fear stood out on his brow, and he hardly dared to breathe, much more to speak, lest the sound of his voice should betray his whereabouts and thus bring his enemies down upon him. The minutes seemed like hours and the hours like days, as he lay there, listening fearfully to every one of the night sounds of the forest. And it seemed to him that he had been there very many hours when at last he fell asleep, and was thus freed from his fears.

Bright and early on the following morning Toby was awake, and as he came to a realizing sense of all the dangers and trouble that surrounded him, he was disposed to give way again to his sorrow, but he said resolutely to himself, "It might be a good deal worse than it is, an' Mr. Stubbs an' I can get along one day without anything to eat. An' perhaps by night we shall be out of the woods, an' then what we get will taste good to us."

He began his walk—which possibly might not end that day—manfully, and his courage was rewarded by soon reaching a number of bushes that were literally loaded down with blackberries. From these he made a hearty meal, and the old monkey fairly reveled in them, for he ate all he possibly could and then stowed away enough in his cheeks to make a good-sized luncheon when he should be hungry again.

Refreshed very much by his breakfast of fruit, Toby again started on his journey with renewed vigor, and the world began to look very bright to him. He had not thought that he might find berries when the thoughts of starvation came into his mind, and now that his hunger was satisfied, he began to believe that he might possibly be able to live, perhaps for weeks, in the woods solely upon what he might find growing there.

Shortly after he had had breakfast, he came upon a brook, which he thought was the same upon whose banks he had encamped the first night he spent in the

woods, and, pulling off his clothes, he waded into the deepest part and had a most refreshing bath, although the water was rather cold.

Not having any towels with which to dry himself, he was obliged to sit in the sun until the moisture had been dried from his skin and he could put his clothes on once more. Then he started out on his walk again, feeling that sooner or later he would come out all right.

All this time he had been traveling without any guide to tell him whether he was going straight ahead or around in a circle, and he now concluded to follow the course of the brook, believing that that would lead him out of the forest some time.

During the forenoon he walked steadily, but not so fast that he would get exhausted quickly, and when by the position of the sun he judged that it was noon, he lay down on a mossy bank to rest.

He was beginning to feel sad again. He had found no more berries, and the elation which had been caused by his breakfast and his bath was quickly passing away. The old monkey was in a tree almost directly above his head, stretched out on one of the limbs in the most contented manner possible. As Toby watched him and thought of all the trouble he had caused by wasting the food, thoughts of starvation again came into his mind, and he believed that he should not live to see Uncle Daniel again.

Just when he was feeling the most sad and lonely, and when thoughts of death from starvation were most vivid in his mind, he heard the barking of a dog, which sounded close at hand.

His first thought was that at last he was saved, and he was just starting to his feet to shout for help, when he heard the sharp report of a gun and an agonizing cry from the branches above. And the old monkey fell to the ground with a thud that told he had received his death wound.

All this had taken place so quickly that Toby did not at first comprehend the extent of the misfortune which had overtaken him; but a groan from the poor monkey, as he placed one little brown paw to his breast from which the blood was flowing freely and looked up into his master's face with a most piteous expression, showed the poor little boy what a great trouble it was which had now come.

Poor Toby uttered a loud cry of agony, which could not have been more full of anguish had he received the ball in his own breast. And, flinging himself by the side of the dying monkey, he gathered him close to his breast, regardless of the blood that poured over him, and stroking tenderly the little head that had nestled so often in his bosom, said, over and over again, as the monkey uttered short moans of agony, "Who could have been so cruel? Who could have been so cruel?"

Toby's tears ran like rain down his face, and he kissed his dying pet again and again, as if he would take all the pain to himself.

"Oh, if you could only speak to me!" he cried, as he took one of the poor monkey's paws in his hand, and, finding that it was growing cold with the chill of death, put it on his neck to warm it. "How I love you, Mr. Stubbs! An' now you're goin' to die an' leave me! Oh, if I hadn't spoken cross to you yesterday, an' if I hadn't a'most choked you the day that we went to the skeleton's to dinner! Forgive me for ever bein' bad to you, won't you, Mr. Stubbs?"

As the monkey's groans increased in number but diminished in force, Toby ran to the brook, filled his hands with water, and held it to the poor animal's mouth.

He lapped the water quickly and looked up with a human look of gratitude in his eyes, as if thanking his master for that much relief. Then Toby tried to wash the blood from his breast, but it flowed quite as fast as he could wash it away, and he ceased his efforts in that direction and paid every attention to making his friend and pet more comfortable. He took off his jacket and laid it on the ground for the monkey to lie upon. He picked a quantity of large green leaves as a cooling rest for his head and then sat by his side, holding his paws and talking to him with the most tender words his lips, quivering with sorrow as they were, could fashion.

20. *Home and Uncle Daniel*

MEANWHILE the author of all this misery had come upon the scene. He was a young man, whose rifle and well-filled game bag showed that he had been hunting, and his face expressed the liveliest sorrow for what he had so unwittingly done.

"I didn't know I was firing at your pet," he said to Toby as he laid his hand on his shoulder and endeavored to make him look up. "I only saw a little patch of fur through the trees and, thinking it was some wild animal, I fired. Forgive me, won't you, and let me put the poor brute out of his misery?"

Toby looked up fiercely at the murderer of his pet and asked, savagely, "Why don't you go away? Don't you see that you have killed Mr. Stubbs, an' you'll be hung for murder?"

"I wouldn't have done it under any circumstances," said the young man, pitying Toby's grief most sincerely. "Come away, and let me put the poor thing out of its agony."

"How can you do it?" asked Toby, bitterly. "He's dying already."

"I know it, and it will be a kindness to put a bullet through his head."

If Toby had been big enough, perhaps there might really have been a murder committed, for he looked up at the man who so coolly proposed to kill the poor monkey after he had already received his death wound that the young man stepped back quickly, as if really afraid that in his desperation the boy might do him some injury.

"Go 'way off," said Toby, passionately, "an' don't ever come here again. You've killed all I ever had in this world of my own to love me, an' I hate you. I hate you!"

Then, turning again to the monkey, he put his hands on each side of his head and, leaning down, kissed the little brown lips as tenderly as a mother would kiss her child.

The monkey was growing more and more feeble, and when Toby had shown this act of affection, he reached up his tiny paws, grasped Toby's finger, half raised himself from the ground and then with a convulsive struggle fell back dead, while the tiny fingers slowly relaxed their hold of the boy's hand.

Toby feared that it was death and yet hoped that he was mistaken. He looked into the half open, fast glazing eyes, put his hand over his heart, to learn if it were still beating and getting no responsive look from the dead eyes, feeling no heart throbs from under that gõry breast, he knew that his pet was really dead, and he flung himself by his side in all the childish abandonment of grief.

He called the monkey by name, implored him to look at him, and finally bewailed that he had ever left the circus, where at least his pet's life was safe, even if his own back received its daily flogging.

The young man, who stood a silent spectator of this painful scene, understood everything from Toby's mourning. He knew that a boy had run away from the circus, for Messrs. Lord and Castle had stayed behind one day, in the hope of capturing the fugitive, and they had told their own version of Toby's flight.

For nearly an hour Toby lay by the dead monkey's side, crying as if his heart would break, and the young man waited until his grief should have somewhat exhausted itself and then approached the boy again.

"Won't you believe that I didn't mean to do this cruel thing?" he asked, in a kindly voice. "And won't you believe that I would do anything in my power to bring your pet back to life?"

Toby looked at him a moment earnestly and then said, slowly, "Yes, I'll try to."

"Now will you come with me, and let me talk to you? for I know who you are and why you are here."

"How do you know that?"

"Two men stayed behind after the circus had left, and they hunted everywhere for you."

"I wish they had caught me," moaned Toby. "I wish they had caught me, for then Mr. Stubbs wouldn't be here dead."

And Toby's grief broke out afresh as he again looked at the poor little stiff form that had been a source of so much comfort and joy to him.

"Try not to think of that now, but think of yourself and of what you will do," said the man, soothingly, anxious to divert Toby's mind as much as possible.

"I don't want to think of myself and I don't care what I'll do," sobbed the boy, passionately.

"But you must. You can't stay here always, and I will try to help you to get home, or wherever it is you want to go, if you will tell me all about it."

It was some time before Toby could be persuaded to speak or think of anything but the death of his pet, but the young man finally succeeded in drawing his story from him and then tried to induce him to leave that place and accompany him to the town.

"I can't leave Mr. Stubbs," said the boy, firmly. "He never left me the night I got thrown out of the wagon an' he thought I was hurt."

Then came another struggle to induce him to bury his pet. And finally Toby, after realizing the fact that he could not carry a dead monkey with him, agreed to it, but he would not allow the young man to help him in any way or even to touch the monkey's body.

He dug a grave under a little fir tree near by and lined it with wild flowers and leaves, and even then hesitated to cover the body with the earth. At last he bethought himself of the fanciful costume which the skeleton and his wife had given him, and in this he carefully wrapped his dead pet. He had not one regret at leaving the bespangled suit, for it was the best he could command, and surely nothing could be too good for Mr. Stubbs.

Tenderly he laid him in the little grave and, covering the body with flowers, said, pausing a moment before he covered it over with earth, and while his voice was choked with emotion, "Good-by, Mr. Stubbs, good-by! I wish it had been me instead of you that died, for I'm an awful sorry little boy now that you're dead!"

Even after the grave had been filled and a little mound made over it, the young man had the greatest difficulty to persuade Toby to go with him. And when the boy did consent to go at last, he walked very slowly away and kept turning his head to look back just so long as the little grave could be seen.

Then, when the trees shut it completely out from sight, the tears commenced again to roll down Toby's cheeks and he sobbed out, "I wish I hadn't left him.

Oh, why didn't I make him lie down by me? An' then he'd be alive now, an' how glad he'd be to know that we was getting out of the woods at last!"

But the man who had caused Toby this sorrow talked to him about other matters, thus taking his mind from the monkey's death as much as possible, and by the time the boy reached the village, he had told his story exactly as it was, without casting any reproaches on Mr. Lord, and giving himself the full share of censure for leaving his home as he did.

Mr. Lord and Mr. Castle had remained in the town but one day, for they were told that a boy had taken the night train that passed through the town about two hours after Toby had escaped, and they had set off at once to act on that information.

Therefore Toby need have no fears of meeting either of them just then and he could start on his homeward journey in peace.

The young man who had caused the monkey's death tried first to persuade Toby to remain a day or two with him and, failing in that, he did all he could toward getting the boy home as quickly and safely as possible. He insisted on paying for his ticket on the steamboat, although Toby did all he could to prevent him, and he even accompanied Toby to the next town, where he was to take the steamer.

He had not only paid for Toby's ticket, but he had paid for a stateroom for him. And when the boy said that he could sleep anywhere and that there was no need of such expense, the man replied, "Those men who were hunting for you have gone down the river and will be very likely to search the boat, when they discover that they started on the wrong scent. They will never suspect that you have got a stateroom, and if you are careful to remain in it during the trip, you will get through safely."

Then when the time came for the steamer to start, the young man said to Toby, "Now, my boy, you won't feel hard at me for shooting the monkey, will you? I would have done anything to have brought him to life, but, as I could not do that, helping you to get home was the next best thing I could do."

"I know you didn't mean to shoot Mr. Stubbs," said Toby, with moistening eyes as he spoke of his pet, "an' I'm sorry I said what I did to you in the woods."

Before there was time to say any more, the warning whistle was sounded, the plank pulled in, the great wheels commenced to revolve, and Toby was really on his way to Uncle Daniel and Guilford.

It was then but five o'clock in the afternoon, and he could not expect to reach home until two or three o'clock in the afternoon of the next day, but he was in a tremor of excitement as he thought that he should walk through the streets of Guilford once more, see all the boys, and go home to Uncle Daniel.

And yet, whenever he thought of that home, of meeting those boys, of going once more to all those old familiar places, the memory of all that he had planned when he should take the monkey with him would come into his mind and damp even his joy, great as it was.

That night he had considerable difficulty in falling asleep, but did finally succeed in doing so. And when he awoke, the steamer was going up the river whose waters seemed like an old friend, because they had flowed right down past Guilford on their way to the sea.

At each town where a landing was made Toby looked eagerly out on the pier, thinking that by chance someone from his home might be there and he would see a familiar face again. But all this time he heeded the advice given him and remained in his room, where he could see and not be seen. And it was well for him that he did so, for at one of the landings he saw both Mr. Lord and Mr. Castle come on board the boat.

Toby's heart beat fast and furious, and he expected every moment to hear them at the door demanding admittance, for it seemed to him that they must know exactly where he was secreted.

But no such misfortune occurred. The men had evidently only boarded the boat to search for the boy, for they landed again before the steamer started, and Toby had the satisfaction of seeing their backs as they walked away from the pier. It was some time before he recovered from the fright which the sight of them gave him, but when he did, his thoughts and hopes far outstripped the steamer which, it seemed, was going so slowly, and he longed to see Guilford with an impatience that could hardly be restrained.

At last he could see the spire of the little church on the hill, and when the steamer rounded the point, affording a full view of the town, and sounded her whistle as a signal for those on the shore to come to the pier, Toby could hardly restrain himself from jumping up and down and shouting in his delight.

He was at the gangplank ready to land fully five minutes before the steamer was anywhere near the wharf, and when he recognized the first face on the pier, what a happy boy he was!

He was at home! The dream of the past ten weeks was at length realized and neither Mr. Lord nor Mr. Castle had any terrors for him now.

He ran down the gangplank before it was ready and clasped every boy he saw there round the neck and would have kissed them, if they had shown an inclination to let him do so.

Of course he was overwhelmed with questions, but before he would answer any, he asked for Uncle Daniel and the others at home.

Some of the boys ventured to predict that Toby would get a jolly good whipping for running away, and the only reply which the happy Toby made to that was:

"I hope I will, an' then I'll feel as if I had kinder paid for runnin' away. If Uncle Dan'l will only let me stay with him again, he may whip me every mornin', an' I won't open my mouth to holler."

The boys were impatient to hear the story of Toby's travels, but he refused to tell it them, saying:

"I'll go home, an' if Uncle Dan'l forgives me for

bein' so wicked I'll sit down this afternoon an' tell you all you want to know about the circus."

Then, far more rapidly than he had run away from it, Toby ran toward the home which he had called his ever since he could remember, and his heart was full almost to bursting as he thought that perhaps he would be told that he had forfeited all claim to it and that he could never more call it "home" again.

When he entered the old familiar sitting room, Uncle Daniel was seated near the window, alone, looking out wistfully, as Toby thought, across the fields of yellow, waving grain.

Toby crept softly in and, going up to the old man, knelt down and said very humbly and with his whole soul in the words, "O Uncle Dan'l! If you'll only forgive me for bein' so wicked an' runnin' away an' let me stay here again—for it's all the home I ever had—I'll do everything you tell me to an' never whisper in meetin' or do anything bad."

And then he waited for the words which would seal his fate. They were not long in coming.

"My poor boy," said Uncle Daniel, softly, as he stroked Toby's refractory red hair, "my love for you was greater than I knew, and when you left me, I cried aloud to the Lord as if it had been my own flesh and blood that had gone afar from me. Stay here, Toby, my son, and help to support this poor old body as it goes down into the dark valley of the shadow of death, and then, in the bright light of that glorious future, Uncle

Daniel will wait to go with you into the presence of Him who is ever a father to the fatherless."

And in Uncle Daniel's kindly care we may safely leave Toby Tyler.

Toby Tyler

illustrated by Louis S. Glanzman, is one of the series of

RAINBOW   CLASSICS

Edited under the supervision of May Lamberton Becker

Typesetting, printing, and binding by

The Haddon Craftsmen

Typography by Peter Oldenburg

Binding pattern by Leo Manso

C   19   5